ten
on
sunday

Also by Alan Eisenstock

Sports Talk

Inside the Meat Grinder

ten on sunday

THE SECRET LIFE OF MEN

ALAN EISENSTOCK

ATRIA BOOKS

New York   London   Toronto   Sydney   Singapore

ATRIA BOOKS
1230 Avenue of the Americas
New York, NY 10020

ISBN: 0-7434-4214-8

First Atria Books hardcover edition May 2003

10 9 8 7 6 5 4 3 2 1

ATRIA BOOKS is a trademark of Simon & Schuster, Inc.

For information regarding special discounts for bulk purchases,
please contact Simon & Schuster Special Sales at 1-800-456-6798
or business@simonandschuster.com

Manufactured in the United States of America

For B, J, K, and Z.

And for all the guys in the game.

Acknowledgments and Author's Note

The classic Hollywood story goes like this: boy meets girl, boy loses girl, boy gets girl. My story follows a similar, though less classic, structure: guy wants game, guy gets game, guy loses game.

I was inspired initially to write that story some three years ago. My thanks to Alice Short for publishing my personal essay, "Losing Their Game," in the September 19, 1999, issue of the *Los Angeles Times Magazine*. A few paragraphs of that essay appear in this book.

The idea to turn the essay into a book came from my agent, Wendy Sherman. Wendy nudged me and nurtured this project every step of the way, from magazine piece to proposal to manuscript. Wendy, every author should have an agent, and a friend, like you. You are the best.

I have a core group of dear friends and devoted family who support me on a daily basis. I can't mention you all but thanks especially to my parents, Shirley and Jimmie Eisenstock; Madeline and Phil Schwarzman; Susan Baskin and Richard Gerwitz; Susan Pomerantz and George Weinberger; Elaine Gordon and Edwin Greenberg; Randy Feldman; Randy Turtle; and the entire Barrabee clan: Loretta, Brian, Lorraine, Linda, Diane, Chris, and Alan.

David Ritz, you are my lifeline. Thank you.

A special thanks to everyone at Atria Books, in particular Judith Curr, Suzanne O'Neill, Felice Javit, and, of course, Luke Dempsey—my *superb* editor—whose insight, intelligence, impeccable taste in music, and twisted sense of humor became necessary on a regular basis.

Finally, I simply could not write books without my wife, Bobbie; my son, Jonah; and my daughter, Kiva. Bobbie, you are my best editor, my toughest critic, my best audience, my best friend, and the love of my life. Jonah and Kiva, you light up my world every day. You are miracles.

Everything in this book actually happened. That doesn't mean that everything happened exactly the way I wrote it. Some events have been expanded or exaggerated and some time frames have been switched around.

With a few exceptions, all of the characters' names have been changed. Some characters are composites—amalgams of two or more real people often embellished with a dash of someone completely fictional. In most cases, physical characteristics and personality traits have been changed, in some cases slightly, in others, totally.

The events depicted here occurred between five and ten years ago. At that time, I had no idea that I would be writing a book about my Sunday basketball game. Therefore, I took no notes, nor did I turn on a tape recorder. On one unfortunate Sunday, a friend did videotape our game. When viewed, the tape revealed nothing but ninety minutes of cursing, grunting, and what can only be described as a deeply embarrassing record of our play.

All of the dialogue, then, comes from memory. I have tried my best to recall and record accurately everything that was said, but due to the length of time that has passed, some conversations and dialogue have been re-created. Every word of dialogue presented here was written to the best of my ability and recollection.

CONTENTS

1.

home court

Los Angeles is burning.

It is spring of 1992. Even though a videotape clearly shows four Caucasian police officers brutally beating and kicking an African-American man named Rodney King, the all-white jury delivers a verdict of not guilty. The four officers are freed. Outraged, people in South Central Los Angeles begin to burn the city down. They set fires and loot stores in their own neighborhoods, then head north toward other areas, such as Hancock Park, where I live.

Less than a mile away from me, buildings burst into flame, windows exploding, panes of glass dissolving into powder. Looters lug television sets out of the rubble that was once an appliance store and dodge police in riot gear. Fear grips my street. People I know, friends and neighbors, reveal that they are armed with handguns and rifles. They are going to keep watch at their front windows and they are going to wait.

"Lock and load," a neighbor tells me.

I have no weapon. I stand guard in my living room, staring in disbelief at the news on television. In the sky above me, helicopters hover, circling rooftops with flames that lunge at their metal bellies. Samy's Camera, five blocks away, shines fiery in the moonlight as a throng of rioters tromp through what was once the showroom, hauling off the entire contents of the store. I move outside to my driveway and watch white ash from Samy's flutter onto the hood of my car like snowflakes.

While my children sleep, I pace, ears cocked to the sound of sirens and blasts I'm sure are gunshots. In the morning, an eerie silence shadows me as I crunch across small hills of glass along the curb. Every car parked on my street has had its windows smashed. I decide to take my family—my wife, two children, and my cousin—and flee. I call for hotel reservations in Santa Barbara. Every hotel is booked. My last call is to the Pancho Villa, a sprawling Spanish hacienda on several rolling green acres.

"I need a room. Do you have anything available?"

"You're in luck," a sweet female voice says. "We have one room left. It's five hundred dollars for the night."

I'm desperate and I'm scared.

"I'll take it," I say.

In Santa Barbara at noon, nursing a margarita, shell-shocked from the city, my home, that smolders two hours away, I consider my life. All of those sure things I once held so tightly in my grasp feel as if they are skittering away. I am forty-three, careening toward midlife. All around me I see other men I know becoming clichés. They are leaving their cushy corporate jobs and taking up carpentry or an Eastern religion, forming forty-something rock bands or training for triathlons. They are buying vintage red two-door Mercedes coupes and having affairs with twenty-two-year-old flight attendants. They are putting everything at risk.

I have tempted fate in my own way. Just a month ago, my wife and I bought a house in Santa Monica, a big house, an expensive house. We looked for two years. We settled on a two-story

New England farmhouse, originally built by the Borden family of Borden Dairy fame. The house has a newly remodeled restaurant-style kitchen and a master bedroom suite comparable to what you'd find in a five-star country inn.

But there are problems. As you walk in, the living room, as long as a bowling alley and as wide as a tennis court, veers off to the left behind haughty French doors. Once inside the vast room you become aware of the slope of the floor, discolored and wobbly beneath a carpet destroyed by the former owners' pets, and you pull your collar up against the room's permanent chill.

"Needs work," I mutter to the empty room, as Bobbie, my wife, entranced by the New England charm, wanders away.

The upstairs master suite sells us. Bigger than our first apartment, it features beamed ceilings of golden pine, a fireplace, a bathroom with double sinks, a bidet, an oversize tub with a Jacuzzi, and behind another French door, a walk-in closet, formerly a bedroom. The only blemish is the hot-pink carpeting, which reminds me of a costume worn by the star attraction in a show I once saw in Vegas called "Eros on Ice."

"That carpet's a do-over," I say, and this time Bobbie shakes her head and utters a tiny *"Duh."*

There are other obvious trouble spots, including a postage-stamp-sized third bedroom, which will need to be opened up and redone for our daughter, and a guest apartment over the garage, which will have to be gutted and converted into my office. I have no vision for makeovers, can't imagine how this will all turn out. I'm ready to walk away.

"We've found it," my wife says.

The search is over, I guess, but I'm not sure. I do love the location. Santa Monica is on the ocean, ten degrees cooler than Hancock Park, with noticeably less smog. I have had my fill of choking on muddy brown air so thick I have to push it away as I jog daily down Fourth Street, toward downtown. I'd much rather run by the beach in the crisp salt air. Maybe take up Rollerblading. I said *maybe*.

Then there is the upstairs factor. I have always dreamed of living in a two-story house. As a child of the early sixties, I escaped nightly into the sitcom households of *Ozzie and Harriet* and *Leave It to Beaver*. In fact, I wanted Ozzie to adopt me. I wanted a father with infinite patience, an appreciation for rock 'n' roll, and a great sweater collection. But that wouldn't be the best part of being a Nelson; the best part would be at the end of the day. I would say good-night to my doting, well-dressed parents and my ultracool, ultrapopular brothers, and I would go *upstairs to bed*. Yes, I am forty-three, and I have never gone upstairs to bed. I want that. I will pay for that.

But mainly this house is about the driveway.

As we stand together, facing the two-car garage, Bobbie slips her hand onto my arm.

"Room for a hoop," she says.

I nod, taking it in, scrunching my mouth like an architect, surveying a high stucco wall on the right side and the open expanse of the backyard lawn on the left. In front of the wall are five equally spaced maple saplings, providing, I'm told by the Realtor, a splash of color in the fall. Behind us is a large, intriguing tree, a carob, its trunk and branches twisted in intricate pretzel shapes. Occasionally, a half-mooned carob pod whaps onto the concrete, leaving a small chocolate blotch. I turn back to the garage, squint up at the apex of the roof.

"We could hang the backboard there," Bobbie says.

"Uh-huh."

"*Or*"—her favorite word—"we could drive a pole right here."

She mashes her foot into the cement as if she were putting out a cigarette. I nod and smile. This could work. I have wanted my own hoop forever.

Again.

• • •

I grew up in a small mill city in western Massachusetts with a hoop attached to my garage. It wasn't a fancy hoop; it was crude and a little too high. My father hammered the rim into a large square of plywood that he'd painted white then drilled into the garage to serve as a backboard. Two houses away, Joey Leighton's father had gone to a sporting goods store and purchased a basketball hoop with a fiberglass backboard, which he had installed by two burly men wearing shirts with their names stitched over their pockets. When these guys were finished, Leighton's hoop protruded perfectly from his garage, the backboard gleaming in the midday sun, held in place by a spiderweb of metal supports, beams, and extensions. From my house, his driveway looked like the Boston Garden. The problem was that Leighton's driveway was narrow, barely big enough for a one-on-one game. My driveway began thinly, then widened out to accommodate a three-car garage. He had the better hoop but I had the better court. No contest. We always played at my house.

There were a couple of hazards. The worst was the left side of my driveway, which dropped five feet straight down into the Zwirkos' backyard. If you attempted a fadeaway jump shot on the left and you faded too far away, you'd suddenly sail out of sight and plummet down, as if you were falling off a cliff, and land with a clunk in the Zwirkos' trash cans.

Facing the hoop from the right side were my back steps, which descended from our closed-in mud porch. A ball clanking off the rim, bouncing toward the porch, had a fifty-fifty chance of shattering one of the windows and a 100 percent chance of bringing my grandmother out of her downstairs apartment. Her name was Gussie. I called her Nana. She was short, buxom, and built like a linebacker. She was from strong Russian stock and regarded every first-generation American with suspicion. She would clomp down the back steps on arthritic knees, grab the ball, hold it tight against her aproned hip, shake her fist at me, and scowl.

"*Alan!*" she'd scream.

"Sorry, Nana."

"If you break window again, you *be* sorry! *You* pay this time!"

"Fine, I'll pay." I just wanted the ball back and for Nana to go inside.

My friends, the other five neighborhood kids my age— Leighton, Kirkhoff, the Zwirko brothers, and Dean Nowak— were staring at me, staring at her. I was eleven and this was humiliating.

"Can I have the ball, please, Nana?"

She tucked it tighter against her hip. "No. You no play. Tell them go home. Go to school."

"It's Saturday," I muttered. "Give me the ball, *please.*"

"*Acchh,*" Nana uttered in disgust, and dropped the ball in front of her like a rotten cabbage. It rolled over to me, and without a word about my grandmother, we continued the game. Nana stood on the steps and watched for a moment, hands on hips. I took a shot. Banked it in.

"*Echhh.*" She shrugged, apparently satisfied that I was at least here, in my driveway, and not roaming the streets with a gang of hoodlums. She turned around and trudged back into her kitchen, where she would oversee three dishes cooking at once—a pot of *shav* (spinach borscht), simmering on the stove next to a tall pot of red cabbage leaves stuffed with hamburger meat, and inside the oven, a slab of flanken, a round cut of roast meat stewing in its own juices—all of which she'd force me to eat an hour before my mother served me dinner upstairs.

Nana died at 103. My parents eventually sold the house. I was long gone. I was slowly making my way across the country, beginning in Amherst, Massachusetts, for college, then Ann Arbor, Michigan, for graduate school, then on to Los Angeles, carrying with me the odd dream of wanting to get paid to make people laugh. At some point, though, that dream became lost. I'm not sure where or how. Drowned out perhaps in a cacophony of compromise and Hollywood politics and the relentless pursuit of lifestyle instead of passion, recognition rather than art.

But if I focus on the reason I came to L.A. and embrace that I am standing here, seriously contemplating buying this four-thousand-square-foot house with six bathrooms and a driveway wide enough for a three-on-three game, I must remember that my dream has come true.

"What are you thinking about?" Bobbie asks me, brushing my sleeve.

"A hoop. I've always wanted to have my own hoop."

"I know. I want you to have one. It's the family game."

I press my thumb against the garage door and, my back to my wife, I wonder, "What are they asking for this?"

She tells me. Seven figures plus.

"And it needs work," Bobbie reminds me.

"Well, sure, what do you expect for that kind of money?"

She grins. "Maybe they'll come down."

They do. They come down more than $200,000. We jump at it. We put 30 percent down in cash. That plus the mortgage on the Hancock Park house leaves us with two mortgages totaling in excess of a million dollars.

It's okay. I can afford it. I'm coexecutive producer of a hot new sitcom and the money is rolling in, no end in sight.

What I can't admit yet, what I don't actually know yet, at least not consciously, is that I am miserable.

It's not because of the two mortgages lashed to my back like two grand pianos. There is something deeper, a hole inside me, related to the midlife crisis I am facing and the numbing sense that, despite all the financial success I have achieved, I have, in fact, achieved nothing at all. The work I do, the television show I produce, and the more than one hundred television shows I have written and produced before, throb through my skull in a low-level hum, accompanied miraculously by an obscene amount of money that I receive every week, an amount that no one could possibly deserve. It's like some crazy game that I've gotten stuck in. I really don't want to do this, but I keep playing and they keep paying and I am scared to death to stop. Because if I stop, I'm afraid I will have to give up everything else in my life. I will have to live my life on spec.

These thoughts come to me in daydreams, mostly when I'm shooting baskets alone at Fairfax High. When I was a kid, shooting baskets in my driveway, my hoop dreams were ambitious fantasies, graphic afternoon novels. In them, I was a college phenom, some days a tricky point guard, other days a slashing forward, sometimes even a lithe and powerful seven-foot center. I would see myself in March Madness, driving and spinning to the hoop, stopping on a dime, spotting up. *Swish!* I was unguardable. I'd score the winning basket in every game, usually at the buzzer. My fantasies took me as far as my rookie season in the NBA, where in my first game I scored fifty against Larry Bird, held him scoreless, and left him shaking his head, gaping at me, wondering aloud, "Who *is* this guy?"

A couple of Sundays before the riots, while shooting hoops at Fairfax, I rewind the tape of my life, stopping at the point where Bobbie and I made the decision to move out West. The choice was either graduate school in Minnesota and settling into academia or moving to California to pursue the Hollywood high life. We went Hollywood. Promised to give it five years. Within a year, I was a writer on *Sanford and Son* and Bobbie was pursuing her Ph.D. at USC.

My basketball dreams are gone, but as I brick one off the front of the rim at Fairfax and chase down the rebound, then pop it in from the left side, jingling the metal net, I fantasize about moving back to New England or taking a shot at New York City. Becoming a *real* writer, my friend Ken, a sitcom writer, calls it, referring to someone who writes articles or short stories or books. This has gone beyond fantasy for me; it is now a full-time ache. But I dare not speak it aloud, not with those two bone-crunching mortgages and my two kids in private school.

Bend my knees. Breathe. Dribble once, twice. Get into my rhythm.

Flash.

I'm sitting in my accountant's office. I'm nervous, uneasy, as he goes over the figures.

"You made a lot of money this year," he announces, pinching the fleshy area between his nose and his lip.

"What if," I say, squirming in my chair, "I decide to move to New England for a year and write a book?"

He blows out a laugh. "You *can't!*"

"I'm serious," I say.

"So am I," my accountant says.

I shoot.

Air ball.

I think about all of this as I stare at a surreal scene before me at the Pancho Villa in Santa Barbara. Twenty or so flabby, pasty-skinned tourists, all of a certain age, stand in a wading pool doing aquatic aerobics led by a twig of an instructor in a blue bathing cap. The people in the pool splash their fleshy biceps in and out of the bathlike water, oblivious or unconcerned, as ninety miles to the south, L.A. chokes on its own fumes. I shake my head and turn away, nearly smacking into Brad, a TV writer I know. He wears dark glasses and a baseball cap to hide his mostly bald head. Brad cocreated a smash sitcom that's about to begin its tenth year. Brad, the lucky son of a bitch, is set for life.

"White flight," he says, indicating us both.

"I just couldn't stay at my house. I was too scared."

"I know. Me, too. I got really lucky, though."

"How so?"

"I got the last room in the hotel," Brad says. "Cost me five hundred dollars a night."

Now, I could let Brad off the hook. I could let him in on the scam that the Pancho Villa is running. I could make him feel better by revealing that he's not alone, that the two of us are a couple of marks, hiding for cover while L.A. smokes.

"Huh," I say. "That's a *rip.*"

"I know. How much are you paying?"

"A hundred fifty," I say. "They gave me a suite, too."

Never liked Brad.

A week later, the riots, or as the mayor insists on calling them, the *unrest,* are over. A prickly calm hangs in the air as those of us who've fled return. No one will deny that buildings in my neighborhood were ablaze and there was insanity in the streets—I have glass from my neighbor's windshield embedded in my shoe to prove it—but those days feel far away, like an episode of a television show I glimpsed while flipping channels late at night before dropping off to sleep. This couldn't have happened *here,* in paradise, where it never rains, it's always seventy degrees, and the breeze brushes your cheek like a kiss. The weather's all wrong for rioting.

Friday at noon, Bobbie and I sit in a stuffy escrow office near our new house, preparing to sign a sheaf of legal documents that will strap us to a thirty-year financial commitment broken down into monthly payments that are more than I made the entire *year* I worked in advertising. The escrow officer has left us alone, stuck to the vinyl love seat in her office, as she scrounges around for a couple of pens and a glass of water. I have a ferocious headache.

"You're sweating," Bobbie says quietly.

She presses my forehead, checking for fever or a pulse. She stares at me.

"You're *pale*. Are you okay?"

"Been better."

"What's the matter?"

What's the *matter*?

Let's start with the *two* houses I will now own, one of which has just dropped two hundred grand in value since the riots, excuse me, *unrest*, five days ago. Talk about timing. We have to do something, change real estate agents, lower the price, offer free gifts, *anything*, to unload that place.

"Here we go."

The escrow officer returns. She has a chirpy telephone operator's voice. She hands me a clear plastic cup half-filled with filmy water. I guzzle it, thanking her with a wave of my pinkie. Through the haze that's dropped in front of my eyes like a curtain, I can barely make her out. I see only nondescript features, a square in a dress the color of lemon ice.

"Ok*ayyy.*"

Back to business. She peers at the mound of legalese in front of her, red *X*'s dotting the first page like drops of blood.

"It simply indicates here what your down payment will be and that you will pay it, in cash, as you've agreed—"

I sneak a glance at the number on, literally, the bottom line. It is a frightening number. Mid–six figures. Is this right? It can't be. I have miscalculated. I look up into the fluorescent light and the room starts to spin.

"I um."

I can't find my tongue. I feel Bobbie's touch on my arm.

"I wonder if we could do this after lunch," she says, her eyes boring into the escrow officer's face.

"Well, I, sure," the escrow officer says. "Is everything—"

"Everything's fine. We just need . . . give us an hour, okay?"

We're up and out before the escrow officer can climb to her feet.

Sitting at an outdoor café downstairs from the escrow office, I slurp vegetable soup. Bobbie, occasionally biting a piece of bread, studies me with emerald eyes, trying to scope me out, get a feel for this latest change I'm putting her through.

"Can you talk about it?" Her voice is kind.

"I don't know," I croak. "I've been going over and over the numbers in my head. I thought we had . . . *more.*"

I feel weak. I reach over and tear off a piece of her bread. It's sourdough and stale. A man squeezes by us, balancing three bowls of bumpy brown chili on a tray. The smell makes my stomach flip.

"If you don't feel right, we can get out of it," Bobbie says.

"And do what? Stay where we are? The neighborhood's not safe. The house is too small. And what about school? We're paying for private school in *Santa Monica.* What are we gonna do, schlep the kids forty-five minutes one way?"

"People do it," Bobbie says.

"We back out now, we'll pay a big penalty. It's in the contract."

"The penalty's less than the down payment."

"Money down the drain," I say.

"A *lot* less," she says.

She's exasperated and tired. I finger her bread and close my eyes, trying to stop my world from spinning.

"I think we should back out," Bobbie says, hard. "When in doubt, don't." Her motto.

"But you love the house."

"I do. But it's just a house."

Her eyes glimmer with the truth. I look deep into them and

see no judgment. She is giving me permission to fail, the okay to walk away.

But I can't.

My upbringing and my gender will not allow me. I am bred to be the breadwinner. The *man,* damn it. I can't shake that. In the sixties, Ricky Nelson was my role model, but in the nineties I have become Ozzie. I am The Dad. Sire of two children, king of the castle, lord of the debt.

"Let's go for it."

"What?"

I draw myself up, push aside the soup, pull out a pen. I scratch numbers on the napkin. Big, scary numbers. I nod and swallow.

"We can do it. See? My income can cover it. And we'll still have savings after the down payment. It's a great house, great neighborhood. We deserve it. It'll be fine."

"Are you sure?"

"Positive."

"But your headache—"

"Gone. It's gone."

"But I want you to be sure. I don't want you to be sick—"

"Honey," I say. "You're right. It's just a house."

I curl my lip into a tough-guy smile, a thin red line. "I can always work in TV. If we need money, it's always there."

"And, I guess," Bobbie sighs, "if worse comes to worse, we can always sell it."

Six months later.

I see a face.

If you connect those two dots, right there, then make a curvy line *there,* yep, in the middle, that's the mouth. Then those two knotholes are the eyes, that wavy line the hair, and that squiggly deal could even be a *hat.* Wow. It's *Waldo.* He's right up there, in my ceiling. Hold on. Is that . . . *water damage?* Just what I need.

Another shit sandwich to swallow. Man. Gotta have Kyle get up there tomorrow and take a look. Wait wait wait. It's a *shadow*. Sure. I see it now. The way the moonlight hits the middle beam through the skylight. Definitely a shadow.

Whew. So . . . Where's Waldo. Bizarre. But not as weird as last night when I saw Larry King at the top of the fireplace. Oh man. What the hell time is it?

I press the alarm clock: 2:13 A.M.

Blinking digital burgundy.

Welcome to my typical night. Home from the show at 11:45, straight to bed, instantly asleep, and, wham, right back up at 2 A.M. It's been this way for. . . ? How long have I owned this house?

So far nothing helps. Medication, herbal or otherwise, speeds me up. Meditating makes me tense. And reading gets me wired, especially the book by my bedside, *Hope and Help for Your Nerves.*

The only thing that seems to work, eventually, is mentally tracing celebrity faces in the ceiling. If I'm lucky, I'll finish a face, then nod off again by three. I wake up for good at six, Bobbie's legs swishing out of the covers for her walk being my alarm clock. I stagger downstairs, swig down half a pot of coffee, and I'm good for the day. Running on fumes.

My semiwaking hours are spent at Sony Studios, where I write and produce *A League of Their Own,* a television series based on the hit movie. The movie starred Tom Hanks, Geena Davis, and Madonna. The TV show stars actors who sort of *look* like Tom Hanks, Geena Davis, and Madonna. And that's where it ends.

Still, CBS has high hopes. They believe the show is going to be a big hit. I've heard executives standing by the bagel table murmuring words like "smash," "monster," and "sleeper."

This is a relief. Let's say *A League of Their Own* becomes another *M*A*S*H* and runs for eleven years. That might be pushing it. Let's be a little more realistic, lower our sights, and say *League* runs seven years like *The Mary Tyler Moore Show*. If I stick with it, we are talking *megabucks*. Set for life.

Which is good because remodeling this house took a lot more money than we thought. Why is that? We had a budget. A drop-dead bottom-line number that we absolutely could not exceed, which we have now exceeded by seventy grand. How did that happen?

I guess because we had choices.

For example: floors.

You can lay a nice level plywood floor in the living room or you can go oak. Plywood is what they use for the newer construction. Those spec houses that are thrown together in a weekend. Cheap and ugly and any minute the plywood could just crap out. Goddamn buffet for termites, too. But oak? Durable, solid, warm. *Classic.*

Fine, fine. Go with oak. Must have oak. It's our *home.* Money doesn't matter. Even when we're talking about a room the size of Kansas, a room that I haven't stepped foot in since we put down the miles of oak over a month ago. *Nobody's* been in there. I could've thrown dirt in there and nobody would've noticed.

Then my office. Have to have a fabulous office. A writer needs an inspiring workspace. We stayed within budget here. Until we came to the cabinets and bookcases. I wanted built-ins all around, filled with books, circling me like a cocoon. I was fine with Ikea, but Kyle the contractor found this guy. Italian kid. Not a carpenter. An *artist,* whose milieu happens to be pine. You have never seen such cabinets. Or such artistry. Or such a bill. I asked Kyle to talk to him. Kyle is six-two, handsome, muscular, with a reedy voice and this annoying habit of sucking in great lungfuls of air when he laughs. He somehow manages to be likable and imposing at the same time. Kyle was pretty sure the Italian guy would give us a break.

"If they no like, I tear them out," the Italian guy said.

"No, no, they *like.* But the price—"

"That ees my price!"

"I know but—"

"THAT EES MY PRICE!"

Okay, so no break on that then. The house, our updated designer faux New England farmhouse in sunny Santa Monica, is finally finished. In celebration, I lie awake, night after night, mouth agape, eyes round as quarters, imagining celebrity faces in the ceiling, the sound of cars whooshing by way up on San Vicente Boulevard like waves breaking onto a beach.

This night, a chilly April breeze bouncing off the carob tree, I sigh. Hearing me in her sleep, Bobbie grunts and knuckles her pillow. I want to talk to her. But what good would that do now? I would feel better, for the moment, and she would feel better for helping me feel better. In the morning, though, she would second-guess the whole move, regret the cabinets in my inspirational office and the oak floor in the barren living room. I would accomplish nothing except to infect her with my panic. Better to carry this burden alone. She's going to find out soon enough anyway.

Because the sheets that we share are soaked.

Drenched in my sweat.

When I fly awake each morning at two, I discover this, to my horror. A second later, I'm shivering. I slide my palm across my forehead and mop it dry. I brush my fingers in front of my nose and inhale the surprising scent of vanilla.

Fear, it seems, comes in flavors.

Yes, I am afraid.

Afraid of . . . ?

It's complicated. This is no simple night terror; this is a twisted paradox of terrors. Starting with two frightful what-ifs.

What if I really do run out of money?

Not likely since *League* has the network's blessing.

Then what if *League* is a hit?

I will have to stay in television. I can't turn my back on set-ting my family for life. I need the show to be a hit. Mortgages, taxes, private school, retirement. I *need* it. But I'm so *stuck.* Trapped by my own . . . *excess?* Is that what this is? I didn't think so. I was just trying to be a good man and *provide.* I kept getting in deeper, denying that I was miserable working in TV. I'm not jaded and I don't feel above it. I just don't want to be here.

But here I am . . . sleepless in Santa Monica, shivering in a pool of my own sweat, my midlife crisis defined in this appalling paradox:

(a) I have to work in television because I desperately need the money.

(b) I just can't work in television anymore.

Hear that rumble in my chest?

It's the hand of death slowly circling my heart.

I hear a faint noise. An echo in a tunnel.

CRUNCH GRIND GRRRRR.

I wake up, one eye at a time. I fumble for the alarm and read 10:23 A.M. Jesus. I haven't slept this late since college.

GRRRRRR CRUNCHHHH.

What *is* that?

My head pounding, crying for caffeine, I clutch the damp sheet around my waist and hop toward the window as if I were in a potato-sack race. I peer through the contorted limbs of the carob tree. Kyle, my contractor, stands, hands on hips, squint-ing into the sun. Manuel, his wide-shouldered Mexican muscle, hunches over a jackhammer. His whole body shimmers as he blasts the machine deep into my driveway, chunks of concrete exploding up and whistling by his ear. Kyle turns, watches, nods, directs. It looks as if they're digging a grave.

An hour later, stoked on three cups of coffee, dressed in T-shirt, shorts, and running shoes, I approach Kyle and Manuel.

They whip around, caught in the act, reddening under sheep-ish grins.

"Damn," Kyle says. "We wanted to surprise you."

"Almost," Manuel says. He is packing a gooey beige cement funnel around a black metal pole, which they've shoved into the depths of their trench. Looming above is a basketball hoop attached to a flimsy backboard constructed, it seems, out of cardboard.

"A basketball hoop," I say.

"*Woo*, got it the, *woo*, first time," Kyle roars, sucking all the air out of the immediate vicinity.

"You remembered," I say.

"Oh *yeah*," Kyle says.

The day Kyle handed us his estimate in a sealed envelope, I told him that the deal had to include a basketball hoop with a fiberglass backboard. Adjustable, so the kids could play.

"I wanted a *glass* backboard," I remind him.

"I know," Kyle says. "Those are crap. They cost twice as much and last half as long. They get all weather-beaten and ugly."

"Uglier than this?"

Manuel coughs out a tiny laugh.

"You don't like it?" Kyle asks. "I thought you'd love it. Take a shot."

He picks up a basketball, which has been lounging against the garage door, and hits me a little too hard with a chest pass. I take a couple of dribbles to get the feel, step back, and launch a picturesque jumper. The ball clangs off the rim. The back-board jiggles like a stripper. Kyle pretends not to notice.

"Well?" he says, beaming.

"*Well?* It *sucks.*"

"Hmm. Maybe I didn't pack the pole in enough cement." He jogs after the ball, scoops it up, turns, and flings a clumsy left-handed jump hook from approximately the foul line. The ball whams off the rim and rockets toward the lawn, the backboard swaying like a windshield wiper. Manuel hustles after the ball, yanks it off the grass, skips once, and drives toward the hoop. No form, all power. He stops and pops. All net.

Swish, sway. Boing, boing, boing.

"Bad," Manuel says.

"Shit," Kyle says, scratching his head as if he had lice.

"Yeah," I say.

Kyle glares at Manuel. Sure. Must be *his* fault. Manuel leans heavily on the jackhammer.

"Shit," Kyle says again.

"Bad," Manuel says again.

"Coffee," I say, and head for the house.

Late that afternoon, the hoop, jerry-rigged in place, immovable, stands majestic in my driveway. I stare at it through the kitchen window and feel a sense of pride. I have my own hoop. I can shoot baskets anytime I want. I *always* got next.

I grab my basketball, jog outside, and start to pop. The backboard is soft and dead, causing more shots than not to drop through the net. I'm used to playground baskets, gunmetal backboards sporting tight rust-colored double rims. Nothing falls unless it's dead-solid perfect. This is better. Shoot, swish; shoot, swish; shoot, *swish.* I'm in a zone. I got the *feeling.* Flush with success, I lower the rim to six feet and I am Shaq. Quick power bursts to the rim, two-handed over my head. *Slammmmmdunk!* I return the rim to regulation and hit thirteen foul shots in a row. Exuberant, I huff into the kitchen, where Bobbie, a silent smile on her face, sits at the table, flipping through the newspaper. I swig a glass of water.

"Nice shooting," she says.

"It's the hoop. It's perfect."

She smiles wider.

"How would you feel about having a game here?" I ask her.

"When?"

"I don't know. Sunday morning, how's that?"

"This Sunday or every Sunday?"

I wipe my mouth with the bottom of my T-shirt.

"You know I've always wanted a weekly game."

"I know. Okay, call some people," she says.

"I think I will."

"No assholes," she warns.

"You're making this tough," I say.

I take a shower and start calling. I phone Phil, Gabe, and Brick, close friends and dads at my son's school. They've already said that if I build it, they will come. They're in. I ask Stewart, the school's director. He's dying to play and knows another dad he can bring. I invite Kyle. He's a nice guy, an inside presence, and he can fix any problems with the hoop. I bump into Duff, my neighbor, mention the game to him. He's good to go. That's eight definites, including me. The game is set for the following Sunday at ten.

The next morning I get the word.

A League of Their Own has been canceled after three episodes.

2.

tip-off

On Sunday, April 25, 1993, the day of the first game, a cool and overcast morning, I'm up at seven and out on my deck, which overlooks my backyard. I lean my elbows onto the white, waist-high railing and admire my hoop.

I'm jolted by a loud *VROOOSH*.

An intoxicating display of a dozen glittery mounds of water rises up in front of me, swan-diving onto the lawn.

The sprinklers.

I concentrate on a continuous, sparkly, moist hill three feet away and I see, remarkably, a rainbow. Even on this soupy April morning, the pecks of water on my face refresh me. I close my eyes, allow the water to dabble at my cheeks, and then it dawns on me.

The . . . *sprinklers?*

Somebody's gonna get killed! I hop off the deck and sprint into the garage, where, maneuvering through an obstacle course of kids' bikes, garden tools, ancient matching stereo speakers the size of twin Hondas, and a mountain of battered and empty Bekins boxes, I locate the faded green automatic

21

sprinkler box. I whip it open, flick the switch off, and return to the driveway. Whew. Dry. Except for one treacherous spot, a small, undulating puddle that slithers toward the base of the basketball hoop, dragging with it a slow, wet, ominous, black tail of water. Have to deal with that.

First, the driveway, which is a mess: caked with dust, littered with crinkled but colorful maple leaves, and dotted with dead carob pods that have crashed into the concrete, leaving a grave-yard of a hundred wizened half-moons. Inside the garage, I dis-cover an old broom left behind by the previous owners. The straw teeth of the broom are few, scraggly, and as misshapen as my third-grade teacher's smile, but it'll have to do. I begin to sweep the driveway free of debris and hazard. I work slowly, methodically, in some determined and demented pattern, like an inmate. Twenty minutes later the driveway is beyond clean; it's *hygienic*. You could eat off it. I bring the broom back into the garage, nearly impale myself on the handlebars of a scooter, lower the door, and go inside to change.

This is my uniform:

Black three-quarters basketball shoes. Full-size kicks are too clunky and nip your ankles; flat sneaks give you no support. True, they are more comfortable, but they look like shit. Black three-quarters are stylish. Wearable on the street, too. Now the shorts: gray, cotton, oversize, not quite baggy. I don't want to look like a rapper. Then a neon blue Ben & Jerry's T-shirt. Significance? I'm an ice cream fanatic. My favorite is Herrell's, but I've worn all my Herrell's T-shirts into rags. Crowning touch: prescription goggles secured around my head with a cloth headband.

Dressed thusly I enter the kitchen. Bobbie looks up from stu-dent papers she's grading and peers at me over her rimless granny glasses. I pretend not to notice. I am so cool, so casual.

"No one here yet?"

"Where did you get those?"

"The goggles? Had 'em made up this week. For the game."

"Huh."

I detect something in her tone.

"What? This is how I play basketball. You don't like the new specs?"

"No, you look great. You look like Woody Allen."

Here it comes. The smirk. She liked that one. She turns back to her papers. I'm dismissed. And then I hear voices coming up the driveway.

They arrive in a pack, as if they've all come together in the team bus. They are dressed for hoop and each guy carries a gym bag. Kyle leads the way, a hulk in a torn-off tank top, arrogantly exposing six inches of rippling stomach. He dribbles a basketball with one hand and carries his bag and a cooler in the other. He walks with Phil—solid, slight bounce in his step, a kind and sage face swathed in a salt-and-pepper beard, immaculately trimmed, capped by snow-white hair cropped close. I met Kyle through Phil. Kyle remodeled Phil's condominium at the beach. The result is so stunning that there are rumors of an appearance in *Architectural Digest*. Phil is one of my closest friends and also the best doctor in the world.

Behind them come Brick, ramrod-straight, powerfully built, bespectacled business guy, walking as always with purpose, a man on a mission, a man on a clock; Duff, tall, thin, angular, lives two streets away, works for a new dotcom having to do with virtual reality; and Gabe, bearded, dimpled, soft-spoken, Canadian, cocoa-colored hair exploding out of a bald head buffed to a high sheen. His day job is gynecologist to the stars.

Bringing up the rear are Stewart, the school head, and Barry, a dad I've seen around. Stewart walks weight forward, toe to heel, as if he's played some ball. No Ichabod Crane, he is broad-shouldered and Brillo-haired. His brown eyes are narrow and squinty, but he listens intently and laughs generously. Stewart's face is dominated by an unfortunate mustache, bushy and sheared off at the ends like Charlie Chaplin's. Barry is obscenely tall, the tallest one here, six-four at least, lean as a pole, with thick black hair primped movie-star back into a perfect wave, gelled I think. I'm guessing he showered *before* the game. Barry is a documentary filmmaker. I overhear him telling Stewart he's going to Alaska to shoot ice formations. Stewart locks eyes with Barry as he speaks, riveted, unflinching, as though Barry were revealing the secret of life.

The guys stop suddenly under the carob tree and stare open-mouthed at the hoop and the court as if confronting a miracle.

"Wow, Alan," Gabe says in a hush. "This is *nice.*"

"Thanks, Gabe."

Duff breaks from the pack, approaches the hoop. He's more than a bit bowlegged and is dressed to the basketball max: kneepads, wristbands, headband, and long, white athletic socks stretched to his calves. He squints up into the net. "Hoop's adjustable, huh? I should put one of these up at my house. What'd this cost?"

"An arm and a leg," I say, looking at Kyle.

"Yeah, right," Kyle exhales. "I threw it in. Comes with the deal when you hire me."

"What are you, high?" I ask him.

He wheezes out a laugh as Phil picks up a carob pod I've missed and flings it aside.

"A little problem on the right," Brick warns.

We turn our attention to the stucco wall, which separates my yard from that of my neighbor, Dr. Klein, a famous eye surgeon and winemaker.

"He's never there," I say.

"I meant, watch out for the wall," Brick says.

A couple of the guys nod and grunt and Duff sidles over to the wall and rubs his hand along that, too. I wonder if after the game he's going to make me an offer.

"Okay," I say, back on track. "I got water, cups—"

"I brought beer," Kyle says, lifting his cooler. "Home-brewed."

"I've had his beer," Phil says. "It's phenomenal."

"Brew it in my garage." Kyle beams. "Brought ale, too."

"Should we have it before or after we play?" I ask.

"It'll be a reward," Stewart says, patting down his mustache.

"So how we gonna do this?" Duff asks, reaching into his bag for a mouth guard.

"Shoot for teams," Brick says with a shrug. It's obvious. The playground way. He picks up a ball and banks a jumper off the backboard. Good form. *And* he got off the ground. Shit.

"I'm ready," he announces.

Kyle climbs onto the deck, slides the cooler under the table, out of the sun. He bounds down the stairs, grabs a ball, shoots a line drive that rattles the rim and rockets back at Stewart, who ducks. Instinctively, the rest of us drift into a semicircle and start to shoot, rebounding misses and giving "change"—another shot—to anyone who makes.

I quickly assess what I'm up against. Brick is smooth and strong, and again, he *jumps,* which is cause enough for alarm. He is easily the best player among us. Kyle, even now during warm-ups, is a careening out-of-control truck. Stewart has certainly played before. He has good rhythm, good form, but shoots inconsistently. Phil has a unique shooting style: he squats, then leaping weirdly as if something's just bitten him on the ass, shot-puts the ball toward the hoop. Incredibly, most of his shots go in. Gabe stands under the hoop and serves as the universal rebounder. Duff is tightly wound and awkward and approaches each shot as if it were the first time he's ever touched a ball. Most of his shots smack the backboard without touching the rim, which is pretty hard to do. He worries me. Barry lays back, uninterested in shooting. At one point he jogs in place. I pass him the ball. He passes it back.

"I'm not very good," Barry says.

"You've come to the right place," I say.

"Never played much basketball. But I'd like to learn."

"He's a runner," Stewart says.

"I can jump," Barry offers.

"Put those two together, you have something," I say. "Take a shot."

I toss him a ball. Barry gathers it in, sighs, then flings the ball somewhere in the direction of the rim. The ball whacks the garage door and ricochets like a torpedo right into Brick's nuts.

"*Ugumph*," Brick says, grabbing his crotch.

"Sorry," Barry says. "I'd better not shoot."

"I'm for that," Brick grunts as he limps down the driveway.

"You want me to call your wife, have her rub it?" Phil asks.

"Je*sus*," Brick groans.

"Phil's a doctor," I say. "You want him to rub it?"

"Maybe later." Brick presses his thighs together, but now he's laughing, a breathy cackle, as his glasses flop onto his nose.

"I don't really play basketball," Barry says.

"Why start now?" Brick says.

A few minutes later, Brick has recovered, and the eight of us line up behind what we decide is the foul line. The first four who make a basket will form a team.

"His house. Big Al goes first," Phil says.

I step up, swish my foul shot. Brick, shooting next, banks his in. The next six guys miss. We begin again with Phil. Squat, leap, shot-put, *yes!* The next five guys miss. They shoot again. Miss, miss, miss, miss, and miss. And two air balls. One by Stewart, although it looked good leaving his hand, and one by Barry, which looked as if he were chopping firewood.

"I have to be somewhere Tuesday," I say.

"I gwanna mick *dis*," Duff says through his mouthpiece. He shoots. The ball sails over the backboard.

"Tim*ber*," Brick shouts as the ball rolls down the side of the roof, onto the lawn.

"Okay," Stewart says, and banks his next shot in.

"That's four," Phil says.

"So soon?" I ask.

"Whata we got?" Brick asks.

"It's us four," I say, rounding up him, Phil, Stewart, and me against Kyle, Duff, Gabe, and Barry.

"Shoot for outs," Kyle says. I do and drill one in from downtown.

"Beautiful shot," Gabe says.

"Take who takes you?" I ask Brick.

"We need to establish some rules, don't we?" Stewart says with a sliver of school director's authority.

"Winner's outs?" I suggest. "And how about we play to seven baskets, by ones."

"If it's tied, you have to win by two," Brick says.

We mark off the out-of-bounds. The lawn to the left, that's easy. The stucco wall on the right, easier still. We determine that the garage door is out and that there are no bounds to the rear. We add that you have to bring the ball past the foul line after a miss by the other team.

We spread out and I find myself guarded by Barry. The other team obviously has no respect for my game. I will have to *school* this six-foot-four-inch ice-filming punk. I check the other matchups. Kyle is on Brick, Gabe has taken Phil, and Duff is guarding Stewart.

I take the ball out, pass it to Brick, who sets up in the high post. He fakes right, spins left, and as he makes his move, slips in the tiny tail of water I've forgotten to sweep away. Brick tumbles onto the lawn, splats onto his ass. *Squish.*

I wince.

"You okay?" I'm there, offering him a hand. He grabs it, pulls himself up.

"You guys are trying to kill me," Brick says.

He shakes his head, reaches down for the ball, dribbles it once on the driveway. Kyle snatches it away.

"Our ball."

"What?"

"You fell out of bounds. Our ball."

"Oh, come *on*."

"Well, *technically,*" Stewart says.

"Technically my ass is bruised," Brick says, hard, then blinks, aware all eyes are on him. He caves. "Fine. Take it out."

It doesn't matter. The game isn't close. Brick dominates Kyle inside and I score three baskets on Barry, getting loose for open jumpers pretty much at will. The first game ever played in my backyard now history, the eight of us head over to the deck for a water break.

"That was good," Stewart says. He's huffing, a droplet of per-spiration dangling in the middle of his mustache like a tear.

"I broke a sweat," Phil says. "Course, I break a sweat putting my shoes on."

"Nice game, Brick," Kyle says, wiping his forehead with a towel he's brought.

"Yeah, thanks, you, too. Kyle, right?"

"Yeah," Kyle says, and they shake hands.

"I wonder," Stewart says. "Do you think it might be better three on three? Four on four is a little tight out there."

"I'll sit out," Barry offers.

"Me too," Gabe murmurs, rotating his right arm. "I'd like to rest my shoulder."

"What's with your shoulder?" I ask him.

"Ah, nothing. Just a slight tear in my rotator cuff."

This stops everyone in middrink.

"Wait a minute," I say. "You're playing basketball with a torn rotator cuff?"

Gabe sniffs, wipes his nose on his forearm. "It's a slight tear. No big deal."

"Ask him if he'll get it operated on," Phil says.

Gabe lowers his voice even further, as if the surgeon's within earshot. "No way. I'm not going anywhere near a cut man. I'll just take it easy. I'll be fine."

"Playing basketball is not exactly taking it easy, Gabe," Brick says.

"It's okay. I'm careful. I'll sit out, watch you guys. I'll play the next game. Stewart's right. Three on three's better."

I look at Phil. "He's playing with a torn rotator cuff."

"What can I tell you? The man's nuts. And if he had the surgery? He'd be fine in a month."

Gabe sniffs, coughs. "I'm not having an operation. I do my rehab, take it easy, warm baths, it'll heal. I don't like doctors."

"You are aware of the irony there," I say.

The guys laugh, the doctors the loudest.

Kyle leans against the house, pushes the wall with his palms, stretching his quadriceps. "Maybe we should break out the beer."

"It's a thought," Phil says.

"You're the doctor," I say.

"How about a three on three, then beer." Stewart the mediator, the educator, the adult.

"I'm sitting out," Barry reminds us.

We scramble the teams a bit, leaving Brick, Phil, and me against Kyle, Duff, and Stewart. This time the game is close and more physical. Kyle, accidentally, I think, whacks Brick every time he drives to the hoop. Forced outside, Brick misses three shots badly. We go down by two then roar back behind Phil, who hits two of his patented squat shots. We go up by one when the doctor fakes a squatter, then drives to the hole, leaving Duff searching for his jock. Ahead by one basket, I go for the kill by trying a short jump shot behind a massive screen by Brick. The ball whams the rim, bounces on the driveway, and sails over the stucco wall, right onto Klein's paddle-tennis court.

"Shit," I say.

"I got it!"

Barry, out of nowhere, is off the deck in one step and, like Spider-Man, begins to scale the wall in a seamless, fluid motion.

"Barry, wait!"

He doesn't hear me. He's too intent on catapulting over to the other side.

What I'm trying to tell him is that the drop from my wall to Klein's paddle-tennis court is at least fifteen feet.

"Barry!"

He stops, his head suspended for a split second at the top of the wall as he looks down. He turns to me, his eyes wide with horror. Then he loses his grip and he's gone.

"YAAAAAAAAA!" he howls. Barry's voice echoes, then evaporates, as he flies out of sight, landing with a distant thump and a tiny "Umphh."

"Ouch," Brick says.

We immediately look at Phil, who shakes his head, unconcerned. "He's fine."

A beat and the ball flies back over the wall.

"Okay," Phil says. "Whose outs?"

His casualness, his *certainty*, breaks us all up.

"Believe me," Phil says, "after twenty years in the ER, I can tell a real injury by the sound."

"Our ball," says Kyle, the maven of possession.

"Ow tick it ow," Duff says, mouthpiece clacking, walking briskly to the foul line.

"I'm fine," Barry confirms from somewhere down below. "But how do I get back up?"

We don't answer him. We're locked in a one-basket death match. Stewart drives. I foul him, preventing a score.

"Nice play," Brick says.

"Big Al," Phil says.

"*Guys?*" Barry from the abyss. And for some reason everyone's looking at me.

"Don't worry about Barry," I say. "If he can make his way

around Alaska, he can figure out how to get out of Klein's back-yard."

Nods all around. We finish the game, my side winning 9–7, and walk back to the deck, just as Barry's head appears at the top of the wall. Grunting, he pulls himself up and over and stumbles onto the driveway.

"See? Told you he'd come back," I say.

"I had to shimmy up the light pole," Barry says, flicking specks of stucco off his forearms and out of his sculpted and rigid hair.

"Break out the beer," Phil says.

Kyle grins, reaches for the paper cups. He pours us each a taste.

I raise my cup. "To Barry."

"To Barry," the guys chorus. Barry, a grin sneaking across his face, gulps his brew down.

"Umm," Barry says, and literally smacks his lips. "This is fantastic beer."

"Thank you," Kyle says. "This is a light lager. The secret is, I add a touch of hazelnut. I've got a red ale, too. It's a tad bitter. New thing I tried."

I sip the beer. The lager goes down with a bite. The aftertaste is both refreshing and dizzying.

"*Ahhhh,*" I say.

Here we are, eight guys sprawled out on my deck, sampling homemade hazelnut beer and bitter red ale after a couple of good sweaty games of hoops . . . *in my driveway?*

Can it get any better than this?

I sneak a look at my kitchen window. Bobbie stands at the sink, watching. I catch her eye and she makes a small cute face, then smiles and turns away. I swirl the dregs in my cup and the sun appears so suddenly it makes us blink.

"We're still playing, right?" Stewart asks.

Grunts, agreement, nods. But nobody's moving. We're basking . . . in the beer, in the silence, in the sunlight, in the company of men.

"Yeah, let's play," Brick says finally, crushing his cup.

We play for another hour and a half, sticking to three-on-three games, alternating who sits out. At one point, Kyle and Stewart, contractor and school head, sit out together, lounging in cushy redwood chairs, eyes toward us, but deep in private conversation. As the rest of us drive and defend, rebound and shoot, a smattering of contractor lingo, terms like *estimate, architect,* and *cost-per basis,* litters the air.

Last game. Teammates now, Stewart and Kyle walk off onto the driveway, still clenched in intimate discussion. Kyle does most of the talking. Stewart is engrossed, enraptured, peppering in an occasional, enthusiastic "Uh-huh" or "Really" and climaxing with a resounding "That's the way I like to work, too." Brick and I volunteer to sit this one out. A man in constant, fast motion, Brick pours himself another beer, takes a moment to cool down.

"This was fun," he says, sloshing the brew around in his mouth as if it were mouthwash. "Did we lose any games?"

"I don't think so."

Brick raises his eyebrows, nods, polishes off the beer, and burps loudly, no attempt to squelch the sound.

"That Kyle's a load," he says, and burps again. "Excuse me."

"You're excused."

"He do your remod?"

"Yep."

"Turned out okay, right?"

"Yeah. But he went over budget. Way over."

"Par for the course," Brick says. "It's because these contractors always come up with extra things to do. They find stuff."

"I know. I call it the 'as long as I'm here' syndrome. As long as I'm here, might as well rip out that wall and put in a new wing."

"That's what happens. You could wait and do it later, but it's cheaper . . ."

And Brick and I say in unison, *"As long as I'm here."*

We nod and grin and look away from each other.

This is a guy thing.

You never want to acknowledge that you and another guy had exactly the same thought in exactly the same words and that you spoke them aloud . . . *at exactly the same time.* If you're out on a date and this happens, this is a good thing. It's evidence that you and your date think alike, you're in sync, possibly even soul mates, and with some luck, you might get laid. When this occurs with two guys, it's simply freaky and should go by as if it never happened.

Finished with the last game of the first Sunday, we convene on the deck. We slug down cupfuls of water and Duff pours the remainder of a bottle over his head.

"This was really great," Stewart says. "So, are we on for next week?"

"Fine with me."

"Is it fine with Bobbie?" Phil asks.

"This was actually her idea."

"I love it," Gabe says, whirling his arm like he's guiding in a plane.

"Well, that's it for me," Brick says, standing abruptly. "Thanks, guy. Good games. See you guys next week." And he's gone, striding down the driveway, his back erect as a colonel's. This is everyone's cue. The guys pack up, tossing towels in gym bags, pulling sweat-soaked T-shirts over their heads, slipping on dry ones.

"Let me help you clean up," Phil says.

"No, no, I got it."

"You know, I was wondering . . ." Stewart. A catch in his throat, a shy expression creeping across his face. "You think I could take a quick look at the work Kyle did in your house? When it's convenient?"

Kyle stands, pushes his chest out, scratches his stomach. "He's thinking of hiring me."

"You?"

"Can you believe it?"

"How's now?"

"Sure," Stewart gushes.

"Go ahead. I'll clean up," Phil says.

I head inside. Kyle and Stewart follow, but stop at the back door and vigorously wipe their feet on the mat. Bobbie, in the kitchen, turns toward them from the stove.

"Umm. What smells good?" Stewart asks.

"Making soup."

"Stewart wants to see what Kyle did," I tell her.

"I'm remodeling my house," Stewart says.

"Be sure to show him the office," Bobbie reminds me.

"Right," I say, heading up the stairs. "First, the kids' rooms. I'll start with my daughter's room, where Kyle overcharged me for building a new closet—"

"Man," Kyle says, "you're killing me."

I give Stewart a quickie tour of the house. We start in my son's room, where my kids are playing a board game on the floor. My son, in kindergarten at Stewart's school, looks up with astonishment when he sees his principal walk into his room. Stewart smiles, immediately engages the kids, asks what game they're playing, gets down with them, down to their level, so he can make eye contact. After a minute of polite conversation, he stands, says good-bye, and leaves. I look back and catch a glimpse of my son rolling over in embarrassment on his rug.

We leave the house, go outside, and climb the stairs to my office above the garage. Stewart lingers here, admiring the built-in cabinets and bookcases, wandering around the room. He nods, narrow eyes half-closed in contemplation, as Kyle gives him a brief history of the space, how it was a frumpy guest apartment before he got his claw hammer into it and renovated it into the showplace it is today.

"And you did this without an architect?"

"Oh yeah. I did all the plans. Never drew them up. Had it all in my head—"

"But as I explained, my job is a lot more involved. I've already hired an architect—"

"Not a problem. I'm easy to deal with. Right?" Kyle looks at me for corroboration.

"Don't look at me."

"Hang me out to dry, why don'tcha?"

"You're welcome. Stewart, you should look at Phil's place, too."

"I already have," he admits shyly.

"His wife's president of the Parents' Association," Kyle says.

"No shit? How about that. You know everything. You guys don't need me."

"We really don't," Kyle says.

And Stewart and Kyle laugh as if they were the only members of an exclusive, secret club.

After a hot, long shower, I join Bobbie in the kitchen for a bowl of thick butternut-squash soup.

"Well?"

I look up in midslurp. "Well what?"

"How was the game?"

She leans in on both elbows. Her green eyes glimmer with more than casual interest.

I shrug, dig into the soup. "Good. Brick was on my team most of the time. He's a good ballplayer. By his count, we won every game. I tell you, though, I'm pretty sore. The shower helped."

"What'd you guys talk about?"

I look at her blankly.

"What's going on?" she asks helpfully. "You know, what's the gossip?" She smiles expectantly.

I shake my head, at a loss. "There is no gossip."

"You were with these guys for three hours. You had to talk."

"Not really." I shrug again. "Soup's great."

Bobbie leans back, folds her arms. "You must've talked about *something.*"

"Oh, yeah. We did talk about something."

Bobbie leans back in. "What?"

"Gabe has a torn rotator cuff."

"And he's *playing?*"

"Yeah. You know Gabe. Nothing stops him. He used to play hockey. Actually, he plays basketball like he's playing hockey."

"A torn rotator cuff. That's bad. What does Sara think about this?"

"You got me."

"She must be upset with him."

"Maybe. I don't know."

"You don't know? You didn't discuss what his wife thinks about his playing with a torn rotator cuff?"

"Nope. Didn't come up."

"I don't believe it." This she says with an edge. Bordering on being pissed.

Frankly, I'm stumped. "Are we having an argument about Gabe's torn rotator cuff?"

"We're not having an argument."

But Bobbie stands up, kicking her chair back with a clatter. She moves away, begins puttering around the kitchen.

"But the games were good," she says softly.

"Yep. Gonna play next week, too. And get this. Stewart might hire Kyle to remodel his house."

"That's a mistake."

"Why? You don't like Kyle?"

"No, he's fine. But he can be a little . . ."

"Controlling?" I suggest.

"And temperamental," she says. "I also get the feeling that Stewart can be a little . . ."

"Temperamental?" I say.

"And controlling," Bobbie says.

We grin at each other.

"Immovable object meets irresistible force," I say.

"Physics 101," says Bobbie.

"Actually, I was referring to Keith Jackson, who used that expression while announcing the Notre Dame–Michigan State game in 1966. Classic game. Ended in a 10–10 tie."

"I am always amazed how you can remember such useless sports trivia."

"All men can do it. It's stamped into our genes. And it's not useless."

"Back to Stewart and Kyle."

"Those two temperamental control freaks? They're made for each other," I say.

"Or," Bobbie says, "they're gonna kill each other."

The next day, Monday, I call G., my former boss, and Sheila, my real estate agent. To be honest, since the demise of *League*, I haven't been actively pursuing television work. The timing's bad anyway. It's April, hiatus for most television shows. The new season won't be announced until mid-May. Right now, most working TV writers are lying on a beach in Hawaii or hotel-hopping across Europe. There will be no television work available for at least two months. This may not matter because of something G. said to my writing partner and me after *League* was canceled.

"You guys want to write a movie? I think I can convince Martin to find one for you."

Martin is a senior partner in, call it Lucky Sperm Productions, and one of the most important movie moguls in Hollywood. A *player,* down to the Armani sport jacket, Fred Segal jeans, Bruno Magli loafers (no socks), spiked hair, and attention deficit disorder. I would love to write a movie for him.

"It won't be for the same money you're used to," G. warns me. "It won't be TV money."

This part scares me. But in my current state of midlife confusion I'm willing to risk it. I need to try something new. I want to feel better about my work. I have had my fill of working in windowless conference rooms, eating cold Chinese food off paper plates, surrounded by a clutch of ten screaming sitcom writers, all desperate to be heard. I share these feelings with my partner. It's the noise, I tell him. It's deafening. I can't hear my own voice. To my surprise, he agrees. I tell G. to convince Martin.

"I'll see what I can do," he says. "No promises."

Sheila is less optimistic.

"We had an open house yesterday and nobody came."

"Nobody?"

"Well, not literally nobody, but nobody with potential. A lot of looky-loos."

"Sheila, I really have to sell this house."

"I hear you. People are still skittish from the riots. Real estate values in Hancock Park have not come back yet. I don't know if they ever will."

"That's very reassuring."

"Listen to me," Sheila says. "The only way we're going to sell this house is if we lower the price."

"By how much?"

"A hundred thousand dollars."

"No way," I say. "I can't. Let's see what happens with another open house or two."

"Looky-loos, I'm telling you. That's all you're going to get."

I hang up from this phone call with a slamming, heavy-metal headache.

• • •

They're all coming back.

I phone everyone Friday and Saturday to confirm and all seven guys say they're playing. Half of them say they can't wait. I'm one of them.

I'm ready by nine-thirty Sunday morning. I've gone to the store, bought more water and cups, turned off the sprinklers, moved the cars out of the way, swept the driveway free of carob pods, dust, and dead leaves, and arranged the water and cups in the middle of the redwood table in a nifty pattern resembling a fort. My pregame ritual completed, I shoot baskets alone, waiting for the guys to arrive. I pop in a jumper from the left baseline, and I hear:

"Yo, dude!"

Dr. Phil. Then I hear laughter, bright *female* laughter. I peer down my driveway and see not only Phil and Gabe, but also their wives, Madeline and Sara.

"Hi, Alan," the women greet me in a duet.

"Women? Ladies? Guys, there's ladies here."

"And bagels," Gabe says, revealing a bulging brown paper bag.

"Helloo," Bobbie singsongs from the deck.

"While you guys are playing basketball, we're going for a walk," Sara says.

"Yes, we're going to be walking and *talking,*" Bobbie says.

"Fine. We'll be playing and eating," I say, reaching into the bag and tearing off a piece of an onion bagel.

"Let me get a knife," Bobbie says, going inside, her friends at her heels.

"And some plates and napkins," Madeline says.

I catch a look from Phil. He rolls his eyes. A knife, plates, and napkins? All of a sudden, it's a picnic. Why do we need utensils? You reach into the bag, rip off a chunk of bagel, dip it in the

cream cheese, stuff it into your mouth, lick your fingers, and
wipe your hands on your T-shirt. Bam. That's it. That's how you
eat a bagel at a basketball game. If you're going to *have* bagels
at a basketball game. Which, by the way, is questionable.

"What do we got, bagels?"

Brick vaults onto the deck, ignoring the three stairs leading
up to it. Behind him is a large tree of a guy wearing a white
headband and a red Viking beard.

"Hi," I say, reaching out my hand. "Alan."

"Ivan Kracjek," the tree says, crushing my hand. "Brick
invited me."

"You two have met, right?" Brick says.

"I don't think so," I say.

"Really? Ivan's in your business."

"Used to be," Ivan says. "Phone stopped ringing coupla
years ago."

For some reason, Ivan finds this uproariously funny. He
laughs, loud and alone, shaking all over as if in spasm.

"He writes action shit," Brick says.

"As opposed to the sitcom shit I write?" I say.

"You know what I mean."

Brick bounds down the stairs, shadowed by Ivan, picks up a
ball, and walks him over to the garage, pointing out the bound-
aries we established last week. Ivan nods as he adjusts his headband, pulls it off, stretches it, then wrestles it back over his pas-
ture of red hair, which sticks up in uneven clusters as if he's just
come from electroshock therapy. Ivan slaps the ball out of
Brick's hand and takes an off-balance fadeaway that drops in. I
tear off another piece of bagel as Bobbie appears with plates,
napkins, and an old knife she's dug out of the bottom of a
drawer. She winks at me and heads back inside. The back door
closes and a second later women's laughter dances out of the
open kitchen window.

Voices cut through the branches of the carob tree and the

sound of sneakers scraping concrete as Kyle, Stewart, Duff, Barry, and Mitch, another dad from the kids' school, come up the driveway. Mitch is ten years younger than the rest of us and built like a lightbulb. He wears wire-rimmed glasses, smiles in a thin line, and seems jittery, nervous, as if he has to take leak. He has a sweet, eager-to-please face, highlighted by droopy brown eyes, reminding me of a beagle. I immediately trust the guy, which means he's probably a scam artist. Then I remember that he's a shrink, specializing in eating disorders, and I feel better.

Brick invades the group, pumps Mitch's hand, and introduces Ivan all around. Kyle puffs out his chest as he and Ivan shake hands in a virtual death grip, grimaces clouding both of their faces. A wedge of bagel tucked into my cheek like a chipmunk, I hop down the stairs and greet everyone.

"Boys," I say, "back for more?"

"Gluttons for punishment," Stewart says.

"Hey, Kyle," Duff says, laying a hand on the contractor's shoulder. "For real. How much would it cost to put up a hoop at my house? But a good one. One with a glass backboard."

"Couple hundred grand," I say. "Right, Kyle?"

Kyle grins, shakes his head, and drills a chest pass at me. I catch it, no problem, and flick the ball over to Barry. Barry lets the ball zip past him and slam into the garage door. He holds up his hand, palm out, the same gesture my father uses when he's had too much to eat.

"I'm not playing today," Barry says. "I'm just gonna watch."

"Seriously?" I say.

"I think I can learn more that way."

"I doubt it."

"Still," Barry insists, "you guys play."

To save time, we decide to let Brick make teams instead of shooting for them. He chooses Phil and me, and pits us against Ivan the Tree, Kyle the Contractor, and Mitch the New Guy. Stewart, Duff, Gabe, and Barry settle into chairs on the deck.

I pull Brick off to the side. "You sure about these teams?"

"Remember last week? We didn't lose a game."

"Yeah, but Kyle and Ivan on the same team? They're sort of *big*."

"Compared to you, yeah. Don't worry about it."

"Who am I supposed to guard? Ivan?"

"Better let me take him. He's an animal."

"Great. Is he at least a nice guy?"

"Not really."

"What do you think?" Kyle says. "We playing *today*?"

"Shoot for outs," Brick says.

I do and miss. Kyle, Ivan, and Mitch get the ball first. They score fast and often and beat us 7–1.

"Good sides," I say to Brick as we retreat to the deck. We descend on the bagels like vultures, and I notice that so far nobody has come near a plate, napkin, or the knife.

"I have a question," Barry says. "Why would you put Kyle and Ivan on the same team? Doesn't that give them a huge rebounding edge, even with you, Brick? What was your thinking there? I'm just trying to learn the game."

"Shut up," Brick says.

For the next hour, Kyle, Ivan, and Mitch rule the court. Mitch, stronger than he looks, plays with sheer abandon and little form. He manages to gobble up a slew of rebounds while missing all of his shots badly, except for one game-winning layup against me.

"Sorry," Mitch says.

"No need to apologize," I say. "When you shoot, you *want* the ball to go in."

"We gotta switch these teams around," Brick says. "Too much size on that team."

"No shit," I say.

"It took me a while but I finally see the light."

"Mind if I try making teams?" Stewart offers.

"Be my guest," Brick says. "You can't do worse than I did."

Stewart thrusts his bottom lip forward, scratches his chin, then lowers his head and musses his hair. Finally, he looks up, nodding with satisfaction as if he's solved a complex math problem.

"Let's try three set teams," he says. "Ivan, Mitch, and Phil. Brick, Duff, and Gabe. Kyle, Alan, and me. We'll keep rotating so everyone gets to play."

"I see," Barry says. "It's like a tournament. Interesting."

"Him I'd like to kill," Brick murmurs next to my ear.

We work it Stewart's way for the rest of the morning. Every game is close. Because of his success, Stewart earns the title of official team-maker, now and forever.

The last game of the morning pits our team against Phil's. I take the ball out, pass it in to Kyle. Kyle dribbles toward the hoop, backs into Ivan, turns, lowers his shoulder, and muscles up a shot. Ivan grunts and swats it away.

"Foul," Kyle says.

"Foul?" Ivan shouts.

"Yes. Foul," Kyle says evenly.

Ivan rolls his eyes, flips the ball to Kyle, who tosses it to me.

"Take it out," Kyle says.

I throw the ball in to him again. Kyle crouches, slides left, and shoves his butt into Ivan's midsection while trying a hook shot. Ivan staggers backward into the garage door.

"Charge," Ivan gasps.

"What?"

"You heard me, bro. That's a charge. Offensive foul. My ball."

Kyle doesn't move. In less than a nanosecond, his face turns the color of a cranberry. Ivan takes one step forward and plants himself an inch from Kyle's nose. And then the staring begins.

Perfect. This is what I need.

A fistfight at my house.

I look at the other guys for help. Sure, like they're gonna get in the middle of this. Phil's leaning against the stucco wall, stretching his calves, which have apparently picked this very moment to tighten up. Brick is watching the scene from the deck, absently ripping and eating a bagel, dry. Nice going, Brick. Bring Ivan, a bitter, oversize, unemployed writer of action shit. He'll mix well. I glare at Brick, hoping he'll read my mind. He smiles, shows me a mouthful of bagel. Asshole.

Then something strange happens.

The blood suddenly drains out of Kyle's face. He takes a step back and grins, yes, *grins*, at Ivan.

"You say it's a foul, it must be a foul."

Kyle picks up the ball and offers it to Ivan as if it's a gift. Ivan looks at the basketball with both confusion and suspicion. The tension that just seconds ago had descended over them like a mist has not only lifted, it's been replaced by a thick cloak of weird.

"Fine," Ivan grunts.

Behind them, the other member of our team, Stewart, clears his throat. Stewart's sudden bout with phlegm leads me to suspect the reason for Kyle's instant and total turnaround.

The remodel.

I'm sure Kyle would like nothing better than to clean Ivan's Nordic clock. But not here, not now. Not in front of a potential employer, the school head, who's waving a mythical report card in his face folded to the conduct page, an imaginary pen poised over the question "Works well with others?" I know Kyle well enough that he's not going to blow an entire career over a charging foul.

Ivan, now on offense, completely ignores the rest of his team. He whips around and viciously slams *his* butt into Kyle's stomach, then, whirling clumsily to his right, gives Kyle a head fake. It's not a particularly effective fake; it looks more like a bad disco move. Kyle doesn't go for it. He rises up and, like a spiker in a volleyball game, hammers Ivan's feeble shot on a fly into Klein's yard.

"I got it!" Barry shouts. Before you can blink, he's off the deck and up and over the stucco wall in a single bound, clearly forgetting the fifteen-foot drop down into Klein's paddle-tennis court.

"YAAAAAAAA!" Barry howls for the second week in a row as he disappears over the wall.

A moment, then a loud crash.

No, not Barry.

It's Brick from the deck. He has dissolved into a gale force of laughter and has fallen over in his chair.

"Ohmygod," he wails. *"Ohmygod.* I, don't, believe, it!"

He's gone, lost it, shaking in hysterical, tearful spasms of laughter as he crawls across the deck on all fours. By now we're all laughing, even Kyle and Ivan.

"Forgot about that drop," Barry calls from somewhere on the other side of the wall. "Wow."

Brick is now crying, his two meaty arms wrapped around his midsection, a coyotelike howl spewing from his lips. He curls up on my deck in a fetal position.

"OHMYGODDD!"

The ball sails over the wall and we start laughing even louder.

For some reason, I glance toward the house. Huddled at the kitchen window, watching us, are Bobbie, Madeline, and Sara. Their expressions are grim, emotionless, scientific. I can read Bobbie's eyes, piercing emerald pools:

Behold the middle-aged male at play. Nine of them. Strewn on the lawn, in the driveway, on the deck. Giggling. Helpless. Slightly insane. And here comes a tenth, a beanpole with good hair, clinging like a chimp to Klein's light pole.

They turn away, having seen enough.

"So next week?" Mitch asks.

Phil, Mitch, and I are cleaning up. Everyone else has gone

except for us and Stewart and Kyle, who have pulled their chairs into the shade and are huddled in conference.

"I guess so," I say to Phil. "Why not?"

"Is it okay if I come back?"

I look at Mitch, thrown by the question.

"What I mean is, I'm not that good."

"None of us is any good," I say. "We all stink. Except for Brick."

"We don't want you to be good," Phil clarifies.

"Yeah, that would mess up the game. Throw off the balance."

"So you guys actually need me."

"Now you got it," I say.

"I really could lose some weight," Mitch says. To demonstrate he grabs his stomach and jiggles two handfuls of flab.

"If you lose weight, will it improve your game?" I ask him.

"I don't think so. I doubt it."

Phil and I nod.

"You're in," Phil says.

"Come every week," I say.

Mitch laughs. "I feel so wanted."

Behind us, Kyle and Stewart stand up, their chairs creaking against the redwood deck. They shake hands and Stewart briefly pats Kyle on the back.

"It's official," Stewart says.

"Yep. Gonna remodel Stewart's house," Kyle confirms.

"Stewart, I warned you," I say.

"I figure if you're still talking to him—"

"I'm here every week playing ball, right?" Kyle says.

"Yeah, but I'm not talking to you."

He, woo, laughs, woo, then lowers his voice and speaks gravely. "Hey, man, I'm sorry about what happened there with Ivan. I just lost it."

"He was out of control. You handled it well," says Stewart, now Kyle's defender, Kyle's *dawg*.

"Still," Kyle says, "I shouldn't let a guy like that get to me."

We all nod in deep, spiritual agreement.

"Okay." Mitch breaks the silence. "Next week then."

He heads off the deck and down the driveway, Kyle and Stewart trailing, now linked in business, shoulder to shoulder, as giddy as life partners.

The school my son attends, Stewart's school, is nothing like the one I—or anyone I have ever known—attended. My memory of elementary school is of square, sterile classrooms filled with rows of metal desks. We sat at attention, alternately bored and petrified, our eyes fixated on the clock on the wall, frozen, it seemed, in time. Before us stood an automaton posing as a teacher who droned drearily through a canned lesson plan and terrorized us if she caught us in less than rapt attention. Educators called this an academic, structured environment; kids called it torture.

In contrast, Stewart's school is dynamic. In fact, it doesn't even feel like school. No sign of academics or structure here, the whole place seems easygoing and loosey-goosey. Kids are mixed together in two-year age groups, taught by women who look like aging hippies or recovering flower children. Everyone is on a first-name basis: kids, teachers, office staff, the cleaning crew, even Stewart. Classrooms are colorful playrooms with beanbag furniture and snuggly lofts lined with bookshelves. Children are celebrated and empowered. They learn to spell inventively, which means any way they want. They'll learn the right way later. The concept here is to learn at one's own pace. What's the hurry? The world is moving too fast, technology is taking over. Damn those computers! Screw the Internet! Slow down, paint a picture, write a poem, compose a song.

Parents are encouraged to be involved. And so I am, reading every week with kids in my son's kindergarten/first-grade class. I read individually with students, encountering a wide range of readers, from kids who are highly advanced to those who cannot recognize even one word on a page. I point this out to my son's teacher, a tall, misty-eyed woman with billowing blond hair that rests braided like a challah on her flowing Native American robe. She laughs agreeably. *That's the way it is here. We embrace academic diversity.* Oh well. My son seems happy enough, although the students in his class appear to be endlessly chasing each other around the classroom in nonstop, full-contact versions of keep-away and tag. To me, he looks a little frazzled in the chaos. I guess that's normal.

"I heard about your basketball game," Challah Head tells me one morning as two kids play tetherball with her hair. "It's great that you guys play. Seriously."

"Well, we try. How'd you hear about it?"

"Stewart. He can't stop talking about it. It's the highlight of his week."

"Tells you the kind of week he must have."

"Seriously," she says, seriously.

Later, walking across campus to my car, I bump into two more teachers and several parents, all of whom want to talk about the game. One woman, the vice president of the Parents' Association, says, "I can't believe you guys are playing *basketball.* I mean, aren't you a little old for that?"

"Probably," I say. "But we do have a doctor on call."

"I know. Phil. Just be careful of Stewart. We can't afford to have him get hurt."

"Don't worry. Usually I guard him."

She sniffs, turns away, not amused.

The school year ends. On its heels blows in a smoggy, hot, hostile summer. In the world outside the game, I wait, on edge, for the screenplay at Lucky Sperm to come through. I endure weeks of meetings being scheduled, shifted around, canceled, rescheduled, and canceled again, all the while being assured by Martin's vice president in charge of development (a twenty-three-year-old Wesleyan grad who answers Martin's phone and brings him coffee) that the only thing required to get the paperwork rolling and a paycheck in motion is a fifteen-minute meeting with Martin. Shouldn't even call it a meeting. More like a formality. The initial meeting, scheduled for early June, is put off until mid-July, then postponed until mid-August after Martin returns from his vacation on Martha's Vineyard, which confuses me since he lives right on the beach in Malibu.

Meanwhile, there are no nibbles on the house in Hancock Park. We bite the bullet and lower the asking price another hundred grand. Sheila calls after a Sunday open house with a spring in her voice I haven't heard in months. There are two very interested parties. Both are coming back for a second look. One is bringing her architect, the other, her mother. At last, two live ones.

Frequently that summer, on Sunday afternoons after the game, Phil, Gabe, Brick, and I continue the day at Mitch's house, where he and his wife, Gracie, host a pool party for their friends and work associates. Their house is a modest one-level California ranch tucked into a cul-de-sac on a street that lurches upward in a treacherous slant. Inside, the house seems oddly like an extension of Stewart's school: kids' art plastered on the walls, LEGO blocks scattered everywhere, colorful plastic furniture surrounding a worn leatherette couch and a wood-veneer coffee table. The kitchen, dining area, and living room are essentially one big room, flowing in an L to sliding-glass doors, which lead to a brick patio and swimming pool that take up the entire backyard.

The theme of the day is always Mexican. Mariachi music tinkles from overhead speakers both inside and out. Multicolored tortilla chips and guacamole dip heaped into clumsily crafted ceramic bowls are omnipresent. Mitch, a game-show host's grin etched on his face, floats from room to room, mixing pitchers of his trademark margaritas and filling any less-than-brimming glass that trespasses into his sight line. The margaritas are tasty and potent and, because Mitch is always pouring, impossible to count. By midafternoon, the mild shrieking of children from the pool is drowned out by the raucous laughter of the watchful but tipsy parents.

On a Sunday on which Phil, Gabe, and Brick are no-shows, I lift myself out of the pool after an hour of hobnobbing with a couple of parents I don't know, a social worker, I think, and a guy whose passions are backpacking and term life insurance. I wind my way past Bobbie and some other people on the patio and pad into Mitch's kitchen. I'm not sure what I want. My head's swimming from innumerable margaritas, and my waistline's surging from the freight car's worth of chips and guacamole I've inhaled all afternoon. Still, I'm tempted to peek into Mitch's fridge. Out of morbid curiosity, I guess. Maybe I just need a moment out of the sun, out of the pool, away from the party.

"Escaping?"

Gracie, Mitch's wife, scoots into the kitchen. She pauses in front of the stove to get her bearings, staggers a bit. She is, like the rest of us, borderline shit-faced. Gracie is maybe five feet tall and squat. Her hair is ink black and stands straight up, not quite spiked, but lacquered in a vague tribute to Annie Lennox. Her speech is educated, snobbish, with a lilt that suggests another place, Monaco maybe. Her brown eyes shimmer with intelligence and drink. She wears a towel with a palm-tree design wrapped around her bottom, and a loose-fitting halter top, a bathing-suit top, I assume, though in two months of Sundays I haven't seen her come close to the pool. Her skin is so white it's opaque. She smiles constantly.

"Hate those margaritas," Gracie says. "Red wine. That's my drink."

She unlatches a cabinet below the sink and pulls out a merlot from Chile. She splashes some into a plastic cup, then looks over her shoulder at me.

"Join me?"

"Why not? Thanks."

"I knew it. I could tell you were a red wine drinker." Her smile widens. She fumbles with another plastic cup on the counter, nearly drops it, laughs, and sloshes red wine into it all the way up to the lip.

"Whoa," I say.

"Bet I could drink you under the table."

"No doubt. I am a lightweight."

She whams her glass into mine. "Cheers."

"Yep. Cheers."

"So," Gracie says, "what kind of father are you?"

"Well," I say. "Huh."

I sip the wine, stalling. I want to tactfully change the subject, talk about school or the weather, but I hear myself say in a distant voice, "I think I'm a good father. I'm, you know, pretty hands-on."

"Hands-on," Gracie says. "Clarify."

"I do a lot of things with the kids. We go to the library every week—"

"The *library?*" She howls. A drop of red wine trickles out of the corner of her mouth and splats onto the counter.

"Yeah, the library."

"That, is, so, great." Gracie slides the back of her hand across her mouth, wiping away red wine and lipstick in one whoosh. "Hands-on, huh? Mitch is, how shall I say this? Hands-*off.* Yeah. I would say that Mitch is hands-off."

This I don't need. I crane my neck toward the pool area. Bobbie is sitting around a table with four other women. They are lost in laughter, an eye on the kids but oblivious to the rest of the party. *Rescue me,* a little voice in my head sings.

"Tell me more things you do. More hands-on things."

Gracie swivels slightly, then reaches behind her to steady herself against the cabinets.

"Well . . ." I'm searching here. Shit. I should never have gotten out of the pool. "I make lunches. Every morning."

"You do?"

I look at her. Her smile fades and her mouth twitches. I wonder if she's going to cry.

"It's no big deal. I slap peanut butter and jelly onto some bread. It's all my son will eat."

"You do that every morning?"

"Yeah," I say, wanting to diminish the importance of this. "Takes like five seconds."

"Maybe you could talk to Mitch. Maybe Mitch would make lunches. He's not very hands-on. Hands-*off,*" Gracie says again. "I have to beg him to do things with the kids. Beg him."

At that moment, Mitch walks in. Gracie chuckles, shakes her head.

"Hey, guys, what's going on?"

"Tell him," Gracie commands me. "Tell him what you told me."

Mitch, the smile still stitched on his face, looks at me expectantly. His glasses are smudged and dotted here and there with what looks like salt.

"Alan makes lunch for his son every morning," Gracie snarls.

"Well," I say quickly, "a peanut butter and jelly sandwich. That's all it is."

"You drive him to school, too?" Gracie asks.

"Yeah, usually, I—"

"I work in the Valley," Mitch says, his voice rising in defense. "It's the opposite direction." His smile remains in place like a plaster theater mask.

"You could make him lunch. Why don't we start there? How about you do that?" Gracie turns to me. She jabs a finger into the air. "See, here's the thing. Mitch doesn't do anything.

Nothing. Not a fucking thing. I'm with the kids, he's on the couch, doing what, I don't know. Watching TV. Reading a magazine. I really don't know. Might say it's an issue with us."

"That's not true, Gracie," Mitch says quietly, his smile cracking for the first time.

"It is true. It is so fucking true."

Man, I want out of here.

"Then, Mitch, why don't you do it? Huh? Why don't you start tomorrow? Make Matthew a peanut butter and jelly sandwich."

"He doesn't really like peanut butter, Gracie."

"Then make him a fucking cheese sandwich. Fuck if I care what you make him."

"I think maybe you've had a little too much to drink," Mitch says.

Gracie stares at him. She starts to speak, thinks better of it, clamps her mouth shut. She shakes her head sadly, then speaks through pursed lips.

"Jesus, I'm tired," she says.

She turns and walks out of the room, a slow, exaggerated walk, almost on tiptoe, as if she's afraid to wake someone.

Martin's office at Lucky Sperm Productions is decorated in a strange mix of Southwestern folk art and FAO Schwarz. The walls are painted in undulating, muted earth tones and are covered with frightening little bumps that you notice only if you mistakenly rub against them. Textured, I think they call it, but to me it looks like a rash. Stationed at five-foot intervals are full-grown, blooming cactus plants that rise and brush the sunset-colored ceiling. Martin's furniture is oversize, jagged, and rock hard. A pinball machine, a Ms. Pac-Man game, Skee-Ball, several life-size action figures in martial arts poses, and a bunch of stuffed animals from various animated movies are scattered around the office.

I squirm in one of the cold Flintstones chairs as Martin peers at my partner and me. Martin is moored behind his desk, a mammoth, sandstone slab the size of an aircraft carrier. Martin is my age but looks much younger. Some part of him is in constant motion, even when he sits. In this case, it's his right foot, which appears to be pedaling an imaginary bicycle.

"So the deal is, you guys want to write a movie and you need my say-so, right?" He suddenly leaps up and jogs around to the front of the desk.

"Right?" he asks again.

"Yes," I say, "we'd love to write a movie."

So far, I'm having a good week. It began with a two-day flurry of phone calls, followed by a frenzied trip to the real estate broker's office, where Bobbie and I scribble our names on the bottom line of several blank offer sheets.

And then it happens.

The house in Hancock Park sells.

The buyers are a Korean couple in their sixties who are purchasing the house for their single daughter. Their offer is $100,000 less than our asking price. We counter by meeting them halfway. They won't budge. I'm insulted. I'm not going to *give* the house away. We come down another $25,000. That's as far as I'm going to go. They counter by going up $5,000, their absolute final offer. If we take this, we'll be selling the house for about half of our original asking price. We grab it. I whisper a silent prayer of thanks, feeling the goddamn monkey climbing off my back.

So come on, Martin, let's keep the good news rolling.

He nods feverishly and sits down in one of his boulder chairs. Instantly, his left leg starts acting up, pumping up and down, out of whack, faster and faster.

"I just wanna be sure you guys can write a movie before I sign off on it," he says. "They tell me you can."

A loud *ping* pierces the room like a heart monitor dying.

"Sorry, guys, gotta take this."

Martin sprints behind his desk and jams the phone against his ear.

"Yeah? Oh, good. Put her through."

He looks up and winks.

"Heyyy. How ya doin'? . . . Listen, here's what I need to know. Who bought the house next door to me? The one to the— wait—*north*. Yeah, north. The big Spanish. . . . Well, find out. . . . I want to know, that's why. I want to know if it's someone I need to be friends with or someone I need to avoid. Find out today. I mean it, because if the person's a dick, I'll lease the place out and buy something else."

He rams the phone down, crawls into his chair, and gets into the lotus position. He rubs his eyes viciously. I wince.

"So, where were we?"

"The movie," I remind him.

"Oh yeah. What are you waiting for? You got the job."

Mitch and his family head to the East Coast for the month of August, discontinuing the pool parties for the rest of the summer. In August, just before Labor Day, we lose our first player.

Barry.

He shows up every Sunday but remains a spectator, watching the games intently without touching a basketball. He eats one bagel a week, dry, and speaks rarely.

"You ever gonna play?" Brick asks him each week.

"I don't know. I've been shooting hoops with my son after school. He's getting better but I'm not."

As if to earn his keep, his weekly bagel, Barry sits at the edge of his chair, poised, ready to scale the stucco wall and return any ball that bounces into Klein's yard. By now he has factored in the fifteen-foot drop and has discovered a light pole farther down Klein's paddle tennis court that allows him a better angle and surer footing while he shimmies back up.

One Sunday, settling into his chair, a dry rye bagel resting in his open palm, Barry announces that this will be his last game. He is departing in the morning for Alaska to begin shooting his ice-formation movie. After the final game of the day, Barry somberly shakes hands with each of us and thanks me for allowing him to sit and watch. I thank him for retrieving the ball.

"Oh, no biggie," Barry says. He smiles and waves his hand in front of his face as if he's brushing away a mosquito. He waits for the other guys to gather their stuff, then walks with them down the driveway in the middle of the pack, his head bobbing above them like a buoy.

Barry will remain in Alaska for several months, during which time his wife will remove their son from Stewart's school and herself from their marriage. I hear this from Bobbie, who hears it from Madeline, who hears it from Wanda, Barry's wife, a petite, energetic woman who offers no details.

"Did Barry say anything at the game?" Bobbie asks me.

"No. Barry didn't really open up."

"Well, it's no surprise. You could see it coming."

At first I'm amazed. *She saw it coming?* From where? The window? I saw nothing. I saw only an odd guy who sat motionless on my deck for months, pecking at a bagel like a bird. But if I conjure up Barry's face and imagine it in front of me as if it were a photograph, I am able to see that his eyes are condensed and pained. I understand only now that he had no real interest in learning basketball. The game was his refuge, an escape from his own bleak Sunday mornings.

I have had no contact with Barry since that Sunday, almost ten years ago. Barry's movie, a forty-minute celebration of ice, surprised us all by enjoying an extended run in IMAX theaters across the country. I never saw it, but those who did reported that Barry's camera work was superb, so effective, in fact, that at certain moments during the film you could feel an icy chill.

• • •

By September, I can count on eight regular players, all of whom appear in my driveway every Sunday without my having to call to confirm the week before. It seems a bit mysterious and magical to me, like a David Copperfield illusion. The guys just *show up*. They bring stuff, too: bagels, muffins, basketballs, a pump, cases of bottled water, a new push broom—and one morning Mitch presents me with my very own electric leaf blower.

One Sunday between games, as we lounge around, the nine of us, in deep, relaxed, manly silence, we share how important the game has become to us. We sit there, luxuriating in our silence, slicing our bagels. Yes. We've grown so comfortable with each other that we've begun using the knife.

The silence lingers and we soak it up like a good steam. Men like silence. We believe in it. We crave it. To us, silence is equal to *peace* and synonymous with *quiet*. Thus the common gender-specific phrase uttered by men in homes throughout the world, usually in the evening and on weekends: "Can I please get some peace and quiet, *please?*"

Men don't want to fill silences; we want to achieve them.

So we're sitting there, the nine of us, slicing our bagels, bathing in our silence, and Stewart, the school head, blurts out:

"I can't wait for Sunday."

We nod as one—a group nod—then we grunt and reach for the cream cheese.

One Sunday, the smell of hickory from a neighbor's evening barbecue still floating above my deck, we pause in the middle of a game as Duff takes his sweet time sending the ball back from Klein's yard. Duff is our new designated ball retriever, a position he's accepted with reluctance.

"Alan, you need to put up a net or something," he grumbles,

boosting himself to the top of the wall with none of Barry's flair.

He blows out a massive breath and eases himself into space like a sky diver. We hear a thump, then *"Shit"* as he apparently comes in for a rough landing somewhere in the vicinity of Klein's paddle tennis net. Then we hear a gasp. Most weekends the Kleins are away, holed up at one of their weekend hideaways, their villa in Napa or their apartment in New York. But this Sunday, the sound of champagne-aided laughter drifts toward us from beyond the stucco wall.

The Kleins are home! We hear Duff's voice, followed by a staccato communal guffaw like that on a sitcom laugh track. Then footsteps and the creaking of a screen door swinging open and clicking shut.

"I think he went *inside,*" Brick says incredulously, on his toes, peering over the wall. The rest of us run over to take a look.

"Here he comes," Phil says after a full minute. Duff waves and we all applaud.

The ball sails over and we instinctively pair off as we await Duff's return. I find myself standing next to Kyle, who shifts his weight nervously, then settles into a crouch. I shrug and scrunch down next to him, my bones snapping loud enough for Klein to hear.

"How's it going?" I ask him.

Kyle dips his head and squelches a laugh.

"Shitty," he whispers, his eyes glued on Stewart, who is planted beneath the hoop practicing layups. "It's going pretty damn shitty."

"Oh, well, I didn't—"

"Stewart's architect is one of the world's greatest living assholes."

I stand up, brush the gravel off my palms.

"Major asshole," Kyle sighs. "Can't work with him."

Kyle stands up, dusts the front of his T-shirt, and says again, as if I haven't heard, "Can't work with the fucking guy."

"Kyle—"

"Hey, man, I don't want to put you in the middle of this."

"Thanks."

"Truth is, we don't even need the architect. But Stewart thinks he's God. Does anything the guy says. It's brutal. The time I'm wasting? *Shitt.* One example. Fucker runs my ass all over the city buying some stupid, high-end piece of crap part that costs three times what it should because it has a European name. I can get the same part for a *third* of the price, but because the brand is obscure or generic, they don't want it. *Same fucking part.* Plus, my friend, we are having some payment issues—"

Now it's my turn to sigh. Loudly. I swivel my head toward the hoop, looking for an escape route.

"So that's how it's going." Kyle suddenly grins and breaks into his high-pitched, breathless laugh. "Aren't you, woo, glad you asked?"

"Yeah. And thanks for not putting me in the middle."

"Dangerous place, the middle. You get squashed."

"Alan, have you seen that house?" Duff. Arriving in the driveway, in the nick of time.

"No, Duff, I haven't."

"Well," Duff says, blowing into his palms, "you should."

"I haven't been invited."

Duff shakes his head, ignores me. "Wait till you see the art. Quite a bit of Far Eastern stuff. He must have a dozen statuettes from Tibet. Bronze and heavy. I know because Ed had me hold a couple of them. They're having a family brunch today. What a spread. Man."

"*Ed?*"

"Yeah. Or Eddie. He prefers Ed."

"What kind of spread? Bagels and lox?" Mitch asks.

"Oh, sure," Duff says. "And omelettes and salads and roast beef and turkey. They had a *huge* turkey, twenty-five-pounder at least."

"Do you have a point?" I ask.

"Are we playing anymore? Or is that it for today?" Kyle. Restless, shifting his feet side to side, eyes turned away from Stewart.

"Whose ball?" Phil asks.

Nobody remembers. I'm elected to shoot for it. I do and hit. Kyle passes the ball in to Brick. Using Brick's screen, I cut to the hoop, gather in Brick's snazzy no-look bounce pass, and blow the layup. Ivan rebounds, swings the ball to Gabe, who throws up a bank shot that's too high off the backboard. I pull down the rebound, one of my two for the morning. I snap a pass to Kyle, who drives the baseline and slings his body into Ivan. The ball bangs off the rim.

"Foul!" Kyle shouts.

"What?" Ivan screams. "You charged into *me!*"

Kyle shrugs. "Foul."

Ivan violently yanks at his maroon Viking beard as if he's try-ing to pull it off, then flips the ball to Kyle. Kyle dribbles left, crosses over to the right, then crosses left again. The ball bounces off his foot and skitters out of bounds.

"You dick!" Kyle yells at the ball.

"Was that off me, too?" Ivan holds his hands out for the ball. Kyle tucks the ball into his hip and glares at him. Ivan's not backing down. He steps into Kyle's face. Here we go again.

"Boys," Brick says, "just play."

Kyle waits a beat, hands Ivan the ball, and backs up to play defense. I drop the ball in to Brick, who flashes to his right and scores over Duff. Game, us. Back to the deck. Kyle walks past us, continues into the house to use the bathroom.

"I saw you talking to Kyle," Stewart murmurs.

"Yeah. We were talking."

"Were you talking about the remodel?"

"It came up."

"Want my side of the story?"

"Actually, I'd rather not—"

"Fine. I understand. I'll just say this. You can tell a lot about a man by the way he plays ball."

"Stewart, I really don't want to get in the middle—"

He picks up his chair and angles it toward me. His speech is hurried and hushed.

"Here's the bottom line. I hired a contractor who hates architects. Hates mine, anyway. Now I happen to like my architect. I've done three projects with him. I trust him. I've had three different contractors but only one architect. A good architect stays on top of things. He makes sure the contractor gives you what you designed. Because, let's face it, a lot of these guys are . . . well, you know what I mean."

"Flakes?"

"I was gonna say assholes, but *flakes* will do."

Kyle comes out of the house, sees me talking to Stewart, and puts his hands on his hips.

"What are you guys talking about?"

"You," I say.

"I bet you are," Kyle says. He scrambles down the stairs of the deck, picks up a ball, and starts shooting, eyeing me like a traitor.

"Last game of the day," Phil says. "Who's playing?"

"I'll play," Stewart says. He kicks his chair back and stretches by reaching both arms briefly over his head as if he's signaling for a touchdown.

"I'm in," Brick says."

"I've had enough," I say.

"I'll sit out," Mitch offers.

Stewart musses his hair, then makes teams of Brick, Phil, and Gabe against Stewart, Kyle, and Duff.

Phil shoots for outs. He squats, lurches forward, and lets fly.

Swish. Gabe jogs to a spot under the shade of the carob tree and takes the ball out. He fakes a pass to Phil, then looks for Brick, who bobs, spins, and darts toward the basket.

I don't see what happens next. It's the sound that jars me, a dull, sickening *thud* that stabs the air. It's a foreign sound, unlike any I've heard before. I squint toward the hoop and see Brick crumple to the concrete in what seems like slow motion. He gasps, then a violent squall of air explodes out of his lungs as if he'd been holding his breath underwater for an impossibly long time.

"Ohhh . . . *ughh,*" Brick moans as Gabe's pass sails over his head. The ball slams into the garage door with a *whap* and bounds away, leaving a dirty black smudge, one of a dozen black smudges that stain the door like Rorschachs.

I can't focus. From my chair on the deck twenty feet away, I manage to make out five blurry basketball players standing in a shimmering tableau around one fallen body, Brick, who's clumped into a question mark on the driveway, writhing as if he's been shot. He grips the base of the black pole that holds the basketball hoop with one hand and holds on to his right leg with the other. His body shakes uncontrollably. He is in shock. I am afraid he might start to convulse.

"My . . . knee," Brick says, his bottom lip trembling. He can barely get the two words out. He speaks flatly, without emotion, as he tries to hold back a whimper. The other players crowd around, unsure of where to look or what to do. Phil kneels over him, a hand on Brick's powerful shoulder.

"Did you feel anything snap? Hear a noise?"

"Yeah," Brick whispers. He is shaking more now. His knuckles turn white as he grips the pole tighter.

"Jesus," I hear someone say.

"Oh," Brick says, exhaling deeply, then merely, "umm."

I am off the deck, standing at Phil's side. My hand, too, goes to Brick's shoulder. He removes his right hand from his leg and squeezes the pole with both hands, one on top of the other. He closes his eyes.

"Oh man," he says.

He won't cry. He can't. To do so would cause him to lose face. He won't do that. He won't show weakness. To a man like Brick, enduring the injury is in itself a competition.

"Get him some ice," Phil says, but the words are at my back as I am already running into the house. I sprint into the kitchen and fling open the fridge as Bobbie, on the phone, watches me.

"What happened?" she says.

"Brick. I think he tore up his knee."

"Oh no. Call you back," she says into the phone, and immediately punches in some numbers. I yank open the freezer and start scooping handfuls of ice chips into a plastic bag.

"Who you calling?"

"Faye."

Brick's wife. I run out the door, jump off the deck, race onto the driveway, and hand the bag of ice to Phil. He lays it gently across Brick's knee.

"Keep it there for as long as you can," Phil says.

"*Shittt,*" Brick says, his mouth flat-lined in pain.

"I can't watch," Gabe says, and turns and walks away.

"You deliver babies," Duff says, tailing him.

"That's different," Gabe says. "Totally different."

"I didn't see what happened," Stewart says to no one in particular.

"It, just, went," Brick gasps.

"No contact?" Mitch asks.

Brick shakes his head, then lets out an earsplitting *"OWWWW!"*

"What do you think it is?" Stewart asks.

"His knee," I say.

A huge, unexpected laugh, breaking the tension.

"Asshole," Brick manages.

"Thank you. I'm here all week."

"I think it's his meniscus," Phil says.

"My what?" Brick says.

"Don't talk. It looks like you tore your meniscus cartilage. You're gonna have to see an orthopod, soon, like first thing in the morning. Figure out your options."

"Surgery," Brick grunts.

"That's one option," Phil says. "But you could get it scoped and be done in a day."

"No more of this," Brick says, slapping at the basketball that has rolled back against the garage door. "I'm done."

"You sucked anyway," I say. Brick laughs, which relieves us all.

"You get it scoped, you'll be back in three weeks," Phil says.

"I'm gonna try to get up," Brick says.

He releases the pole, places his palms on the driveway, and pushes himself to a sitting position. His eyes look glazed over. Brick glances at his right knee and his leg begins to vibrate. He bites his lip and tries to raise himself up. He moves a couple of inches and collapses back onto his butt.

"I can't," he says.

Within seconds, Kyle and Ivan are on either side of him, their arms lashed around Brick's shoulders and under his arms. They nod to each other and lift Brick up. Brick braces himself against them, applying only the slightest pressure onto his right foot.

"*Agghh!*" he screams. "Shit! Fuck!"

"Bring him to that chair," Phil says.

Kyle and Ivan guide Brick to a beach chair that someone has set up on the lawn. Brick carefully pivots on one foot, as if he's afraid of being called for traveling. Kyle and Ivan lower him into the chair. Brick lands with a thump and looks up at us, stunned.

"Jesus," he says. "Jesus."

"I think I have some crutches at my house," Duff says. "From last year, when I broke my ankle skiing."

"He's gonna need 'em," Phil says.

"I'll drive you home," Stewart offers.

"Don't go to any trouble. I can crawl," Brick says.

We laugh eagerly.

"What happened?" I ask.

"I really don't know," Brick says. "I cut to the basket and my knee just buckled. It just went."

"Keep the ice on it," Phil says. He picks up the bag of ice, which lies in a tiny puddle near the base of the pole. He places it back on Brick's knee.

"Whew," Brick says. He blows out a smoke ring of relief. His muscular body, quivering out of control moments ago, begins to steady itself. The rest of us, as if in a cartoon, share a collective sigh. Duff and Mitch step aside and Bobbie appears, phone in hand.

"What happened?" She locks eyes with Phil.

"Torn meniscus cartilage," he explains. "He'll be okay. He might have to have surgery. That's my guess, anyway."

Bobbie nods, then says softly to Brick, "Faye's on her way. She'll take you home."

"I think I have crutches he can borrow," Duff says.

"That's okay. We already got some from another friend of ours," Bobbie says.

"Boy," Duff says, laughing, "talk about *efficient*. Jeez."

"Well, I'm not gonna wait around for you guys to get it together," Bobbie says, whipping the cordless-phone antenna around like a sword, her green eyes flickering.

"Okay," I say, "Mitch, you wanna come in for Brick?"

Silence.

"I'm kidding," I say. "A little meniscus humor."

But nobody's laughing.

• • •

At twilight that Sunday in September, I lose myself in my driveway by shooting hoops. I dribble once, twice, bend over, get low, dribble, *whap whap whap,* lower still, *whap whap,* look up, exhale, and swish in a foul shot. The ball rolls back to me, I gather it in, breathe out, take another. Off left; hustle over, pick up the ball, start to shoot, and see Bobbie standing, hands on hips, head tilted, watching me from the deck.

"That was Faye," she says, meaning the phone. "Phil set Brick up with a surgeon he knows. He's going in first thing in the morning."

"He'll get it scoped, right? Isn't that what Phil said?"

"That's what Phil's hoping."

I blow out a thin stream of air. "Quite a weekend."

"Oh yeah. The fun never stops."

Bobbie leans over and drums her long fingers on the railing surrounding the deck.

And then silence. Not the good kind.

"Take a shot," I say.

She hesitates, but head still tilted, mouth moon-shaped, she walks barefoot off the deck toward me. Her foot lands on a fallen carob pod. She dances over it and arrives at the ball. Standing carefully at an angle to the right of the hoop, she places the ball close to her shoulder and, not unlike Phil in his signature squat, heaves her shot up, off the backboard, and in.

"Yesss," she shouts, a fist in the air.

"Nice shot," I say, and set up for a jumper.

"Hey. Change."

I stare at her. *"Change?* Where did you get that?"

"I hear you guys. Come on. Some change."

I grin, bounce the ball over to her. She collects it in, moves to the other side of the hoop, same angle, and banks one in from there, too.

"Oh *yeah.*"

"Change?"

"Come on, pal, I'm on fire, don't ice me."

I toss her the ball, and for the next full minute my wife stands in her spot and banks in shot after shot, a succession of four-foot layups, ten, fifteen, in a row.

"Not bad, huh?"

"Imagine what you'd do with shoes," I say.

A step back, another shot, and "Ooh," as the ball shanks off the rim, a miss, surprising us both.

It's gotten dark suddenly, and with the night comes the heaviness I've felt all weekend but have so far refused to speak of aloud. Neither of us has dealt with it, really. When we got the word, we both ducked for cover, dodged the inevitable by embracing convenient distractions such as hanging out with the kids, work, the Sunday basketball game. Maybe under cover of the night, I will be able to broach the subject.

"Getting dark," I say.

"I can still see," Bobbie says. Her feet slapping on the cool concrete, she heaves a short jump shot accompanied by a small, sexy grunt. She watches curiously as the ball swirls around the rim a half dozen times, then plops into the net.

"I think I want to go in," I say.

"Couple more, then we will."

Even in shadows I can see that Bobbie's face is flushed with joy and accomplishment, her eyes wide soft green circles. Bobbie gets this way when she's clicking on all cylinders. Which is most of the time. She knows only one speed: breakneck.

"So?" I say quietly. "Now what?"

Bobbie shoots, bank . . . *good.* She allows the ball to curl through the net and roll onto the driveway, all the way to the carob tree.

"Well," she says.

"Yeah." I slide into my clunky way of bringing up the subject, which is, "Nice kick in the ass, huh?"

But she's already there, on topic. One of the many reasons I love her.

"We have to *strongly* consider changing real estate agents," she says.

"I know."

"These things are always awkward *but.*"

I blink at the sky, grateful for the dark. I clumsily lay an arm across my wife's shoulder and pull her gently to me. She rests her head against my chest, her hair lightly brushing my cheek. She smells of herbal shampoo tinged with sweat.

We have nothing to say. Not since noon yesterday when we learned that the sale of the house has fallen through. The Korean couple has been denied a loan by an obscure bank. Something to do with their daughter's credit rating, not theirs, but when we suggested trying a different bank or a mortgage broker, they refused.

"They're ashamed," our real estate agent explained. "Their agent says they've lost face."

"But they can try again—"

"They won't. It's dead." Then with a voice not even attempting to hide her annoyance and defeat: "I don't know what to do. We're running out of options. Maybe lower the price again, have another open house. I'm open to suggestions."

"Right now, though, we just have to hang in there," Bobbie says to me, Sunday in the dark.

"All we can do," I say. A hollow voice in the night. Canned, prefab words instead of tears.

Bobbie leans up and kisses me on the cheek.

Holding hands, we walk slowly into our house.

3.

trap

I'm soaring.

My elbow brushes the net, juts past the rim, on the way up as I guard MJ, sewn to him like his shadow. He's quick for his size and slick. But I'm quicker and trickier.

He's lost me, so he thinks. His head whipsaws back and forth looking for me. Can't find me. He focuses then on the hoop and picks up his dribble. He can try the jumper now, bank it off the left side. Plenty of room. And I'm gone. Nowhere to be seen. Vanished. MJ can relax, set up, take his time. He pumps. Spots up. He's confident. No. Make that *arrogant*. He lets it fly.

And there I am.

A missile. Out of the sky. Neon Ben & Jerry blaring off my T-shirt. Goggled like Horace Grant. Airborne. Feels like I jumped off a trampoline. Fingers splayed, my left hand reaches up . . . *up* . . . *UP.* I graze him, but MJ doesn't complain. He's too stunned to call a foul. Ticky-tack anyway.

Then I whistle my palm forward as if I were throwing a fastball and *SWATTTT!* The ball flies out of MJ's hand and plops right into my teammate's astonished arms. He knocks down the layup as I return to earth. The smallest second of stunned silence. Then a roar, and a laugh somewhere, probably from Brick on the deck cradling crutches across his lap, and someone shouts, "He's a goddamn jumping bean!"

I hit the ground in a slow-motion crouch, superhero style, both feet crunching the concrete. MJ's back is to me. He can't face me.

"Who's your *daddy?*" I want to shout, but I restrain myself.

This is the tape that runs in my head now, into which I drift at various times during the day: in the car driving on errands, in the office when I should be working, in bed late at night when I should be sleeping. Watching my own inner highlight reel has replaced sketching celebrity faces in the ceiling. Sure, some weeks I have to reach to find a highlight. Not this week. This week is worthy of the archives. Wide-eyed, triumphant, I relive in instant replay and stop action, with expert analysis by me, the one and only blocked shot of my life.

It happened on a surprisingly humid late-October Sunday. And of course, MJ is not Michael Jordan, superhuman NBA great. He is Michael Jessup, thirty-year-old junior movie agent. This MJ is a bear of a man, a lumbering, gentle giant who wears tortoiseshell glasses, a baseball cap flipped backward, and a hesitant half-smile.

Throughout the Sundays of the game, several guys, among them MJ, will float into the game, play for a time, then move on.

Ivan, the hulky, savage, flame-bearded writer of action shit, is one. Out of the blue, Ivan gets a deal to write and direct a movie for a Christian organization. Ultimately, his film, a well-told, heartfelt drama threaded with the requisite amount of morality, attracts the attention of Robert Redford. The film opens the Sundance Film Festival, receives a prestigious audience award, and is purchased by a well-known production company for the largest fee ever paid for a movie at the festival. Ivan rockets from obscurity in my driveway to a two-picture writing and directing deal with Redford. His head spun around by his storybook success, Ivan quits the game and shaves his beard. In that order.

Others who play for a time, then leave, are:

Vora, an athletic and polite twenty-two-year-old from India who lives in an apartment next to Stewart's school. Vora shows up for eight weeks in a row, dominates, then disappears, looking for, I assume, younger and faster competition.

Henry, an estate planner, and the tallest player in the history of the game, plays for a few months before injuring himself in a collision with Duff. Henry displays flashes of brilliance, but for the most part remains an indifferent player. He seems distracted. I bump into Henry a couple of weeks later. He tells me he has experienced a "financial reversal" and has had to sell his house, a massive Tudor just three streets away from me.

Buddy, a stand-up comedian from Boston, joins the game when my daughter and his daughter strike up a conversation near the self-service frozen-yogurt machine at the Souplantation, a family-friendly buffet restaurant. Buddy is funny and full of energy. As a basketball player, he is a wonder. A man of physical prowess and an array of dazzling moves, he has no ability whatsoever to make a basket, not even a layup.

"I can't fucking shoot," he says, his voice packed with misery.

"I wonder why that is," I say.

"Because I fucking *stink,*" he says.

Buddy stops coming when he injures himself in a collision with Duff.

Finally, there is Monk, who plays once, arriving one Sunday slouching under dark sunglasses and a stocking cap yanked down to his eyebrows. He clutches a brown paper grocery bag.

"Hey, guys," Monk says. "Do me a favor. Don't tell my wife I was here, okay?"

No one questions Monk as Stewart inserts him into the first game. Monk is skilled and hard-nosed, bordering on reckless.

He dives for every loose ball, powers through defenders to the hoop, and rattles in a blizzard of line-drive jumpers. His team wins easily.

"Good game, Monk, good game," we say, impressed. Monk is a keeper.

Monk waves in response, suddenly unable to speak. He slumps over to a lounge chair, plops down, then tumbles over the back, breathing in a frightening, raspy, hip-hop rhythm.

"You okay?" Phil is there, kneeling at his side.

"Need . . . my . . . bag," Monk gasps.

I race to the deck, return with Monk's grocery bag. He stuffs his hand in, removes a worn, lime green, plastic cone resembling a miniature tuba, and slams it up to his mouth. In a few moments his shoulders sag in relief and, dreamy-eyed, his breathing circling normal, he drops the inhaler back inside the bag.

"I really shouldn't be playing," he says.

"Maybe you better call it a day," Phil says.

"Yeah." Then, looking longingly toward the hoop, Monk says, "I'll just play one more."

"You do and I'll tell your wife," Phil says.

Then there are those who stay:

Ben, a doctor, head of infectious diseases at Children's Hospital. Ben is married to our kids' pediatrician, Nikki, Bobbie's regular walking partner and our good friend. Ben is brilliant, funny, high energy, a marathon runner, and Steve Martin's clone. He's known for a deadly hook shot from deep in the corner and for bringing a terrific assortment of muffins. Some Sundays, Ben comes to the game *after* he's jogged ten miles. On those days he will eat two giant blueberry muffins and still run your ass into the ground. Humbling.

The others are dads at Stewart's school:

Jack. Lawyer #1. Environment. Father of my son's best friend, Jack is a skilled player with a boxer's build and a deadly outside shot. A presence on the court. Jack is well-read, loves old movies, American history, especially Civil War battles, and is always tuned to the History Channel. Off the court, he is shy and tentative, a low talker, bringing new meaning to the term *soft-spoken*. Jack is among the nicest guys in America.

Wally. Lawyer #2. Entertainment. A wide body with a handsome baby face. Wally is like family, kind of a cousin. Wally can take you inside, hit the occasional jumper, set a bone-jarring pick. He tries to be a fashion plate—baggy shorts, backward baseball cap—but fails. Doesn't have the body for it. Too round and too white. No matter what, Wally arrives an hour late for the game, always with a different excuse: "I ran out of gas on Pacific Coast Highway"; "I set my clock an hour *ahead* instead of an hour back"; "The neighbor's dog ate my shoelaces." By the third month of excuses, no one's listening and no one cares. It's Wally. He's late.

Big Sam. Lawyer #3. Criminals. Big Sam has defended some of the worst people on the planet and gotten them off. Hideous scumbags and killers you've read about. "Jesus," you wonder, "who would ever stoop to defend this piece of shit?" Big Sam, that's who. Passionate about every person's right to a fair trial and dogged about winning in court, he's considering a return to the public defender's office, where he started. A very tough player. Played linebacker in college. Plays hockey *now*. Big Sam has a barrel chest, a barrel belly, thinning strands of gray hair that brush his forehead like a tiny field of wheat, a gentle, boyish face, and a booming voice. *Love* Big Sam.

Danny. Lawyer #4. Real estate. The White Shadow. Danny's by far the best player in the game. He's rail-thin and taut as a rope, with zero percent body fat. He's got droopy eyes, a high forehead, and a beak of a nose, but you mix all these features up and somehow Danny is a handsome man. He has a weird laugh; he throws his head back and roars silently. You always want to be on Danny's team because he's so good, he makes you better. Danny hates to lose. He'll crush a plastic water bottle or shove a chair in disgust when his team does lose, which is next to never. Danny has it all going on. He's smart, funny, and often brings me great surprise gifts like old Johnny Hartman CDs and all of the *Ultimate Fighting* videos, uncut. Such an amazing guy, but I know he has a dark side. I'm determined to find it.

"I heard this report on the radio," I say to him one Sunday. Danny, Phil, and I, having just vanquished our opponents, wait for next on the deck. "One out of every three men likes to dress up in women's clothing. Now, I don't do it."

"I gave that up in med school," says Phil.

"So, Danny, I guess that leaves you."

Head thrown way *way* back in a long silent laugh.

On any given Sunday, there can be as many as thirteen of us, including Brick, who now plays wearing an intimidating black metal knee apparatus right out of *RoboCop*.

"Did you watch the operation?" Phil asks. "You can see the whole thing right there on the monitor."

"I know that," Brick snorts. "No. I did not watch."

"It's fascinating," Phil says.

"I actually closed my eyes. I'm a tad squeamish."

"Me too," says Gabe.

"Are you sure you went to medical school?" I ask him.

"I'd watch," Big Sam says, his voice thundering through the neighborhood. "I'd be curious."

"Was it bloody?" Duff asks, his face scrunched up tight like a fist. Guy reminds me of Yoda, only taller. Similar skin color, too.

"I don't know if it was bloody. I didn't *watch*," Brick says, squirming in his chair.

"It's not that bloody," Phil says. "See, what they do is—"

"Can we *not*?" Brick pleads.

"What's the matter with you? I thought you were Mr. Macho," Big Sam bellows.

"I don't want to relive my knee operation. Once was enough."

"Let's change the subject," Ben says.

"Please," Gabe says.

"Hey, guys," Big Sam roars. "Remember the time Jack had that loose piece of bloody skin hanging off his nose and Phil just ripped it off? That was great. He grabs the dead skin like this and yanks it right off. *Rrrrppp.* Man, that was funny."

"Uhhhhh," moans Brick.

"Alan, quick, think of something else to talk about before Brick passes out," Danny says. He begins dribbling a basketball through his legs unconsciously, *rap rap rap,* waiting for me to bail out Brick, grinning, *rap rap.*

"Nothing medical," Brick says. "No hospitals, operations, doctors—"

"Popular culture? How's that?" I say.

"Wonderful," Brick says. "Fabulous."

"Okay. Movies." I pause, wait for the subject to sink in. "Brick, in your opinion, who is the better actor, Jim Brown or Freddie 'the Hammer' Williamson? Take a moment."

Brick nods gravely. "A very difficult question."

The guys hum in agreement. Thoughtfully, Brick tears off a piece of onion bagel. He massages it with the tips of his fingers as he contemplates his response.

"I'd have to say Jim Brown."

"Interesting. And why is that?" I ask.

"Because of *The Dirty Dozen.* The Hammer has only done genre films. Until he appears in something more meaningful, I'd have to go with Jim Brown."

"Dirty Dozen also featured a fine performance by Trini Lopez," Mitch reminds us.

Brick glares at him. "Where do you get Trini Lopez? He's not an athlete. He's a *singer.*"

"I stand corrected," Mitch says.

"All right," Danny says, dribbling crossovers now, right to left, left to right, ball a blur, eyes on me, on Brick, never on the ball. "Who's the better actor, Kareem Abdul-Jabbar or O. J. Simpson?"

"That's an unfair comparison," Brick says. "Kareem has no body of work."

"Even so, O.J. is so *bad,*" Gabe sniffs.

"So who is the best actor, overall?" Duff asks.

"That's easy," Ben says. "Alex Karras."

"No one comes close," Jack whispers.

"Mongo," Mitch says, referring to the character Karras played in *Blazing Saddles.*

"He's in a class by himself," Danny says.

"Should've won the Academy Award," Big Sam rumbles.

"Mongo," Mitch says again.

We chew in reverence.

One evening in November, nine dads—Brick, Phil, Mitch, Gabe, Danny, Jack, Wally, Big Sam, and I—converge at Stewart's school for Back to School Night, when we parents view samples of our kids' work and listen to Stewart's teachers wax poetic about their curricula.

Moving through the campus with Bobbie, I intermittently pass the guys from the game. I feel a different energy among us now, something more familiar and personal. After all, I have smelled their sweat, heard them swear, learned the noises they emit during moments of exertion, shared their laughter, watched them bleed. It feels strange to encounter them this evening, in this setting. I'm used to seeing them Sunday mornings in shorts and sweaty T-shirts. Tonight they've come from work, attired in jackets and ties or pressed pants and dress shirts. They seem stiff and formal, as if they're in costume.

I also get the feeling we're being watched. There are eyes on us, the eyes of our wives, of other dads not invited to play, of their wives, and of the teachers who've heard about the game from Stewart. They are the people on the outside looking in, at us, at me, the man who hosts Stewart's now famous Sunday basketball game. This is Stewart's Night at Stewart's School and we are, the nine of us, Stewart's Men. It's a little heady, but mostly uncomfortable. And although nothing is expressed aloud, I feel a deeper connection with Stewart, as though I myself am back in school and part of the popular crowd, the ruling class. Odd since I never really ran with that crowd and my gut tells me that neither did Stewart.

As parents flip through their children's poetry and artwork, confer with teachers, or corner Stewart, their expressions vary from quiet satisfaction to pop-eyed gapes of panic. Stewart is a master of calm, an effusive host, a convincing salesman. In this progressive school, 10 percent of the parents moan incessantly that their little Johnny or Janie is in fifth grade and can't read, while 10 percent gush like Kool-Aid–guzzling cultists. Can't do much about the former, don't have to worry about the latter. The parents in the middle 80 percent are the concern, the ones who demand the most attention and reassurance. Progressive education requires some hand-holding and, in Stewart's words, "a leap of faith." Academically, your kids will get there, he promises, but they will get there at their own pace, happy, loving to learn, and oozing self-esteem.

At the far end of the playground, Bobbie sits at a picnic table in conversation with Challah Head and two moms I don't know. Stewart, head wagging, a half-grin curling beneath his sawed-off mustache, shuffles over to me, hands thrust deeply into his pants pockets. The night has turned cool and he exhales a slow, frosty breath.

"So," he says, "we have to talk."

"Okay."

"We have a situation."

We are standing in an open blacktop area illuminated by the

overflow of a nearby flickering streetlamp. Behind us, a flimsy, eight-foot, portable basketball hoop casts a creepy moonlight shadow like a pall over us.

"What's the problem?" I ask Stewart.

Stewart's half-grin expands to full length. Even in the dark I know it's a nervous smile.

"Kyle is taking me to arbitration," he says.

"Shit."

"Yeah. It has really turned to shit."

"What happened?"

"Call it a difference of philosophies. Or a difference of working styles. Or a personality clash. I don't know. Maybe all these things. The bottom line is my architect and I approached the job one way and Kyle approached it another. Let me give you a few examples . . ."

Stewart's rolling now, ticking off a checklist of Kyle's inadequacies as a contractor and a human being, speaking in a low, insistent, steady drone. He never raises his voice, but he might as well be screaming. Finally, Stewart stops, mainly, I think, to catch his breath.

"When's the arbitration?" I ask.

"The date's not set yet."

"What a nightmare."

Stewart removes a hand from his pocket, plops it onto his head, and musses his hair. "I'm not sure what to do. That's why I wanted to talk to you."

"Well," I say, "the arbitration—"

"I'm talking about the game," Stewart says.

"The game?"

"I don't know how I can play with Kyle anymore."

"Oh," I mumble.

A hand to Stewart's head. Muss, massage, muss. "I look forward to playing so much. The game is, well, it's really my whole social life. I work so many hours, so many nights, and as head of an elementary school, frankly, I don't have a lot of male friends. A couple of guys on the board of directors, that's it. My friends are the guys in the *game* . . . plus it's about the only exercise I get."

Stewart jams his hand back into his pocket, rocks on his heels, then says, "Have you noticed when I make teams, I don't put him with me anymore?"

"Now that you mention it—"

"Never put him on my team. *Never.* For a couple of weeks I could deal with him on the other team, but no more. It's become impossible."

"I guess I can understand—"

"I can't be on the same court with him. And it doesn't matter how the arbitration comes out either. That won't help. Win, lose, it won't matter. The two of us, oil and water . . ."

His voice trails off. I am not only in the middle; I am in the middle and about to be crushed.

"You're saying you don't want Kyle to come anymore."

"No," Stewart says. "Oh, no. I'm not saying that. I'm saying *I* can't play with him." His voice cracks. "You said you understood—"

"I do understand, but—"

"I'll stop coming. That'll solve it. That will make things easier. I'm serious. If you want, I'll stop coming."

"You're asking me to choose between you and Kyle."

A beat. "Well, yes, I guess. If you put it like that, I guess I am. I don't know what else to do. I feel horrible . . ."

He's waiting. He wants me to choose now. Tonight. Back to School Night. His playground, my pick.

In the next instant, I am gone, plucked from this spot into the front row of my own private screening room where I am watching this scene, watching Stewart and myself, standing across from each other.

The camera zooms in. Our faces on the screen explode into

extreme close-up, dusted by the moonlight, the rest of us swallowed into the blacktop. I stare at my own magnified face, shriveled in incomprehension. Stewart's small, brown, unblinking pebble eyes bore into mine, waiting.

My head tilts as I consider this man. I don't really know him. Yet, every day, without a second thought, I give my son over to him. For the bulk of his waking hours, Stewart's school is my little boy's universe. This man standing before me, this man who has just ambushed me on his playground, profoundly affects my son's emotional, intellectual, and moral development. He will have an everlasting impact on how my son will see the world. I don't just rely on Stewart; I trust him with my son's life.

Suddenly I wonder, if I choose Kyle, will Stewart take it out on my son?

I do know this. If I choose Kyle, only Phil, Brick, and Gabe, my closest friends, and Duff and Ben, who are unaffiliated with Stewart's school, are certain to stay in the game. The rest of the dads will leave with Stewart. No way they'll take the chance of alienating the director of their kids' school. The game's not *that* important.

Did Stewart plan it this way? Is he that calculating? Did he at least know that, by asking me to choose, he's offering me no choice at all? This was a done deal from the beginning. It was, as my mouth curls into a crooked ironic smile, academic.

The screening room dissolves and I slip back into my skin. My journey, departure and return, has happened in the blink of an eye, but it feels as if I have been gone for the weekend. I am exhausted.

Here, now, in the present tense, I look into Stewart's eyes. He gazes back at me with kindness, sympathy, and concern. I am relieved. My son was never part of this. Stewart would never use my son or any child as a bargaining chip. I have to believe that.

Somehow I feel that Stewart has been with me on my journey all along, riding shotgun, manipulating me where he wants me to go. I swallow hard, trying to conjure up some deeper force within me, groping for an inner guide to help me find the strength to do what's right. I flinch because I know that doing what's right and doing what I have to do to keep the game intact are not the same thing.

"I'll tell Kyle not to come," I say.

"You sure?" Stewart asks, threading his pinkie through a path in the center of his mustache. "Because, honestly, I'll stop coming."

"No. I'll ask him to leave."

"I don't know what to say. Thank you. I really appreciate . . ."

Stewart steps forward and hugs me.

"I'm so sorry," he says.

After a beat, he steps out of the embrace but leaves his hands resting on my shoulders.

"This means a lot," Stewart says.

"Give me a week or so."

"Oh, no, of course, it doesn't have to be this Sunday."

"Okay."

"It'll be a better game without him," Stewart says.

Someone calls his name.

"Alan, excuse me." He moves away from me and joins a short, well-dressed man with a goatee. They stop at what looks like a center jump circle crudely drawn in chalk. The man says something and Stewart laughs.

I stand off to the side feeling as if I've been punched in the stomach.

On Saturday, after a month of guilt and procrastination, we fire Sheila, our real estate agent, and hire Kay, a Mary Poppins clone who comes complete with British accent and a flowery, shlumpy dress. Kay specializes in Hancock Park, has lived there her whole life, and despite her appearance is reputedly a hard-ass.

"We have to sell this house," I tell her.

"Oh, we *willll,*" Kay sings. "I promise we *willl.* Before the New Year, too."

She pronounces *year* "yare."

"Great."

"The first thing we have to do, of course, is lower the price."

"By about how much?"

"A hundred thousand dollars," she chirps.

"Why the fuck not?" I sing back.

Yeah, sure, why the fuck not?

Typical Saturday night. A video with the kids. Take-out Chinese. A crisp sauvignon blanc. Kids asleep by nine-thirty. Bobbie and I in bed by ten. She, flipping channels with the remote. Me, a zombie, contemplating the ceiling. My breathing, meantime, has fallen into an alarming rhythm. My heart thumps, *pa-pa-pa,* revved up like an outboard motor, then abruptly recedes to just above the rate of a cadaver. I rest my hand on my chest as if I'm saluting the flag.

"I can't believe Stewart put you in this position," Bobbie says. "He and Kyle should work it out themselves."

"Kyle's taking him to arbitration. They're barely speaking. How are they supposed to work it out?"

"Then you should all talk it out together."

I stare at her.

"What?" she says.

"We're not like you. We're not *women.*"

"So you have to do Stewart's dirty work? You have to be the bad guy?"

"Yes."

"That makes *no* sense."

"It's the way it is."

"But it's everyone's problem," she says. "Can't you see that?"

"No. A crappy thing happened between two guys at the game. Both guys still want to play. But they can't anymore. And because the game is played at my house, because it's my game, I have to clean up the mess. I don't like it. In fact, I hate it. But what else can I do?"

Bobbie takes this in, accepts it reluctantly. "How are you going to tell him?"

"I thought I'd ask him to come by Monday morning for coffee."

"You want me to be here?"

"If you want."

Ka-thump. My heart thrums, turbos into passing gear. Electrified, my fingers hop off my chest.

"Actually," I say, "it'd be great if you were here."

"Then I'll be here."

"Thanks."

Bobbie touches the sleeve of my T-shirt. "You're not alone in this, you know?"

"I know."

Then I blurt out, "Shit," and whack my pillow.

"There is no good way," Bobbie says.

I'm finally asleep.

It took sketching two famous faces in the ceiling plus the repeated visualization of me knifing down the lane and hitting a reverse layup over Duff to get me down for the count sometime after midnight.

Then the phone rings. I jerk straight up into a sitting position. I gaze drunkenly at the blurry, jangling phone for a good ten seconds before I reach over and press the receiver to my ear. For a moment, I think I'm in a dream.

"Hello?"

"Alan?"

"Yes?"

"This is Simone? I live next door to your house in Hancock Park?"

"Oh. Simone. Hi."

"I'm calling because your sprinklers came on this morning at eight o'clock?"

"Yeah?"

"Well, they're still on? I think maybe a pipe burst."

"What time is it, Simone?"

"Two-thirty A.M. My backyard is like totally flooded? It's a *swamp.*"

"Oh great."

"I tried to turn them off myself? But I couldn't. You probably have to do something from inside the house. I don't know. But I think you really better come over and turn off those sprinklers? You know, before the water starts coming into my house?"

"Shit."

"I'm sorry to call you so late."

"No problem. I only get two hours of sleep anyway so I was pretty much finished for the night."

I hang up the phone, page my plumber, wake him, and somehow convince him to meet me at the house in an hour.

God knows how much this is gonna cost.

Monday morning I brew a pot of coffee and put out a spread of bagels and cream cheese, muffins, jellies, fresh orange juice, and fresh fruit. Sunday night I'd made the call to Kyle.

"Tomorrow morning is great. I have to be in Santa Monica anyway to drop off a bid. Need another gig after finishing up your *buddy's* house. What's this about?"

"I just need to talk to you."

"Very mysterious."

In the background, something clanks and a child wails.

"Wonderful. My kid just dumped brown shit all over the carpet. *Ericcc.* I gotta go. See you tomorrow."

• • •

Kyle is a half hour late. Calmly, quietly, but undeniably *present,* Bobbie sips a cup of coffee and sifts through the morning paper. Impatient, nervous, I retreat into silent, inconsequential puttering—rearranging the bagels and the fruit, sweeping the kitchen floor, sorting the recycling, changing the trash compactor bag.

Finally, the doorbell rings. Bobbie attempts a reassuring smile. I begin the slow walk to the front door. Just as my hand settles on the door handle, the doorbell rings again, rattling me. I pull open the door. Kyle, looking flushed and in a hurry, leans a heavy forearm against the doorframe.

"Hey."

"Hey, Kyle. Come on in. I made some coffee. Got some breakfast."

"Thanks, I ate. I can't stay anyway. I have to get back home. Hey, Bobbie."

She has slipped next to me, undetected. "Hi, Kyle."

"Traffic was a mess this morning. Took me an hour to get over here. Pain in the ass."

"You had to be on this side of town anyway, right?"

"Actually not. Right after I spoke to you I got the call. The kiss-off. They went with someone else."

"I'm sorry . . ."

"They, woo, probably talked to Stewart. Or, woo, you."

He laughs. Bobbie gently presses her palm into the center of my back.

"You know I'm taking him to arbitration?"

"I heard."

"He won't pay me. Guy owes me a shitload of money, too. I did the job. Did everything he and his crazy architect wanted and then some. And now he's stiffing me? Have you seen his house?"

"No."

"It's a showplace. Well, you know the work I do. I don't have to tell you. And he's withholding my *check?* What a horror show this turned out to be."

Kyle kicks a stone off my driveway with a battered leather workboot. He raises his eyes, catches mine. "Uh-oh. What's up?"

It just trips out: "Kyle, I have to ask you not to come anymore."

"What? To the *game?*"

I nod. "Yeah."

"You're kidding me, right?"

"Stewart can't play with you."

"He told you to kick me out of the game?"

"No. He told me to make a choice."

"He told you to . . ." Kyle blinks as if he's got something in his eye. "I don't believe it. You're choosing him over me?"

"What else can I do? My son goes to his school. I'm always there, reading, helping out, I see Stewart every day—"

"You're actually doing this. You're kicking me out of the game."

"Alan's in this awful position, Kyle," Bobbie says.

"Do you two know how fucked this is?"

"I do know. I really do. I don't know what to say. I feel terrible. Believe me. You have no idea how bad I feel. But Bobbie's right. I'm in this position—"

"*You're* in this position? Okay, fine. Don't even . . . just . . . Fuck you. Okay? Fuck both of you."

He pounds his fist against our doorframe, then charges down the driveway. I stand in the open doorway. My legs suddenly feel distant and wobbly. I lean against the inside wall of my house, afraid that I will fall. What I just said to Kyle, what I just did, seems like a scene from someone else's life. I swallow and a grim, sour taste rises into my mouth.

Bobbie's palm returns to my back. She lightly circles my shirt.

"I don't feel so great," I say.

In my imagination or twenty yards away, I can't tell which, Kyle climbs into his shiny silver pickup and slams the door. He

flicks on the ignition and the engine grinds once and fires.
Then he floors it. His tires scream down my street.

I close the door, wander out to the deck, and begin clearing
away the food.

"I heard," Phil says on the phone.

"Who told you?"

"Kyle. He left me a message while I was dropping the kids at
school. He had lovely things to say about you."

"I bet."

"This sucks," Phil says. "I really liked his beer."

I grunt.

"That was a joke."

"I know. It was very funny. I'm laughing inside."

"I never had a problem with him during construction, did
you?"

"Phil, I invited him to play basketball with us."

"Amazing how it all turned to crap. And now they're going
into arbitration. I will say, I couldn't see them playing together
much longer. They're not even talking."

"Slow as I am, I just started noticing that," I say.

"Me, too. Gabe says they haven't been speaking for weeks."

"He caught that?"

"Gabe notices everything."

"He never said anything."

"Would it have mattered if he did?"

"No, I guess not." I sigh into the phone. "I've had better
mornings."

"Your *bris* was a better morning."

"Hey, Phil."

"Yeah?"

"What would you have done?"

He doesn't hesitate.

"The same thing," he says.

Then he takes a beat.

"Yeah," he confirms. "I would've done the same thing."

On Sunday, nobody mentions Kyle. No one points out that he's absent and nobody asks where he is. It's not as if he's vanished; it's as if he never existed at all.

Sitting out with Brick, I pull at a bagel, pop tiny pieces into my mouth.

"Done for the day," Brick announces. He bends over and begins unclasping his knee brace. "That must've been tough," he says, not looking up.

It takes me a moment to register that he's talking about Kyle.

"Oh. Yeah."

"You had no choice."

"Well, I felt kind of squeezed."

"He was out of control."

I shrug.

"Gotta piss."

Brick heads into the house.

And that is all anyone says about Kyle's short-lived career in the game.

Fifteen words.

I'm not sure what I want, but I know I want more. More discussion, more connection, more sympathy, more agreement that I did the right thing, more remorse from Stewart. Just . . . more.

I feel my feminine side fighting through. I want to gather the guys around the table and say, *As you know, I have asked Kyle to no longer play in our game. It was a difficult decision and a horrible conversation. I think it's important to talk about this. Let's go around the table and, one by one, share a fond memory of Kyle. And, Phil, it has to be about something other than his beer.*

I know. Never gonna happen. I don't *want* it to happen. But fifteen words beginning with "That must've been tough" and ending with "Gotta piss"?

Something wrong there.

My dear friend David, author of nearly thirty books, many of them acclaimed as-told-to autobiographies, is looking to build a gym in his backyard. No freestanding structure is in place, so he will need an entire building constructed from scratch. His previous contractor, a wild-haired, fast-talking, coke-sniffing David Crosby look-alike, has fled to Las Vegas to become a blackjack dealer. David wants to know if I'd recommend Kyle for the job.

"Absolutely," I say. "He's a good guy and he does good work. He finished on time and on budget."

"I'm waiting for the *but.*"

"You're right. There's a but."

I tell him about Stewart and the arbitration and how I asked Kyle to leave the game. When I finish, David says, "Sounds like a personality thing."

"I honestly think it was."

"I want to meet him," David says.

I camouflage my sigh of relief in a cough.

Every morning at the crack of ten-thirty, my writing partner scales the stairs to my office, balancing his briefcase with a cardboard carrying tray stuffed with two Grande Lattes, which poke up like stubby styrofoam goalposts, flanking a bagel or a muffin, or on certain decadent mornings, a chunk of coffee cake. We settle in and bullshit about sports and show business while we snack. Time flies. We break for lunch. We read the trades. We take a walk.

What we don't do is work.

I can't somehow, can't find the words or the motivation. Despite my desperate need to make a living, I am paralyzed.

This is no mere midlife crisis. This is a whole life crisis, based on the deep, throbbing possibility that everything I have done in my work life for the last twenty years will be revealed to have been a brutal mistake. I am stunned that I am now stuck, in this place, struck impotent and mute. What happened? How did I get here? I wanted to simplify my life. Instead I have overextended myself, committed to doing work I clearly don't want to do. Hell, can't *get* myself to do. Instead I stand frozen, watching chunks of my savings peel off and tumble into space like shingles falling off a decaying roof.

Two weeks before Christmas, Martin calls from his car en route to his workout. He wants the script. I look at where we are in the screenplay—a small mound of dialogue rests across the top of page 42 like a skullcap—and I lie. I tell him we're just cutting and polishing. Almost there, have it to him in a week, ten days tops. Two weeks at the latest.

Propelled by buckets of caffeine, we crash through the rest of the script. I don't remember one second of that frenzied process, but we deliver the screenplay in ten days and retire to my office where we wait for Martin's reaction, wait for the second-draft notes, wait for our agent to get us another movie to write, and I wait wordlessly for the screaming to stop in my head.

David and I meet for lunch at an outdoor café on Larchmont Boulevard in Hancock Park, my old neighborhood. We sit for a while, catch up. He tells me about the latest R&B celebrity he's chasing down and asks me about my switch from sitcoms to screenplays.

"Don't ask," I say.

David shakes his head.

"I know," I say. "I should write something of my own. An article, a book proposal, something."

"I didn't say a word," David says.

"I'm not ready, David."

"All right," he says, hitting the *t*. His voice is soft, soothing, and clings to a trace of Dallas drawl. "We should order."

He whips off his sleek black owl-rims and peers at the one-page, laminated menu.

"It's on me," I tell him. "Belated birthday."

"Okay. Thank you very much."

"My pleasure. Order anything you want. Just keep it under ten dollars."

"That's the other thing," David says, lowering the menu.

"What?"

"You'll be fine, writing alone. You'll make a living."

"I suppose, because I won't be splitting the fee."

David grins. "That's not why, man."

He pauses and speaks so quietly that I have to lean forward to hear him.

"You'll make a living because you'll be doing something you *love*. You'll be following your heart."

David picks up his menu again. He brings it close to his nose and studies it as if it were a final exam. I stare off into the street. The world around me—car horns squawking, dogs barking, a skateboard rumbling by, the sting of perfume, the punch of strong coffee—batters my senses. David smiles at me, the kind of smile he'd give to someone who's lost and asking for directions. Our laminated menus flap in our hands.

"You'll know when you're ready," he says.

We order lunch and a pot of peppermint tea. David taps his spoon into his open palm as I pour.

"There's something I have to tell you," he says.

He takes a deep breath.

"Kyle's wife has an inoperable brain tumor."

I blink once, twice, trying to get my bearings.

"He's been unbelievable," David says. "He's finishing the

gym. And it's beautiful. I don't know what the problem was with the other guy . . ." David's voice trails off.

"Two little kids" is what I manage to say.

"Real little." David circles his hands around his teacup. "Like four and two."

"Jesus."

"They did chemo. They got some of it, couldn't get all of it. She's very sick. She's not . . . it's really horrible, man. She doesn't have much time."

"How much?"

"They don't know. The doctor is saying six months."

"My God. This is unbelievable. How old is she?"

"Thirty-five."

I can't speak. The squeak of our server's shoes, the clatter of silverware scraping nearby dishes, a customer's high-pitched laughter, bubble in the background.

"What is he going to do?" I ask finally.

"He says he just wants to be with her, and, you know, wait."

I nod, stunned, numb. "This is just . . ." I shake my head.

"Yeah."

"Shit," I grunt, and I blow my nose into my napkin.

"I'm gonna have a combination Christmas party and grand opening. Will you come?"

"Of course. Why wouldn't I?"

"Well, Kyle's gonna be there. I wasn't sure, you know . . ."

"I'm going to come," I say.

"That would be good," says David.

When I get home, I call Phil. He already knows. Kyle has called him at work seeking advice and referrals. Phil and I talk for a half hour, trying in vain to get any kind of grip on this information. We finally hang up and retreat into our families. At night, once the kids are in bed, Bobbie and I talk about Kyle, his wife, and his kids. We are both devastated. On Saturday, we write Kyle a note wishing him and his wife strength.

On Sunday, as soon as the guys arrive, I tell them about Kyle's wife. My voice cracks as I stumble through the news. I hadn't expected this. I clumsily clear my throat, and thankfully, Phil jumps in. As he speaks, my eyes search for Stewart's. His head is down, his eyes fastened into the grain of the redwood table. His fingers clutch the handle of a plastic knife, which he absently stabs into the wood. His knuckles are as white as cream cheese.

"My God," someone says over Phil's words, and then someone else says, "Fuck."

"She's so *young,*" Jack says. His voice is a bleat of pain and incomprehension and protest.

I glance at Stewart again. He shakes his head, a heavy, sad gesture, but still he remains locked in a staring match with the table. He is now the one caught in the middle. But he doesn't *say* anything, and to me that feels saddest of all.

"Bobbie and I sent Kyle a note," I say. "Maybe we should all send him a card."

"Yeah. Something like 'We're thinking of you,' something like that," Wally says. "Sign it, 'The Guys in the Game.' "

"I'm sure we have a card. Bobbie always has cards around."

"It's true," Phil says. "She's like Hallmark."

"Should I see if she's got something?"

"Absolutely," Gabe says.

"A blank card. That's what I'm talking about."

"A card's a good idea," Brick says.

Stewart nods.

When I emerge from the house two minutes later with a couple of choices and a pen, no one has moved from the deck. I pass around the cards. The guys study them, front and back, as if they are contracts. Finally, we decide on one, the plainer one. It has a simple boxy design on the front. Earth tones. Manly.

"What should we say?" Big Sam asks.

"Wally said it," I say. "How about just 'Thinking of You?' "

"Good," Phil says. He begins to write. I snatch the pen away.

"No offense, Phil. You write it, it'll look like a prescription."

"Good point," he says.

Grunts of agreement.

That afternoon, and each night during the following week, nearly every guy in the game calls me. The conversation with Brick is typical:

"This is fucked," Brick says.

"Really fucked," I say.

Brick sighs, then sips and swallows from what sounds like a hot cup of coffee. He exhales.

"It's so *tough*. The man is going to be a *widower*. Can you imagine? The responsibilities of raising a family on your own? Does he have help? Can he afford help?"

"I don't know. Probably not."

"What's he gonna do? He has to work. He's gonna have to hire someone or put the kids in day care."

"All these practical things you don't think about at first."

"Could you picture yourself in that situation? Je*sus* Christ. You have to ask why. Why is this happening?"

"You do ask those questions."

"What can you say?"

"Nothing. There's really nothing to say."

"That's just it," Brick says. "There's nothing you can say."

We don't speak for what feels like a minute. I start to wonder if he's still there. Finally, Brick sips again, swallows, coughs.

"Man," he says. "Shit."

We stay on the line in silence, waiting for the other to hang up.

Holding on . . .

•   •   •

Christmas Day. David, sporting a festive red-and-green sweater over his thick, heavily muscled chest, greets Bobbie, the kids, and me at his front door with hugs all around.

"Come on in, y'all. We've got food, drinks, you know the drill."

We do know the drill, having shared twenty years of parties and dinners and evenings together with David and his family. He steers us inside his warm English Tudor home—polished tongue-and-groove floors, burnished ceiling beams the color of semisweet chocolate, Art Deco furniture accented with muted pastels, and bookshelves built into every wall. I feel as if I've wandered into my favorite bookstore in Berkeley. Normally jazz engulfs us from speakers hidden in the ceiling, but tonight our sound track is Nat King Cole and Ray Charles crooning Christmas carols.

We maneuver through a maze of guests and cruise the dining room table, which is decorated with boughs of holly and platters of vegetarian curry. My kids gravitate toward the family room and David's extensive windup-toy collection. Bobbie nods at me and drifts into the kitchen toward some friends.

"Want to see the gym?" David asks me.

"You bet."

"You won't believe it. This guy Kyle's a motherfucker. He *slammed* it. I have never seen anyone work so hard. Friday was his deadline. He beat it by a week, down to the last knob. And it is *beautiful.*"

We swing through the back door and out into the backyard. We walk through a narrow garden, past a cluster of musicians who look vaguely familiar. I smell freshly mowed grass and recently rolled pot.

"Whoa," I say, stopping at a small building. "This was not here before. We have an entire *edifice.*"

"I'm *telling* you. He did this whole thing from scratch."

David opens the door, reaches inside, clicks on the light. We walk into one large square room that looks like a small-scale fitness club, Gold's for one guy. An island of pulleys, bars, and benches sits in the far corner. A treadmill, StairMaster, and stationary bike hug the left wall; free weights—barbells and dumbbells—snuggle in a metal rack along an entire wall of mirrors. Black vinyl exercise mats cover inch-thick, gray-speckled carpet. The gym glistens with chrome and smells like a leather jacket.

"Heaven," I say.

"I am one happy guy. I never have to leave my house."

"You have everything you need on the premises. Except a grocery store."

"That's next. I'm going to dig up the backyard, put in a Trader Joe's."

I move inside and rub my hand along the smooth mahogany finish on the frame of one of the double doors.

"These doors," I say.

"Home Depot."

"Come on."

"I'm serious.

"Amazing." I stroll over to the rack of free weights. "All right, what do we have here?"

I reach down and haul out two twenty-pound dumbbells. I back up a couple of steps and take a deep breath. I raise an eyebrow and slug through three awkward biceps curls.

"Oh *yeah*. Got a little burn there. Okay. That's enough." I replace the dumbbells with a clunk. "I'm all dressed up. Don't want to get sweaty."

"I know what you mean."

"What else you got here?"

"Tell you what," David says. "You hang here, put on some music, try the stuff out. Make yourself at home. I have to mingle."

"You don't have a sauna or anything, do you?"

"Hot tub. Right outside the door."

"You've given me an edifice complex," I say as David goes.

I squeak over the black floor pads to a CD player on a shelf protruding from the far wall. I pluck *Al Green's Greatest Hits* from the top of a tiny tower of CDs and pump it up. I plop down on the hard rubber seat of the Universal system, adjust the weight, yank the metal bar down to my chest, and begin doing a few light, uninspired pull-downs.

I close my eyes and try to shut out everything but my breathing. I work the bar slowly. Inhale. Pull down. Exhale. Release. Inhale . . .

The door opens and Kyle walks in.

He wears a black T-shirt, black jeans, and a red Santa Claus hat. He holds two paper cups. He walks over to me and hands me one. "I call this Arizona Red. My new lager."

I raise the cup to him, sip it, and make a face. "Got a bite."

"Oh *yeah.*"

I stand up and impulsively we hug. We slap each other on the back, then break apart clumsily.

"I got your card. Got the card from the guys, too. Thanks."

"Kyle, I'm sorry—"

"Sorry is for when it's over, man. And it's far from over."

"That's just what Gabe said."

"Woo, Gabe. Hockey Night in Canada. How is Gabe?"

"Same. You know. Gabe."

"*So* clever with words. No wonder you get the big bucks."

"Yeah. If you only knew."

Kyle struts through David's gym. He stops in the center and raises his arms as if giving a benediction.

"Well? Huh? Give me some *love.*"

He cups a hand to his ear. Waiting.

"It's a showplace, Kyle."

"All *right! That's* what I'm talking about! There was nothing here, you know. Nothing. I had to build this whole thing. Build a *structure.*"

"Come on. Manuel did all the work. You sat around and drank beer."

"You been talking to Stewart?" He laughs.

I just shake my head. "I'm sorry how that all went down."

Kyle shrugs, takes another sip of his new lager. "Trying not to think about that enormous pain in my ass. Leaving it all up to the arbitrator. There are more important things in life, my friend."

"Yeah," I say, then a shadow creeps into my voice. "How you doing, Kyle?"

"Taking it slow." Kyle winks into the wall of mirrors. "This could be my last construction job for a while."

"I can understand that."

"It's not just my wife. It's the whole thing, you know what I mean?" He looks at me as if we're both in on something.

"Not exactly," I say.

"I don't want to do this shit anymore. I'm good at it and all. And I like this kind of job. The kind where you build something from scratch and you see the whole idea through. That's rewarding. But I got into this business because I saw there was a void. Lotta fuckups out there. Look, I'm different from most contractors. I went to college. I can relate to most of my clients. We can *talk*, about movies, music, politics, whatever. I can draw up a plan, I have a good eye, a good design sense, and I'm responsive. I call you back. I follow through. There are just too many shitty parts. Hustling for jobs, dealing with assholes, chasing people who owe you money and won't pay you. It's getting to me. Life is too short, man. Time for a change. I'm gonna do something else."

"Which is?"

He raises his paper cup. "Beer. Gonna brew my own beer. Matter of fact, I'm looking for investors. I think David's in. By the way. *David.* Now, that guy is the best. I can't thank you enough for hooking me up with him."

"No big deal."

"You don't hook me up with him, I'm probably still pissed at you. Now, if you want to really get on my good side, invest in my microbrewery. Get in on the ground floor."

"Can't do it right now, Kyle."

"Oh, the brush-off. Fine."

"I'm not brushing you off. It's about cash flow."

"I hear you. Well, keep it in mind."

"I will."

We polish off our beers, crush our cups. We stand together for a few seconds, and then I ask, "How's your wife?"

Kyle clears his throat, and when he speaks, his voice trembles. "She's doing chemo. Got one more session left. She's been really sick. Lost all of her hair. Check this out."

He pulls off the Santa Claus hat. His head is completely bald, pale, egg-shaped, and shiny.

"I shaved my head, too. In solidarity, man."

He raises his fist. I smile and raise mine, too.

"I kinda like it," he says. "In fact, I may keep it. What do you think?"

"You look like a giant penis with ears."

"Woo, Dumbo the Flying Erection."

This knocks him out. He laughs until he's bent over. He finally straightens up and adds, "Better than being called a big prick."

He laughs again. Catching his breath, Kyle sniffs and takes a seat on the stationary bike. He pedals absently.

"I found a building," he says.

"Where?"

"Culver City. I think I'm gonna go for it."

"You're serious about brewing your own beer?"

"No. I'm *passionate* about it. I spend all my free time planning, crunching numbers, dreaming up new recipes. Why should I keep being a contractor when my heart's not in it? I am burned-out, man. What am I waiting for? *Someday* I'll do what I really want to do? One thing I learned through this. You got no idea how long you got. *No* idea. Someday. Fuck that. What if someday never comes?"

I say nothing. The only sound in the room is the whir of Kyle pedaling on the bike.

"Say something, man."

"I'm just thinking about what you said. It actually makes sense."

"Watch those compliments. I don't want to get full of myself."

"I know. You're Mr. Modest."

"Hey, you know what we're gonna do, soon as my wife feels better? Hopefully around New Year's?"

"What?"

"We're going to Hawaii."

"Which island?"

"I don't know. Some of 'em. All of 'em. As many as we can. My wife's never been. She said the one thing she wants to do before she dies is go to Hawaii."

Kyle begins to pump the bike hard. He slides his palm over his shaved and sweaty head and leans his elbows onto the handlebars.

"Have you been?"

"Three times," I say. "Been to Maui, Oahu, and Kauai. Kauai's my favorite. It's paradise."

"Kauai, huh? Gotta go there. Got to check out paradise."

"That you do."

He closes his eyes, lost in reverie and a stream of perspiration that pours unchecked down his forehead and over his eyelids. He presses down on the pedals, pumping ferociously, forcing himself to rise into a crouch above the seat.

"I'm gonna go inside," I say.

"Check you later," Kyle says.

He grits his teeth and his pedaling becomes manic, frenzied, then, suddenly spent, he stops. His eyes still jammed shut, he cradles his head on his fleshy forearms, which rest on the handlebars. His breathing comes in gasps, then abruptly slows to a heavy doglike pant.

His eyes still closed, imagining perhaps another life, one filled with health and Hawaii and his own microbrewery in Culver City, Kyle begins to pedal again, deliberately at first, then with more power, finally exploding into a sheer, frightening fury.

I sneak out of the gym like a thief.

Kay, the hard-ass Realtor with the British accent, comes through.

"Ta *daa,*" she warbles one morning when I pick up the phone. "It's *Kay,* of course. Your *savior.*"

"You have news?"

"How would you like to sell a house today?"

Oh, would I ever. Screw the price, too. Let's grab what we can get and head for the hills.

"Believe me, we don't want this one falling through," Big Sam says on Sunday.

"Yeah. We'd rather not live through that again," Danny says.

"Why? Was I an asshole?"

"Oh no, you weren't an asshole—" Ben says, stopping himself.

"That's not the right word," Phil says.

"You were a little *manic,*" Mitch suggests.

"Obsessive," says Gabe.

"Compulsive," says Wally.

"I thought he was an asshole," Brick says.

"Whose outs?" Duff says.

Sunday night, the guys call me with recommendations for carpenters, painters, plumbers, and termite companies to repair, replace, spruce up, and fumigate whatever the new buyers want. I hire them all. I'm taking no chances.

Escrow closes right before New Year's. I am now the proud owner of only one overpriced house. The sigh of relief booming from my gut is like a gunshot.

"I told you I'd sell your house before the New *Yare.* Well, *too-dles,*" Kay sings, pirouetting out of my life.

On that Sunday, Phil arrives with champagne, which we have the good sense to keep on ice until we're through playing for the day. At the crack of noon, Phil pops the cork and fills each of our paper cups. He holds his up.

"To owning one house," he says.

"To the return of cash flow," I say.

"To a good New Year," Ben says.

"Yes. A safe one," Stewart says, then adds quickly, "and a healthy one."

We drink and crush our cups in unison.

The New Year, January 1994, begins with a chill. Temperatures at game time dip into the thirties. Meteorologists on CNN and zany weather clowns on local TV discourse endlessly about the weird climate conditions, which they coin the Arctic Effect. One morning it actually *snows* in the San Fernando Valley.

It doesn't stop us. Neither rain nor sleet nor snow. We don't miss a Sunday. In defiance, Big Sam, embracing his tough Detroit upbringing, shows up one Sunday in a tank top.

"Let's play shirts and skins," I say.

"I'm skins," Big Sam says, and snakes out of his top.

In January, my movie-writing career limps forward. Martin faxes me five single-spaced pages of rewrite notes on the screenplay. My partner and I flail through the morass, hand in a second draft, and while we wait for the studio to give us notes on that, get hired, incredibly, to write a screenplay for another company. I don't stop to figure out why. I start to believe that a steady flow of film-writing assignments lurks right around the corner. I have to believe this because I don't know what else to believe in.

• • •

As the temperature begins to rise, I get a call from David. Kyle's wife has passed away. Blessedly, her death was swift. Kyle and his wife did take their trip to Hawaii. They visited a couple of islands but cut the trip short when she began to feel weak. On the flight back to Los Angeles, she suddenly became violently ill. Calming herself, she nestled her head against Kyle's shoulder, closed her eyes, and died in his arms. A small, private funeral ceremony was held for immediate family only.

After I hang up with David, I call Phil. He offers to phone half of the guys in the game, including Stewart. I call the others. Some guys want details; all absorb the news stoically, expressing shock and sadness.

"The things you take for granted," Big Sam says on Sunday, thudding up the driveway, Phil and Danny on the wing. "Your health, living to a ripe old age . . ."

"Talking about Kyle's wife," Phil explains to me, arriving at the deck. Today we are a contingent of nine. We are, all of us, measured, deliberate. A heaviness presses down on us, a soupy, thick cloak.

"Very sad," I say lamely.

"I can't imagine," Gabe whispers.

"Puts everything into perspective," Ben says, speed-talker, cutting to the crux. "What's really important."

Mitch nods. "And *time*. How you spend your time. It's not about work, not business . . ."

"The connections you have with people," Phil says with a half smile at Gabe, Brick, and me, his closest friends.

Brick fastens the last strap of his knee brace. "It's so fucked. I mean, how is Kyle gonna deal with, you know, *life?*"

We pause communally, our heads strangely bowed in a kind of silent devotion. I sneak a glance at Stewart. He catches my eye, turns away, focuses on wriggling a sweatband over his wrist.

"It's hard," Stewart says finally, his voice hoarse, as if someone's got his hands around his throat.

We pause again, all of us, busying ourselves with pregame preparation, stretching, double-knotting shoes, massaging gobs of suntan lotion onto bare arms and legs, dribbling basketballs on the deck, distracting ourselves from further discussion of how one deals with death, unwilling to expose or share our feelings of grief.

Instead, we head for the hoop and shoot around, desperately wanting to escape in a game.

The following Wednesday afternoon, I am helping Bobbie prepare dinner when the doorbell rings. I open the door to a tall, skinny man about ten years older than I am. He wears glasses and smiles shyly. His eyes sparkle when he speaks as if he's recently applied eyedrops.

"Hello," he says. "I'm your neighbor. Ed Klein."

The Ed Klein? The mythical doctor and winemaker from beyond the stucco wall? He of the massive house, expensive Tibetan artwork, and thrilling Sunday brunch?

"Ed," I say. "Alan Eisenstock. Nice to meet you. Come on in."

"Oh no, thanks, I'm on my way out."

"Ed, about our Sunday basketball game. I hope we're not disturbing you—"

"No, no, it's fine. I'm hardly ever here anyway. But about climbing over the *wall* . . ."

His eyes flutter. He removes his glasses and wipes them on his shirt.

"I'm sorry. The ball sometimes bounces—"

"I know. That's why I'm giving you this." Ed reaches into his shirt pocket and pulls out a key tied to a worn piece of twine. "It's to the outside gate. This way you can just walk into my backyard and get your ball."

I'm thrown and surprisingly touched. "This is very . . . helpful. Thank you."

"It's nothing. What are neighbors for?"

"Sure you don't want to come in for a drink?"

"Thanks. I really have to run."

"Well, okay. Thanks again for the key."

"Don't mention it," Dr. Ed Klein says as he lopes down my driveway.

"Who was that?"

Bobbie, phone in hand, appears behind me.

"That was our neighbor. Ed Klein. Get this. He just gave me a key to his gate. We don't have to climb over the wall anymore."

"That's great." She scrunches her forehead. "And weird."

"And weird."

Bobbie tilts her head toward the phone. "Guess what today was?" A flickering of jade eyes.

"The arbitration," I say.

"That's right."

"Well?"

"I just spoke to Madeline. The arbitrator came over to Stewart's house to see Kyle's work and to hear both sides of the case. The arbitration started at three."

"And?"

"It was over by three-twenty."

Bobbie pauses for effect.

"*Well?* Who won?"

Bobbie drops her head for a second, allowing a strand of tawny brown hair to spill over one eye. I step back and look at her. And wait.

"Kyle," she says finally. "Kyle won."

She blows the hair out of her face and heads back into the kitchen.

4.

wnba

The death of Kyle's wife crushes us.

Her passing clams us up, stuns us into a period of stony silence. We don't know what to say to each other, so we say nothing. Stewart's legal entanglement with Kyle complicates things further. Stewart knows it would be bad form, even callous, to discuss the loss of the arbitration at the game. Privately, though, he fumes, eagerly presenting his case to us one-on-one, explaining why the arbitrator went against him. But Sunday mornings, we stay stuck in silence and occasional small talk. We choose instead to throw ourselves into ball, raising the play to a new level of intensity, denying the undercurrent of confusion, frustration, sadness, and helplessness that simmers beneath us, unspoken, but deeply felt.

Finally, the silence is shattered by music.

One Sunday morning before the game, two men deliver to our back door a karaoke machine, the main entertainment for my son's birthday party later in the afternoon. We set the machine up on the deck near the door leading to the kitchen. It lurks there, steady and inviting, a hulking robotic presence with a chrome pate, darting neon blue-and-pink grin, and two microphones dangling on either side like emaciated arms.

The guys flock to the machine as they arrive, drawn to it as if it were a new car I'd just purchased. At times like these, all men become mechanics. We stare at the thing, nod our approval, rub it, poke it, press its buttons, fiddle with its switches, blow into the microphones, consider its heft, inspect its back, and of course, examine its innards.

"I was recently in Japan on business," Wally reports, pressing his pale round mass against the railing on the deck. "Everybody sings karaoke there. It's part of the culture. One night, I was taken to this bar that had a karaoke machine. I got completely bombed on sake. Before I knew it, I was standing in front of everyone in the restaurant singing old Motown songs. I'm up there going, 'Sugar pie honey bunch . . . can't help myself.' I probably looked ridiculous."

"You?" Danny says. "Not possible."

"I would've paid money to see that," Phil says.

Wally laughs. "Hey, I wasn't that bad."

"Wow. They have everything," Big Sam says, flipping through the song list that rests in a plastic binder on the table. "I think. I don't have my glasses."

"Let me see," Danny says, bending over in midstretch.

Duff slides his chair close and pokes his head next to Big Sam's until they're practically cheek to cheek. Duff suddenly stabs the page with his finger. He laughs. "Oh gee. Remember this one?"

"Always a crowd pleaser," Danny says.

"Well?" Big Sam says, his eyes traveling from Duff's to Danny's and back again. "Should we do it?"

"No," Duff says.

"Why not?"

"*Now?*" Duff asks.

"Absolutely," I say.

"Come on, Brick, you're in this, too," Danny says.

"Sorry, I don't sing."

"You have to," Danny says. "Especially this one. It's for power forwards only."

"I will if you will, Brick," Duff says.

"We want him to do it," Danny says.

"It's the *anthem,*" Big Sam roars. "I insist."

Brick pauses, then rises to his feet. "In that case."

Posture sharp as a knife, Brick peers over Big Sam's shoulder at the song lyrics, his glasses riding his forehead. He laughs.

"Oh yeah, this is perfect," Brick says.

"Alan, hit one oh six," Big Sam says. "And don't look at the song."

"I wouldn't think of it."

I punch in the three numbers.

The karaoke clicks its tongue and begins its search for the anthem. As the machine works, Duff, Brick, Big Sam, and Danny snuggle into a line. These four are the enforcers, our strongest inside players, our toughest rebounders, our most feared shot blockers. To remind us, they each flex a biceps, pose as if they are the finalists for Mr. Universe.

A whir, a hum, the song begins.

A distant rumble of thunder, getting closer.

The power forwards raise their hands, exposing their palms, and morphing instantly into Diana Ross and the Supremes, shout and sing, *"STOP! In the name of love . . ."*

Danny steps forward, stealing a microphone for himself. Instantly, he *is* Diana Ross, his baritone soaring into a glass-cracking falsetto. Big Sam, Duff, and Brick crowd around the other microphone, challenging each other with brutal dance moves, content to sing backup.

Suddenly, Ben uncoils from his chair and launches himself into the middle of the pack, a frenzied go-go guy. Damn, Ben, the marathon-running Steve Martin clone, can *dance*. He swivels his hips, corkscrews himself into a crouch, and springs *up* facing the opposite direction. He's doing *choreography.* Behind him, less than supreme, Big Sam, Duff, and Brick struggle to mimic his steps, try a spin, circle the wrong way, tangle up, and crash into each other. Big Sam shakes with laughter.

"This is great," he rumbles. "This is too *great.*"

The rest of us stomp our sneakers, beating time on the table, on the railing, on the floor, singing along: *"STOPPP! In the name of love . . ."*

The song ends and "Diana and the Supremes" bow. We leap to our feet, roaring, whistling, applauding. Danny, Brick, Duff, Ben, and Big Sam, arms around each other, bow and stagger away, overcome with breathless laughter.

"Okay. We got one," Mitch says, indicating himself, Jack, and Gabe.

"Gabe?" Phil says, shocked.

"I know. I hate stuff like this."

"Hate it," Phil agrees.

"But those guys set such a low standard. I figure, what the hell?"

At the machine, I say, "What's it gonna be, boys?"

"Are you, uh, sure you want that one?" Jack mutters to Mitch, pointing at a song on the list.

"Yeah, that's fine. You?"

"Whatever you want."

"It's up to you."

"I don't care."

"Guys, you're not picking out furniture. It's a fucking song," I say.

"Okay, okay. One twenty-eight, Mr. DJ," Mitch says.

I punch in the code and we wait briefly before the Coasters, then Mitch and Jack howl, *"Fee fee fi fi fo fo fum . . ."*

Jack leans his compact, sturdy body into the song and with surprising fervor bleats: *"Charlie Brown! Charlie Brown!"*

We're all on our feet, clapping and stomping along to Jack

and Mitch tearing up the song, finally screeching, *"CHARLIE BROWN! CHARLIE BROWN!"*

"WHY'S EVERYBODY ALWAYS PICKING ON ME?" sobs Gabe.

We rush and surround Phil, Jack, Mitch, and Gabe. Except for Big Sam, who is leaning into the carob tree, laughing so hard he's crying.

"One more!" I shout. "All of us this time."

"I'm not doing another one," Gabe says.

"Come on," Phil says.

"Everybody," I say. "Stewart, Wally . . . ready?"

"What's the song?" Stewart asks.

"You'll recognize it," I say, locating the song on the list, then darting my fingers over the selection keys.

Before anyone can protest, the intro music to a classic R&B song rains over us.

" 'Love Train'!" Ben says.

"By the O'Jays!" Danny says.

"Oh *yeah,"* Big Sam shouts.

"Yeahhh!" Duff screams, doing a couple of deep knee bends, which I'm pretty sure are dance steps.

Instinctively we cluster around the karaoke machine and sing the first verse of the song with passion.

"Take it, Dr. Phil!" I shout.

"No!" he shouts back.

"Come on, it's a love train!" Jack screams, his shyness out the window.

"Welll," answers Gabe.

And we all sing: *"Love train, love train . . ."*

The music swells and we follow Ben, our dance captain. He shimmies his shoulders, glides two steps forward, backs up two more, dips and slides to the right, to the left, all the while miming pulling a train whistle. Giddy, clumsy, but as determined as guys in a Broadway chorus line, the rest of us follow, howling, singing, ranting.

Tentatively we join hands, then lock arms around each other's shoulders and waists, the whole team, a dozen basketball guys dancing, crazed, caught up in song, wailing, *"Ride! Ride! . . ."*

"YEAHHH," answers Gabe.

From then on, we talk.

All the time. Constantly, continuously. Before, between, and during games. Some Sundays it feels as if we talk more than we play. We tear off pieces of bagels, rip out the hearts of doughy blueberry muffins, swig our water and freshly squeezed orange juice, settle in, and blab. Most Sundays when we finish playing for the day, the guys stay and we talk some more.

We talk about sports, stocks, politics, religion, travel, movies, books, music, plays, TV shows, mortgages (fixed or adjustable), restaurants (best high-end and favorite hole-in-the-wall), wines (white or red, California or French), cars (new, used, to buy or lease), favorite junk food, best and worst memory of college, first and worst time getting drunk, best and worst concert-going experience, best and worst drug experience, last drug experience, best and worst investment, favorite holiday, favorite city (American or foreign), favorite route to take into and out of the San Fernando Valley, encounters with the police, most recent and most successful fistfight (Big Sam's was three weeks ago; mine was in the third grade), job stress, coworkers, partners, in-laws, wives (admirable qualities and amusing anecdotes only), kids, pets, weird family members who are currently visiting and won't leave, and where to get an all-wool Italian suit with a vest and two pairs of pants for $99, including alteration. Two topics are conspicuously off-limits: how much money we make and sex. At some point, Danny tells us his joke of the week and Phil brings us behind the scenes of the ER, always more harrowing than anything seen on the TV show.

"I had a guy this week, sixty years old, businessman, comes in wearing a suit. He's got abdominal pains. I tell him to take off his clothes, put on a gown. Guess what he's got?"

"Do I want to hear this?" Brick asks.

"Nipple rings," Phil says.

"I do not want to hear this," Brick says.

"He forgot to take them out."

"Jesus *Christ,*" Brick howls.

Phil grins. "There's more."

"I know I don't want to hear *this,*" Brick says.

"You don't," Phil says.

"Is he gay?" asks Gabe.

"Possibly," Phil says. "Because he also had a penis ring."

A chorus of moans, groans, laughs, and coughs.

"*Owwww,*" Brick says, and shoots off the deck. He grabs a ball, takes a shot, and turns back to Phil. "Why would anyone do that?"

"You have one, don't you, Sam?" I ask.

"Yeah. But I don't wear it on Sunday."

"That is sick," Brick says.

"It's just like getting your ears pierced," Jack says softly. We all look at him. He lowers his eyes. "So I'm told."

"That's gotta hurt," Duff says.

"It wasn't that bad," says Jack.

"And that's my ER story of the week," Phil says.

"Ladies and gentlemen, Dr. Phil. He's here all week," I say.

"Try the veal," Phil says.

"Anyone want to play basketball?" Big Sam asks, heading toward the hoop.

"So Bill Clinton dies and is on the elevator going up to heaven," Danny says.

"Wait, wait," Big Sam says, jogging back to the deck.

Nobody's moving. Except toward the bagels and juice.

• • •

Around this time, we institute a tradition: our annual basketball banquet.

We hold the first of these yearly dinners one Sunday evening at six in the private room of a Chinese restaurant, eleven of us sitting elbow to elbow around a circular table, mesmerized by a wobbly lazy Susan stacked with egg rolls and fried wontons, revolving hypnotically in front of us. The meal follows, pre-ordered by Phil, several courses of recently clubbed crustaceans in sizzling sauces presented to us by a parade of waiters holding metal trays aloft like shot puts.

Tipsy on beer, we pick up the conversation we began that morning: a discussion of how we were personally affected by the Vietnam War. We share reminiscences of the late sixties and early seventies—psychedelics, the Beatles, Woodstock, free love, our more or less hippie lifestyles, the draft lottery, and like most of us who attended college during that era, our passionate opposition to the Vietnam War.

With one exception, none of us served in the military. Mitch missed the draft because he was too young, Big Sam because he was too old, and Gabe because he was Canadian. Brick, Danny, Wally, and Duff were not drafted because of high lottery numbers. Phil was granted a deferment because he entered medical school. Stewart applied for and became a conscientious objector.

I was awarded lottery number thirty-six. Soon after, I was sent by bus to my local draft board, where I was ultimately forced to undergo *three* separate physicals, all of which I failed with flying colors. Even though I have worn glasses since the first grade, the result of record-breaking astigmatism, a team of army ophthalmologists insisted that I could read the eye chart, a target length away, without my glasses. Finally, after examining my eyes for literally hours, they gave up and reluctantly stamped a medical deferment across my draft notice, sending me straight to graduate school instead of boot camp.

The one member of our game who did serve in the military was Jack. He speaks now in a small, trembling voice.

"I had a very low draft number, number fourteen, I think. I decided to enlist in the army. I was terrified of going to Vietnam. I knew I was going to be drafted and everyone who was drafted went to Vietnam. I was told that if I enlisted, I had a chance of being sent to Europe. So I did. The army was just hell. I hated every minute of it. I'll never forget the day I got my orders. We were in our barracks, maybe fifty of us, all lined up. One by one we were handed a folded slip of paper. I opened mine up and read it. It said I was going to Germany. I couldn't believe it. I wanted to scream, but of course you couldn't. I glanced around and I could tell who got orders to go to Vietnam just by the look on their faces. Their eyes were sunken. They all died a little right then. I got lucky."

Jack stops, takes a small breath. For a moment the only sound in the room is the whir of the lazy Susan.

"What did you do in Germany?" Stewart asks.

"Military police," Jack says.

We all chuckle.

"I know. It was a joke. I was essentially a security guard. I spent two years guarding a room full of files. But, thank God, I didn't have to go to Vietnam."

Jack drops his head and swallows.

"I think about the guys who went, guys I knew who didn't come back, and the guys I knew who did, what they went through . . .

"Yeah," he says, low, his words skimming the table, "I got lucky."

Monday morning, January 17, 1994, the earth cracks open.

I am asleep. And then, right before it happens, almost as if I've had a premonition, I am awake, blinking through a haze, bracing my body for an ambush. There is a muffled rumble in the distance, then a loud growl coming from somewhere beneath us. The house begins to sway, back and forth, as though the foundation is resting on a giant seesaw. Our bed shivers and the house slides again, back and forth, back and forth, a ludicrous adult ride, once, twice, three times, four. I lie in bed, immobilized, panicked, absurdly twisting the sheet for protection. The room ripples out of focus. I don't know how much time passes. Thirty seconds, forty-five, a minute? I have no idea.

The swaying stops and Bobbie and I both shoot out of bed. The floor feels as if it's moving, although I know it is not. I run into my son's room. He lies breathing in blissful, innocent sleep, stretched out in the bottom of a massive bunk bed made of oak plank, probably the safest place in the house. I run into my daughter's room. She is awake, bleary-eyed, cradled in Bobbie's arms, their heads nestled against each other, cheek to cheek below an antique light stanchion fastened to the wall. I want them out of there. As if by telepathy, Bobbie hears my warning and ducks our daughter's head under cover of her thick patchwork quilt.

It is dark. I leave my daughter's room, go back into ours to get my bearings. I want to know the time. My guess is that it is around three in the morning. I know this much. This earthquake is the biggest I've ever felt, more violent and more sustained than the shakers we've experienced before, those perfunctory ten-second tweaks of earth that freak out visitors and fill us residents with feelings of toughness and superiority. This is different. And then, on cue, the ground coughs and the house sways again.

"Come into our room," Bobbie whispers to our daughter. Her voice is soothing, just above a whisper, and like two girls at a sleepover, my wife and daughter rush across the hall and dive into our bed as the swaying subsides.

I squint at the clock and realize only then that we have no electricity. I try the light switch to be sure.

"Power's out."

I reach under our bed and fumble for the flashlight we keep there. I find it, try it, never expecting it to work. Surprise. A shaft of light bleeds white onto our carpet.

"Check downstairs," Bobbie says. Calm, commanding, in crisis mode.

Trailing three steps behind the light, I follow the flashlight's beam out to the hall. The light cuts the darkness enough to lead me down the stairs. I clop uncertainly from one step to the next. I reach the bottom of the stairs, place my palm on the wall, and rub my way down the hallway. I locate the French doors that lead into the dining room and go in. Every window has been blown open. One oversize hand-painted wineglass lies shattered on the floor, a jagged, multicolored mess. Other than that, everything seems intact.

The phone rings, jarring me. My eyes are adjusted to the dark now and I inch into the kitchen, where I fumble for the phone. The silence on the line baffles me. Then I remember that our inherited, elaborate, and expensive phone system is electrical and, therefore, dead. The phone jangles again, echoing through the dark house. The sound is coming from the guest bedroom, from the one phone in the house that's connected independently to a wall jack. I make my way in there and grab the phone on the seventh ring.

"Hello?"

"Alan?"

"Yes?"

"It's Murphy."

Murphy? My crazy friend, the radio DJ. Of all the times . . .

"Murphy? Where are you?"

"I'm here, man, in Massachusetts."

"What time is it?"

"Seven-twenty A.M. Four-twenty your time. Are you okay? Is your family okay?"

"I think so—"

"Good. You're on the air."

"Wait a—"

"We are on the air, live, with Alan Eisenstock in Los Angeles. Alan, can you tell us what happened?"

"It's an *earthquake.*"

"We know that. They say the epicenter is Northridge."

"Really? My wife teaches at Cal State Northridge."

"How close is that to you?"

"Too close."

"They're calling this a seven point two on the Richter scale. That is a major, *major* shaker. Do you have much damage?"

"I'm not sure. We don't have any electricity. I can't really see anything. I know we lost a wineglass but I don't know what else—"

"And everyone's fine?"

"Yeah. Everyone's okay. I don't know what it's like outside."

"Amazing. So what are you writing these days?"

"What am I *writing?* My *will.*"

"Ha *haa.* Well, take care of yourself. Mind if I call you again for updates? Maybe do a regular feature. Call it . . . *A whole lotta shaking goin' on.*"

"Murphy—"

"Thanks, man. That's Alan Eisenstock, live from Los Angeles, right in the heart of the devastating Northridge earthquake. Back with more of *Murphy's Law* after this."

I stare at the phone, then climb back upstairs. The kids are sleeping again.

"Who was on the phone?" Bobbie asks.

"Murphy. I was just on the radio."

"No."

"Yes."

"Tell me this is a dream," she says.

"It could be," I say.

● ● ●

I call Brick, who lives three streets away.

"Are you guys all right?"

"We're fine. I think we lost a vase and that's it. Faye's sister is a total mess, though. She's here now because her apartment basically caved in."

"Are you kidding me? She lives half a mile away."

"Tell me about it. I mean, physically she's fine. Emotionally, another story. She's lucky she's alive. She could've been buried under all the crap she's got over there. I'm going over now to help her clean up. This makes you seriously think small town in Vermont."

"It's surreal."

"Hey, how's the basketball court? Did Kyle's hoop hold up?"

"That's what's on your mind?"

"I'm just wondering."

"If the hoop can survive Phil's bank shots, it can survive this."

"Point taken."

"Do you have electricity?" I ask.

"Yeah. You?"

"Our power's out. I can't get through this day without coffee."

"I'll make a pot. Come on over."

The drive to Brick's house is in direct contrast to what has just happened. The day is crisp, cloudless, and sunny, the kind of mid-January day that propels people to abandon the deep freeze and dirty slush of East Coast winter and move west to Eden. Eden, as we eventually find out, comes with a price—riots, smog, rock slides, brushfires, blondes, and earthquakes.

When I get to Brick's kitchen, there is more unreality. Everything seems so *normal*. His kids slurp cereal at the kitchen table. They giggle, talk of school, swat at each other. The smell of coffee sweeps through the air.

"My sister is a wreck," Faye says as she pours me a cup. "Her windows are all shattered, the cabinets flew open and all her dishes fell out and smashed onto the floor. Bookshelves collapsed. It was like a bomb went off in her apartment."

It's hard to picture the devastation Faye describes in the midst of this typical Americana.

"She may have lost everything," Faye says.

I blink, uncomprehending. Collectively, our two families have escaped the worst of this disaster, losing between us a vase and a wineglass.

As I fill my thermos full of coffee, Brick and Faye's sister, Debra, come in from the back door. Debra's eyes are crimson from crying.

"It's just unbelievable," she says, three words I know she's sick of hearing herself say.

"Have you driven down Montana?" Brick asks me.

"No. I came right over here."

"Before you go home, drive down Montana. Take a look."

He leans his elbows across the center island in his kitchen, lowers his head, removes his glasses, squeezes his eyes closed, and pinches the bridge of his nose.

"Man," he mumbles, "what a morning."

An hour later, I creep down Montana Avenue in Santa Monica, a two-mile stretch of restaurants and coffee hangouts sandwiched between expensive antique shops and exclusive clothing boutiques. As I drive, I scan the stores on both sides, or what's left of them. The street has been ravaged, the windows of every store blown out. The sidewalks and street are littered with glass and rubble and dust. The ceilings of some stores have collapsed *in*, ridiculously, as if they were constructed out of cardboard. A few dazed store owners methodically sweep up the glass on their sidewalks while others start to pick through clumps of inventory they've pulled out from inside. Farther down, near Montana and Fifteenth, two men wrestle a massive oak armoire to a standing position, then struggle to maneuver it through a gaping glass wound that only hours ago was their front window.

This is a movie. It must be. This street, Montana Avenue, is where I live, daily, outside of my house. I walk here, shop here, eat lunch, drink coffee, and read in these coffee shops. I bring my kids here for ice cream. I fill my prescriptions here. I get my hair cut here. What would have happened if the quake had hit a few hours later, during business hours, with throngs of people on the sidewalks, shopping, on their way to work, eating in those restaurants?

As I drive farther down Montana, toward the beach, it gets worse. The stores here are gutted. Empty shells. My head begins to pound. I need coffee and I need to go home. I turn up Seventh Street, head back along San Vicente, and I notice a common thread of destruction among all these million-dollar homes: the chimneys. Every one is either leaning at a precarious angle, sheared in half, or completely gone, leaving only a jagged brick nub. Zigzag trails of bricks lay strewn along rooftops or scattered in uneven and random mounds on the ground.

Houses without chimneys.

The image follows me home.

When I get to our house, I cross the street and take a look at our chimney. It's still there, in its place, erect but askew. A few months ago I would've gone inside and immediately called Kyle. Things have changed.

When I come inside the kitchen, Bobbie is on the phone with Faye. At least our power is back on. I put the thermos down on our counter, take a cup out of the cabinet, and fill it for Bobbie. She smiles, mouths, "Thank you," and goes back to Faye.

"I know. Oh, thank you, Faye. Alan just arrived with the coffee. . . . Absolutely. Let's check in hourly. . . . Yep. That's what it's all about. Talking, communicating with each other, staying in touch. . . . I love you, too. . . . Okay. Wait. Hold on." She hands me the phone. "Brick."

"Well?" Brick sighs into the phone.

"Devastating."

"Incredible, isn't it? Fucking incredible."

"Hey, have you checked your chimney?"

"Oh *yeah,*" Brick says. "I got up on the roof. I gave it a little nudge with my shoulder just to see if it was intact. I nearly knocked the whole thing over."

"You got up on the *roof?*"

"You better get up there, too. Check yours."

"Me? I'm not getting up on any roof. I get dizzy changing a lightbulb. You know how I am."

"It was pretty cool up there. I felt like Dick Van Dyke in *Mary Poppins.*"

"Yeah. Chim-chim-cheree."

Putting on a cockney accent, Brick sings, *"A chimney sweep's lucky, as lucky can beee."*

"You're singing now?"

"One must. What do you call this?"

"Gallows humor," I say.

"Right on. The other line," Brick says. "Probably Debra. Later."

I hang up and join Bobbie in the family room. She has on the news. She leans forward on the couch, watching intently.

"Where are the kids?"

"Upstairs," she says. "Playing Monopoly. They're thrilled they don't have to go to school."

On television, a reporter with a pained look on his face stands in front of a pancaked building in Northridge.

"That's the university," Bobbie says.

Where she teaches.

"An apartment building collapsed a few blocks from school," she says. "At least three people are dead."

She reaches for my hand and knits her fingers through mine.

The rest of the day consists of aftershocks, phone calls, visits from friends, and horror stories. A gas line breaks near Seventh and Montana, and the residents, among them Ben and his family, are asked to evacuate their homes. The houses in that section of Santa Monica, an area closer to the beach, sustain the most damage. The soil there is softer, rumored to have once been marshland, while our houses have been built into bedrock.

Awakened by the quake, Ben had run into his daughter's room. A bookcase had suddenly rocked away from the wall and begun to pitch forward. A shelf had ripped out of the bookcase and jackknifed toward him. Instinctively, Ben had shielded his face. The shelf had caught him on the forearm and cracked his wrist.

"I was fortunate," he tells me on the phone. "I caught it on my wrist instead of on my head or in my eye. It's just a small break. I'll be back playing in a few weeks. Meanwhile we're moving into my mother-in-law's house until the city fixes the gas line."

Other people are not so fortunate. A family who lives two streets away from Ben (the dad is a screenwriter I know; his daughter attends Stewart's school) moves out of their home an hour before their house explodes. Within a month, they pack up what remains of their belongings and relocate to New York.

I call everyone in the game. Other than Ben, we have escaped any serious injury or loss. Mitch's big-screen TV toppled over and crashed onto his living room floor. Phil lost some dishes and glasses. Danny's chimney fell off. Brick offers to climb up and take a look.

• • •

By Sunday, the earth has calmed down and we meet for basketball as usual. But this Sunday we talk about moving away.

"Where would you go?" Mitch asks. "I'm not moving back to Philly, that's for sure."

"Yeah. Shitty weather," Big Sam says.

"No," Mitch says. "Shitty family."

"After this week, Sara and I would consider leaving," Gabe says softly.

"Really?" Phil asks.

"Well, for a lot of reasons. Not just this. Although this is the major reason."

"Why else, Gabe?" Stewart asks.

"First of all, it's so damn expensive here. You can get a great house in Montreal in an equivalent neighborhood for a fraction of what you pay here. And the crime rate is so much lower. We've been talking about it."

"You're never going to move," Phil says. "You love your house."

"That's true. I do love my house."

"He's never gonna move," Phil repeats, slapping his palm on the ball. He shakes his head, allows the ball to trickle out of his hands and roll onto the lawn.

"I'd move," I say.

"Yeah, just like I will," Big Sam says. "You're not going anywhere. Even after this week, L.A. still beats everywhere else by a mile. My friends in Detroit call me. They want to know about the earthquake. How it felt. Was I scared. I tell them, 'You have no idea. It was like a bomb going off. I was scared out of my mind. This is the worst place on earth. I can't believe I'm staying here. Only reason I am is that I'm so *entrenched*. Career, kids, wife's family. I'm stuck.' That's what I tell them. It's bullshit."

"Nice guy, Sam," Stewart says.

"Hey, I don't want any more people moving out here. Too overcrowded as it is. Look around, boys. We're wearing shorts and T-shirts, outside, about to play basketball. This is *January*.

Do you remember January in New York? I remember January in Detroit. I'll take an earthquake every ten, fifteen years in exchange for this. In a second."

No one speaks. Meanwhile, Bobbie is inside our house scraping together four earthquake kits with the same efficiency and ease with which she throws together a salad. Each kit consists of enough prepackaged and canned food and bottled water for a week, a flashlight with extra batteries, a wrench designed specifically for shutting off the gas valve located at the curb in front of our house, and family photos of our loved ones on the East Coast, since we'll be out of touch for a while. She places the completed kits throughout our house, strategically, in safe, accessible, earthquake-proof locations.

"Alan," Mitch asks, "would you really move?"

"I might."

"He's been threatening to move since the first day I met him," Phil says.

Danny stands up, leans on the railing on the deck, and starts to stretch. "Where would you go?"

"Back to New England," Phil says. "We've had this conversation a million times."

"First of all, as Gabe says, real estate is much cheaper. You can get a huge house on an acre of land for a couple hundred thou. Maybe less. Second, you can send your kids to public school. No offense, Stewart."

"No offense taken."

"Then there's the air. In New England, you can actually *breathe* it."

"It's not so bad in Santa Monica," Duff says feebly.

"Come on. Have you ever been in an airplane above Los Angeles? Have you noticed the air? It looks like shit. Literally. You feel like you're flying above a giant layer of crap."

"You would move because of the lousy air quality?" Phil says.

"Then you have your totally fucked-up values," I say.

"Oh, here we go," Big Sam says.

"Wait. I agree with him," says Stewart.

"Listen," I say with a passion that surprises me, "I know a guy who moved to Westport, Connecticut, shortly after his kid went to a friend's bar mitzvah and the bar mitzvah boy was led into the party by the Laker Girls. They did a twenty-minute dance routine finishing up with the hora."

"The Laker Girls did the hora?" Gabe asks.

"That's a little over-the-top," Brick says.

"Why wasn't I invited?" asks Big Sam.

"Those values are everywhere," Wally says. "Including Westport, Connecticut."

"Not the Laker Girls," Duff says. "The Laker Girls are not in Westport."

"You know what I mean."

"Those are the values of a lot of people here on the West Side," Mitch says.

"You mean us?" Danny says.

"Yes. Us," I say. "We no longer have to keep up with the Joneses. We have to top the Joneses."

"We *are* the Joneses," Danny says.

"Affluenza," Stewart says. "The disease of affluence. I see it every day."

"You need that disease to keep you in business," Brick says.

"Some of it," Stewart says, "but most of my parents aren't that way."

Now he gets the look.

"I said *most.*"

"The question is, what would you do back East?" Phil asks me.

"What I'm doing now," I say. "Write."

"Would your partner move, too?"

"No," I say. "He wouldn't move. But I wouldn't write TV or movies."

"What would you write?" Gabe asks.

"I don't know. Articles, books, sonnets. Or I'd teach or open a bookstore. I'd figure something out. I'd make a living."

An awkward silence suddenly descends.

"He'll never move," Big Sam says flatly.

Actually, Bobbie and I have talked about it. We have discussed creating a new life on the East Coast. We fantasize about this every summer when we visit family in New England and travel through the small, quaint towns of Connecticut and western Massachusetts. We sometimes window-shop in real estate offices. We envision ourselves settling in Madison or Guilford in a rambling clapboard house right on the beach overlooking Long Island Sound, Yale our backyard, New York an hour by train. Or raising our kids in an authentic Victorian on a patch of land in the Berkshires, surrounded by pine trees, antique shops, and gentle, aging hippies strumming acoustic guitars in Alice's Restaurant. Now is the time for all good fantasies. The kids are young, my wife is willing to relocate and look for a new teaching job, and work-wise, I'm capsizing.

"Why don't we look into it?" Bobbie has offered, more than once.

I'm the one who holds us back. I'm the one who can't pull the trigger. I'm the one who's frozen. Surprising, given my own personal earthquake, churning within me constantly, shaking my soul.

On this Sunday, the one following the Northridge earthquake, creaking from stasis, the guys and I rise slowly to our feet and begin to dabble in pitiful, cursory stretching. We bend, barely, breathe strenuously, groan loudly, and run, ridiculously, in place. We exit the deck, and three of us scatter, collecting the basketballs that lie around seductively, one hugging the garage, one sunbathing on the grass, and one lolling on the driveway, and we lumber onto the court in a pack. There we heave up halfhearted jump shots, never actually leaving our feet. After a while, we pick up the pace and move with surer purpose, even showing, on occasion, some bounce. Blood pumping, energy unleashed, we begin to run to spots, break for the hoop, muscle inside, box each other out. Mitch puffs out a laugh, Big Sam playfully shoves Jack, Brick glares at everyone. Stewart steps to the side, studies us, rests his chin in the cup of one hand and claws through his hair with the other, conjuring up teams.

We're getting ready to play.

All is well.

One Sunday, Duff shows up with his wife, Andie. She is blond and pretty and walks on the balls of her feet like an athlete. She is dressed in sweats because she has come to play.

"You guys know Andie, don't you?" Duff asks.

A few of us do and mumble hellos. The two that have never met her, Ben, recovered from his broken wrist, and Jack, smile widely as if they're on a job interview. Even though Andie is taking crisp chest passes from Duff and draining jump shots from the side, I don't think it has sunk in with us yet that she is here to *play*.

"So you're a ballplayer?" I ask.

"Oh yeah. *Love* basketball. Used to play all the time. Coached our kids at their rec league this summer."

"Huh," I say, because that's the best I can do.

Phil, Gabe, and Brick join us on the court.

"Hi, guys," Andie says. She smiles winningly and approaches them. She's not going to hug them, is she?

Yep. She hugs all of them and kisses Phil.

"Andie," Duff says, and hits her with a bounce pass. Andie grabs it and sinks a short jumper.

"Nice shot," Phil says.

"Okay, Stewart, what are the teams?"

Brick. Down to business. No small talk today, no bullshit, no bonding. Just the feeling that today is about to be off-the-charts weird and the sense that most of us want it to be over. I notice that Stewart's entire face is furrowed. Where do you put Andie? Whom do you match her up against?

"Let's see," Stewart says. "Teams."

He's vamping. He has no idea.

"How's this?" Duff says. "Me, Andie, and Stewart against Brick, Phil, and Alan."

"Good, that's good," Stewart says. "Perfect."

"Unless, Stewart, you want to do it a different way."

"No, no, perfect, Duff, perfect."

"Great. Shoot for outs."

I do and pump it in. Our ball.

"Take who takes you," Brick says.

The other team breaks from their defensive huddle. I prepare to toss the ball in to Brick. I want to see the matchups. Duff takes Brick, Stewart is on Phil, and—you could've bet on this—Andie is guarding me.

Why? Why does she have to guard *me?*

I have nothing to gain and everything to lose.

The bigger question on everyone's mind is . . . why is she here?

I kick the ball in to Brick and sprint to his flank to get the ball back for a shot. The idea is to run my defender into a Brick screen, which is like running into a wall. But today I just don't think I should do that. Instead of running Andie into him, I go wide and fly past him. He looks at me as if I've suddenly gone senile and haplessly flicks a horrible pass way over my head and out of bounds.

"Our ball," Stewart announces.

"Sorry," Brick mumbles.

"My fault," I say.

On any other Sunday that exchange would've gone like this:

Me: "Who you passing to, dickhead?"

Brick: "You, numbnuts."

Not today. Today we're on our best behavior. Today we're polite. Today we're coed.

Now I'm on defense and I have to guard her. Fine, but . . . where do I put my hands? I can't hip-check her. That would be awkward. That would be wrong. I don't want to harass her. Can't try to disrupt her by shouting, jabbing my fingers toward her waist. That would be obnoxious. I'll just keep my hands to myself, right here at my side, and play religious defense, which means pray that she doesn't get the ball.

Duff passes the ball to Andie first thing. She dribbles right, looks for her husband, lays the ball off to Stewart, cuts toward the hoop, takes a bounce pass from Stewart, and tries a layup.

Now. I don't care where my hands are.

She is not going to score off me.

I am all over her, reaching up to block that shot. Plenty of body contact. Serious body contact. Bumping, smacking, whacking, and I don't know where. I'm not thinking about it. She should call a foul on me but she doesn't. And damn it, after all this, she shoots over me. But I bother her enough to alter her shot. The ball sails too far right. Brick yanks down the rebound, guns a pass to Phil, who dribbles twice, squats, and shoots.

Yesss.

We take the lead.

We never look back. I stick on Andie like glue. She gets another couple of shots off, but none fall in. Duff manages two hoops and Stewart scores one off Phil, but we win, 7–3.

Relieved, we jog back to the deck.

"If we'd lost that . . ." Brick mutters to me.

"I resent your tone," I mutter back.

"Oh?"

"You're implying that it would've been my fault."

"I'm implying no such thing."

"Why are we talking like this?"

"Because there's a spy," Brick says.

On the deck, those of us who've played reach for the water and cups. I start to wipe my nose with the bottom of my T-shirt. I catch Andie looking at me and I stop. I tear off a square of paper towel from the roll I keep on the table and delicately dab at my right nostril.

"That was good," Andie says. "I broke a sweat."

"Huh," I say.

She pours some water into a paper cup, slugs it down, like a guy for chrissakes, then glances at us.

"So what happens next?"

"Oh, we play another game. And then we play again. That's all we do. We just keep playing. One after another. Stewart makes the teams."

"I see," Andie says.

"That's his sort of unofficial job," Phil says. "I have no idea how he got that job. How'd you get that job, Stewart?"

"I have no idea," Stewart says.

"Yeah, see," says Phil.

"Okay. Who wants to sit out the next game?" Stewart asks.

Every hand goes up.

"You guys can't," Stewart says to us. "You're winners."

"Andie and I'll sit out," Duff offers.

"We got next," Andie says.

Duff laughs loudly at this for reasons I can only guess.

"Okay, then," I say, and jog onto the court. Brick is right behind me.

"Did you fucking invite her?" he asks me.

"Fuck no."

"Duff just brought her?"

"Apparently so."

"She's not a bad player," Brick says. "She's actually pretty good. She almost scored off you."

"Shut up."

Phil picks up a loose ball, shoots it. He glances at the deck.

"Did Duff tell you she was coming?"

"No," I say. "Surprise."

"What do we do?" Brick says.

"What can we do?" says Phil.

"We have to do something," Brick says. "Because this is not going to work. It's not that she's bad—"

"It's just not right," Phil says. "Maybe if we knew she was coming. Why am I having a hard time with this?"

"It's not the same with her," Brick says.

"You want me to say something?" I ask.

"Absolutely," Brick says.

"It should be me, right? It's my house."

"It has to be you," Brick says. "Who you gonna talk to? Her or Duff?"

"I don't know," I say. "Phil, you say something. You're a doctor."

"What does that have to do with anything?" Phil asks.

"You're used to giving people bad news."

Big Sam rumbles over, lifts a ball, and slings it at the hoop as if he's throwing a baseball. The ball clangs off the rim. The backboard vibrates. I cringe.

"She schooled you, boy," Big Sam says to me.

"Then you guard her. You figure out where to put your hands."

"Why'd he bring her, anyway? Tell her to go home."

"Phil's gonna talk to her."

"I never said that," Phil says.

"Can you imagine if I showed up with Faye?" Brick says.

"What about if Bobbie came out here in sweats and said, 'I got next'? How would that go over?" I ask.

"Bobbie would kick your ass," Big Sam says.

"That's not the point," I say.

"Let's play. It's cold out here," Phil says, hopping on one foot.

"It is cold. My nipples are getting hard," I say.

"*Shh,*" Brick says. "She might hear you."

"Jesus," Big Sam says. "We can't even have a serious conversation with her here."

A few minutes before noon, after the longest Sunday ever, Duff and Andie get up to leave.

"Well, this was really great," Andie says. "Thanks a lot, Alan."

"No problem."

"See you guys," Duff says.

"Bye," Andie says, and they walk together down the driveway. There is dead silence.

"What was that?" Danny asks.

"You think she's coming next week?" Jack asks, panic in his voice.

"I think she's coming every week," I say. "Every week from now on. Next week Duff's bringing his daughter, too, and the following week his mother-in-law's in town—"

"That was uncomfortable," Stewart says.

"The energy was completely different," Wally says.

"We couldn't *talk,*" moans Gabe.

"We can't have her here again," Ben says.

"Phil's gonna talk to him," I say.

"You keep saying that," Phil says.

"Don't you guys think that Phil should say something?"

"I think *you* should," Brick says.

"Keep out of this," I say.

"Anybody want to play basketball?" says Big Sam.

And so we play, a long, intense game to 11, all of us rotating in, each of us trying to understand the morning.

"Why do you think she did it?"

It's four o'clock Sunday afternoon and Bobbie and I are sitting in front of the fire, sipping a hearty syrah.

"I can't speak for her," Bobbie says. "I don't really know her."

"Was she making some sort of feminist statement?"

"I don't think so. I think she just wanted to play basketball."

"But why play with us?" I whine. "In our game?"

"That's the issue. She came into your turf, uninvited. She trespassed. She crashed the party."

"Exactly. If Duff had asked if it was all right for her to come, I would've said no."

"You sure?"

"I'm pretty sure," I say through a sip of wine.

Bobbie tucks her legs under her and looks into the fire. The flames start to fizzle. I get up and poke the wood. The fire crackles and blue flames shoot up. In about a minute, I've got a roaring fire going. I settle back onto the couch.

"Good job," Bobbie says.

"Thanks. This is my idea of camping."

"I know. Mine, too."

I put an arm around my wife's shoulders. She leans into me. After a sip of wine, she says, "To me the issue is that this is your special time with the guys. You guys need it; you look forward to it. You carve this time out of every week, without fail, to get together and do what guys do. Play sports, bond, talk, whatever. I know you need it, just like I need my women's walk every Sunday and Madeline needs her book club. For some reason, Andie didn't see it that way. But I don't think it's a gender thing. I really don't."

"So it's about privacy?"

"It's about respecting your game. Do you think Phil would show up at Madeline's book club?"

"Never."

Bobbie slides her glass onto the pale, pine, antique map chest that functions as our coffee table. "The question is, now what? What are you going to do if she comes back?"

"You don't think this was a onetime thing?"

"I don't know. What were the games like?"

"They were okay. They were different. You play differently with a woman."

"How?"

"We were very self-conscious. Guys were concerned about being too rough. Nobody said anything, but I could tell. The games were a little more subdued. I was also very careful about what I said."

"Were you nice to her?"

"No. We spit, we scratched, we swore. Of course we were nice. We were on our best behavior. Which is not what I look forward to on Sunday. On Sunday I look forward to being gross and nasty. We all do."

"You think she felt welcome?"

"I don't know. I didn't offer her wine or cheese or anything. But she played as much as anyone, if that's what you mean."

"Did you talk to her?"

"Sure."

Bobbie gives me a look. I back down.

"Well, okay, kind of. She was sitting there. You had to include her in the conversation. You would anyway. She's intelligent, she's interesting. She's Duff's wife."

I lock my hands behind my head and I sigh. Deeply. "Why the hell did she have to come?"

An hour later the phone calls start.

"What are we gonna do?" Phil asks. "Nothing against Andie—"

"Oh, no. She's perfectly nice. But the game—"

"Not the same," Phil says. "Not our game."

"You think she's gonna come back?"

"Do you?"

"No," I say.

"Why not?"

"A feeling. I think she was checking us out. Testing us. Making some kind of statement."

"Which is?"

"I have no idea. That she's as good as we are? That women and men are equal in all things? Maybe she's upset that Duff has a Sunday thing and she doesn't."

"She has her book club," Phil says.

"That's not every week. It's every month."

"Maybe she feels that Duff's taking quality weekend time away from them." Phil's phone beeps. "Hold on. Call waiting."

"I hate call waiting. It's rude."

"I'm a doctor. Get over it."

He puts me on hold. Through the phone I hear his voice crackle in a distant echo, "Hello? . . . Hey. I'll call you in a couple." The phone clicks back. "Dude? You still there?"

"I'm here."

"That was Stewart. He wants to discuss the WNBA."

I sigh. "I guess I have to say something to Duff."

"Well, Stewart agrees with you. He thinks it was a onetime thing. If it is, then she had her one time and she's not coming back."

"Meaning?"

"Meaning if she's not coming back, why do we have to do anything?"

I switch ears. My right one is starting to throb. "So we should wait and see."

"That's what I think. Wait and see."

"Do nothing," I say.

"That's right," Phil says. "Unless she comes again next Sunday. Then we have to say something. Obviously."

"To Duff?"

"Yeah. He had to feel how uncomfortable it was."

"You would think. He sure didn't look uncomfortable. He seemed like he was having a good time," I say.

"Seemed to me like he was tuning out."

"Maybe you're right. He had a goofy smile on his face all morning. Looked like he was drugged."

"Maybe he was."

"So. Wait and see."

"That would be my advice," Phil says.

"Do you think she's coming back?"

"Can't read it."

"What's Gabe's take?"

"Gabe didn't like playing with her but he preferred her to some of the guys we play with."

"I can see that. What about Big Sam and Brick?"

"That precinct hasn't reported in yet."

"Jack and Mitch seemed pretty mum."

"They would be," Phil says.

I toe my floor, polishing a circle around a knothole. "The old wait-and-see. Okay. I'll give it another week."

"And how's this for an offer?" Phil says. "If she comes back, *I'll* talk to Duff."

"Seriously?"

"Yep. I'll make the call."

"I thought it was my house, my game."

"Fine. You call him. Better if you do it."

"Wait a sec—"

"Whoops. There's my other line. Gonna take this, dude."

"Phil—"

He's gone.

Hate call waiting.

An hour later, I'm foraging through my Sub-Zero in search of satisfying junk food when the phone rings again. Cradling a box of Wheat Thins and a plastic container of guacamole that's turned a suspicious shade of taupe, I pick up the phone. Brick.

"Yo. Spoke to Jack and Danny and ran into Ben at the market. We've got to do something."

"I spoke to Phil."

"What did he say?"

"He spoke to Gabe and Stewart."

"And?"

"Word is she's not coming back."

"That's the smart money?"

"Yep. We're going to sit tight and see what happens next week."

"That's the plan?"

"Unless you got a better one."

"No. I like it. It's a good plan. The old wait-and-see. Let's go with it."

"Some problems fix themselves," I say.

"Most of 'em, usually," Brick says.

Bobbie is astonished: "You're not going to do *anything?*"

We are in bed. The room is dark except for the pale blue glow of the Sunday-night news.

"You're not gonna say anything to Duff?"

"That's the plan."

"That's not a *plan.*"

Her eyes, emerald searchlights, angle up toward the ceiling. She blinks in frustration, groping for the right word. "That's *moronic.*"

"It's *smart*. It's the only way to handle this."

Nodding. Not in agreement.

"Bobbie, we don't have to do anything because she's not coming back."

"And if she does?"

"She won't."

"If she *does?*"

"If she does, we'll deal with it then."

Bobbie lowers her voice to a shadowy whisper. "Let me get this straight. You guys are willing to endure another lousy Sunday because you won't talk to Duff?"

"It's a calculated risk. But we're willing to take it."

Bobbie rolls her eyes. Something's just clicked in. "You know what I think? You guys are afraid of confrontation."

"That's ridiculous."

"You are. All of you. You're wimps."

"You're talking about successful attorneys, doctors, business-men, educators. These are type-A guys. How can you call us wimps?"

"Because you won't deal with this. I can't understand why you guys won't tell Duff that while you like Andie, she shouldn't play in your game. It's a guy's game. She stepped over the line."

"I agree with you. We all agree with you. But there's no rea-son to talk to him. Because she's not coming back."

"Why not?"

"I'll tell you why not."

"I want to hear this."

"Because she made her point."

"And what is her point?"

I squirm under the covers. I clear my throat. Scratch my cheek. Buying time.

"Well?"

"I don't know," I say.

"You don't know?"

"No."

Bobbie and I stare straight ahead at the TV screen. Neither of us knows what's on.

"Do *you* know," I ask, "her point?"

"No."

"Aha," I say.

Bobbie cranes her neck toward me. I can't look at her. I

don't think I've ever used the word *aha* in adult conversation before.

"Fine," she says. "It's your game. Handle it any way you want."

"If this were your game, if it were a women's game, what would you do?"

"If a woman brought her husband or boyfriend to our game, either we would all discuss it openly right then or one of us would take her aside during the first game and talk about it. We would deal with it immediately. We'd never let it go for an entire Sunday, never mind an entire week! We would talk it out and we would *deal* with it."

"We are dealing with it," I say, my voice starting to take off.

"If you say so."

Bobbie craters her pillow with a slam of the back of her head and hones in on the weather report. She raises the remote in front of her and waggles it from side to side like a switchblade.

"And you're wrong about confrontation—"

"I want to hear the weather." With a flick of her thumb, she boosts up the volume, drowning me out.

Feel a cold front coming in.

Duff comes alone on Sunday.

Tall, gangly, and mum, he warms up as usual, bricking his share of jump shots and chomping on his mouthpiece. Nothing is said about Andie. We remain deep in wait-and-see mode. Even as Stewart reveals the teams for the first game, I expect Duff to announce that Andie is on her way.

But Andie does not come. Not after the first game or even as I prepare to take the ball out for game two.

"So, Duff," I say cool as a rock star, "Andie coming?"

"Oh *no,*" Duff says as if I've asked him to lend me money. "That was a onetime thing. She wanted to check out the game. She just loves to play."

Overzealous communal wails of "She's a good player" pelt Duff like hail.

"Oh. I almost forgot." Duff jogs up the steps to the deck. He rummages through his duffel bag and produces a paper plate tented in Saran Wrap. "She baked you guys cookies."

"Umm," Stewart says.

"She just wanted to thank you for letting her play."

"Totally unnecessary," I say.

"Andie's great" is sung now with evangelical fervor.

"What do we have here?" Big Sam says ripping through the Saran Wrap.

"Chocolate chip and oatmeal raisin," Duff says, beaming.

"Thank her for me, Duff," I say, trying to elbow my way in for a cookie. It's like trying to fight a flock of pigeons for a crumb.

"Andie is known for her cookies."

"Huh," Brick says. "I'm known for the size of my dick."

Big laugh. I tear off a piece of an oatmeal raisin and lob it at Brick. He catches it in his mouth.

Applause.

Got our game back.

5.

road trip

In the spring of 1995, a swarm of helicopters dots the sky above the basketball court. There are dozens of them, distant iron bugs, their full metal stomachs painted with logos from the local news. They whir overhead, suspended, nearly synchronized, treading the air. A collective low-level *pocketa pocketa whap whap grrrrr* floats down from the mouths of their engines as shrill as the screech of a million fleeing locusts.

The choppers are hovering over O. J. Simpson's house on Rockingham Drive, less than a mile away. The occupants of the copters are on a surrealistic stakeout. They seek any morsel of media op—a glimpse of the aggrieved family, Gramma fixing supper over the stove, the kids engaged in PlayStation battle, Kato Kaelin blow-drying his hair. Most amused by the media storm is Big Sam, who is good buddies with all of the participants in the trial.

"Known Lance for years," Big Sam says, swiping cream cheese across his bagel.

Lance is Judge Lance Ito, the presiding judge at the trial.

"Nice guy. Good judge. Not used to this kind of attention, though. Has to be careful he doesn't let Johnnie run the show. Johnnie is pretty charismatic."

Johnnie is Johnnie Cochran, Simpson's lead attorney.

"Soon as Johnnie came on, Bob Shapiro got pretty much aced out. Course Bobby's not a trial attorney. He had to give it up to Cochran."

"Give what up?" I ask.

"The spotlight, *boychik*. The *spotlight.*"

Big Sam laughs, stuffs a hefty wedge of bagel into his gaping mouth.

"Doesn't the prosecution have them by the balls though?" Ben asks.

"You would think. Marcia and Chris—"

"Clark and Darden," I explain to the others.

"—have a ton of evidence. A *ton*. I've never had that much evidence. I've never *seen* that much evidence. I'm being serious." Big Sam uncaps his water bottle, gulps down a river. "Ahhhh." He backhands his bottom lip.

"It ain't about the evidence, though," Big Sam says. "It's about the jury."

"I heard that Cochran said all he needs is three black jurors," Duff says.

"That's not true," Big Sam says.

"It's not?"

"Nope," Big Sam says. "He said, 'All I need is one.' "

It's their voices.

Ben in the lead, speed racer, peppered *ha ha* with his *tee-hee* laugh. Bristling with white-hot spirit, whiz-kid-like brilliance.

Danny. Wit. Dripping sarcasm. Cut you through the teeth of a smile. Can't believe he said *that* while dazzling with astounding Slinky moves.

Jack . . . bashful, soft, almost sweet. You want to lean in to hear because what he says has body. And sometimes bite.

Gabe . . . thoughtful nurturer, deliverer of life. Bass and

treble . . . calm, still . . . not an angry word, even when he's pissed.

Duff, out of key, but only occasionally so discordant you'd want him to lip-synch; Stewart, teacher, generous, joyous, encouraging, makes you want to go on.

Brick and Big Sam, tough-sounding thugs, emotions bulging out like biceps. First in the foxhole, these two. Would die for you if they loved you. Maybe even if they had nothing better to do. The court is their foxhole now . . . deep radio voices holding us all like a basket, piercing you one-on-one.

Mitch and Wally. Laid-back listeners for fear of sounding a sour note. Unaware that they're safe here. Unknowing that we would never hear anyone's sour note unless it's turned.

And Phil. Long Island candy-store twang. Funny bone sharp as a scalpel, heart as big as The City. Lean on me, his voice says. When I get the Bad News, when I need The Truth, I want to hear it from Phil. He'll know how to tell me.

Together the voices meld into one voice, one sound, a sound we know:

The E Street Band.

A Mamet play.

A poker game.

Sports pages rustling on a commuter train.

What we say matters much more than who says what.

On Sunday, when we're rolling, I can't tell the voices apart. Couldn't tell you who's talking. Don't want to know.

Don't want to get that close.

After all, it's just a game.

They leave reluctantly. They linger, pretending to help me clean up, but they're going through the motions, flipping a lone crushed paper cup into my outstretched plastic Hefty bag or flicking invisible bagel crumbs off my picnic table. They want to stay.

Some guys leave and come back. Duff, for example. There are Sundays when, late in the afternoon, dressed in street clothes, he returns, once with a bottle of wine, another time with a book he thinks I might like to read. One Sunday midafternoon, Duff knocks at our door with his mother, a former high school art teacher with long, flowing silver hair and a glowing, welcoming smile that makes her look vaguely Native American, as if she were about to offer us a new variety of corn. Instead they greet us with an eight-foot-high tepee that she has built from scratch and painted herself.

"My son has outgrown this," Duff says. "I thought your son might like to have it. Keep it as long as you want."

The mother smiles again, gloriously, and behind her, Duff beams as if to say, "What a woman. What a tepee."

"I'm sure my son would love this," I say. "What kid wouldn't want to have his own hand-painted tepee? Would you like to come in for a drink?"

"Well, sure, thanks," Duff says, "but we can only stay a few minutes."

Two hours later, Duff and his mom are gone and I'm in the garage, shoving crap around, trying to find a place for the tepee. My son stands off to the side, looking at me as if I'm a lunatic. Finally I stand the tepee up in an open area I've cleared between a couple of bookcases and my old stereo speakers.

"There," I say. "All set."

My son shrugs and heads out of the garage.

"Where you going? Don't you want to play in this?"

He shrugs again. "Maybe when I'm older."

"Hey, Alan," Duff calls to me the next morning while I'm hauling my recycling down to the curb. "How's your boy like the tepee?"

"Can't get him out of there, Duff. He wanted to sleep in it last night."

"My boy was the same way," Duff says.

• • •

Between-game conversation the next Sunday leads me to a sig-
nificant sociological discovery.

There are two types of men:

Those who love Home Depot and those who think Home
Depot is hell.

Phil, Brick, Danny, Big Sam, and Duff belong in the first cat-
egory. Stewart, Jack, Gabe, Mitch, Wally, Ben, and I make up the
other group. We're into bookstores, CD stores, coffee shops,
and calling repair people.

"Hey, Brick, what kind of varnish you using on your deck?"
Big Sam asks.

"No varnish. Just a water seal. I picked some up cheap at
Home Depot."

"The only place to go for drill bits," Duff says.

"They have a marvelous selection," Brick says, his voice lilt-
ing like a radio pitchman's. "I'm at the Depot every weekend.
It's my home away from home."

"Which one do you like?" Duff asks. "The one in Burbank or
the one in Playa?"

"Tough call. The Burbank store is bigger, but Playa's more
convenient."

"See, I'm lucky," Phil says. "I work in Burbank and the other
one's five minutes from my house."

"They just opened one in Hollywood," Danny says.

Brick's eyes get wide. "Really? Where?"

"Sunset and La Brea," Danny says. "It's not as big as the one
in Burbank, but the layout's much better. And the staff is very
knowledgeable. Field trip?"

"Abso*lute*ly," Brick says. "In fact, let's go this afternoon. Who's
coming *with*?"

Big Sam and Phil start clamoring like kids who've been
invited to Disneyland. Brick winks at Sam.

"Big Al, you coming with us?"

"I've been to Home Depot, Brick. Once. With you. Don't take this wrong, but I'd rather stay home and chew off my own foot."

"I'll take that as a no," Big Sam says.

"Hey, guys," Brick says, "on the way back, maybe we can stop at Fisher Lumber."

"If there's time," Duff cautions.

"Don't want to shortchange the Depot," says Big Sam.

"You may want to rethink this, Alan, now that we might stop at Fisher Lumber," Danny says.

"It's tempting, but I have to gut an animal for dinner."

Brick wads up his paper cup and slings it at me. I shake my head along with the men in my group, the bookstore and coffee guys.

The real men.

One Sunday, Mitch is the last to leave. He stands awkwardly, swaying from foot to foot. He begins gathering empty water bottles to occupy what look like trembling hands.

"Mind if I have a glass of water?" he asks.

"Sure, Mitch, no problem."

He falls heavily into a chair on the deck while I head into the kitchen, open the fridge, and take out a bottle of water. I go back outside, hand it to him.

"Thanks. I'm so thirsty." He swigs down half the bottle. "Oh man, that was good. I don't know why I'm so parched."

"You just played three hours of basketball."

He grins. "That could be it." His mouth folds into a crease. "I'm not keeping you from anything, am I?"

"Nope. Got no plans."

"Because if you have something to do . . ."

"Gonna hang out today and do nothing. Stay as long as you want."

"Well, maybe for a little while," he says.

A half hour later, while Mitch is inside using the bathroom, Bobbie ladles her homemade soup into a bowl.

"Are you okay with Mitch being here?" I ask.

"Sure. I like Mitch."

"He's a nice guy," I say, and then Mitch is there, popping out onto the deck with us, rubbing his hands together.

"Soup looks great," Mitch says.

"Do you want a spoon?" I ask. "Or are you going to drink it right from the cup, the way it was meant to be drunk?"

"What do you think?" He picks up the cup and sips the soup like a cup of coffee. "Incredible."

"Thank you," says Bobbie. "It's a combination of carrot and tomato. Sure you don't want a spoon?"

Mitch looks at me.

"Real men do not use spoons," I say.

"Is that so?" Bobbie says.

"It's in the manual."

"I've always liked soup," Mitch says. "Ever since I was a kid."

Bobbie leans against the table. "Where'd you grow up?"

"Philly. South side."

"I have cousins in Philadelphia," I say. "They grew up right near Temple University."

"That's my neighborhood. I haven't been back in a while. My dad lives in Florida now."

Bobbie and I nod and Mitch takes another hit of soup. He drops the cup down onto the table with a clunk that startles us. He wipes his face with a napkin.

"Listen, if you guys have something to do . . ."

"We don't, right, honey?"

"Nope," says Bobbie. "It's a lazy Sunday. Nothing going on."

"I'll leave in a little while," Mitch says. "Polish off the soup, then I'll hit the road."

"I have some warm bread in the oven," Bobbie says.

"I'll leave right after the warm bread," says Mitch.

"That reminds me. Better check on it." Bobbie says and hustles into the kitchen.

"This soup is really delicious," Mitch says in a hush as if he'd been lying before and is only now telling the truth. He pushes his soup cup off to one side and sighs deeply. He gently pats his stomach and laughs nervously. Then using his hand as a visor, he shields his eyes from the nonexistent sun and grimaces.

"Things not so great at the ranch," he says.

"Oh?"

"Yeah. Not so great. Gracie and I are splitting up."

"Oh, Mitch, I'm sorry. I didn't—"

"No, that's okay," Mitch says. "Don't tell Bobbie yet, okay? At least not until I leave."

"Sure, I—"

And Bobbie is back with a basket of steaming sourdough bread, which she places in front of Mitch.

"More soup?"

"If you have it, I'd love it."

She whisks his cup off the table and heads back into the kitchen.

"Gracie wants to be alone with the kids today," Mitch says. "That's why I can't go home. I don't want to be there with her." He swallows. "I didn't know where else to go. I thought since I was already here, playing basketball . . ."

"Mitch, I'm glad you stayed."

He nods somberly.

Bobbie comes back with Mitch's second helping of soup. She catches my eye and immediately knows something's up. She also knows that she has to leave us alone.

"Well, I'm going to go inside and grade some papers," and she's gone like a blur.

"It's been going on for a while," Mitch says. "Gracie thinks I'm a terrible father. Well, you know. You heard her. I honestly don't know what she's talking about. I have a great relationship with my kids. It's crazy. That's all I can say. It's crazy."

"What are you going to do?"

"Get a divorce. Sell the house. Mess up my kids. The usual."

I don't say anything.

"If I sound pissed, it's because I am. I'm sorry."

"Don't apologize. It's all right."

"Fuck if I know what she wants."

"You think maybe she's seeing someone else?"

"I have no idea. She says she isn't. I know she'd rather be at work than at home. I don't know. Maybe there is another guy. Good luck to him."

He squints at the cloudless sky.

"Maybe I'll go to a movie or something. Get out of your hair."

He sighs, rubs the bridge of his nose.

"You want a glass of wine?" I ask.

Mitch grins as if we're two kids about to play hooky from school. "Kind of early, don't you think?"

"It's six o'clock somewhere," I say.

"Homemade soup, warm bread, wine. You've got it made."

I open a bottle of wine and pour some for the three of us. As I pour, Bobbie asks softly, "Are you and Gracie all right?"

"Actually, we're splitting up. How did you know?"

"I had a feeling."

"She's good," Mitch says to me.

"Oh yeah."

"It's been brewing for a long time. It became kind of official this week."

"Her idea?"

"Yes. I'm willing to try to work things out, but she's made up her mind. She can be strong-willed."

Mitch drifts over to my CD player, looking to change the subject. He bends over and flips through a cluster of CDs that have the player hemmed in. "You like jazz?"

"Yeah. I'm no expert, though. I recently got into it."

"I've always loved jazz." Mitch's tone suggests that with the loss of his marriage he has also lost his love of jazz. "Got some good stuff here."

He plucks a CD from the pile. "Miles Davis. *Kind of Blue*. One of the best jazz albums ever."

Mitch flips his glasses onto his forehead. He reads the CD cover. A smile flashes across his face like someone turning on a light.

"Miles Davis, Paul Chambers, James Cobb, Bill Evans, Cannonball Adderley, and on tenor sax, John Coltrane. Amazing musicians. Mind if we put this on?"

"Not at all."

"Well, I'm gonna check on the kids and prepare my lecture for tomorrow," Bobbie says, looking at me.

"Thanks for everything, Bobbie," Mitch says.

"Mitch, take care of yourself," she says, and sweeps out of the room. I head over to the CD player.

"I'll just finish my wine, listen to some Miles, and then I'll go."

"Stop with that," I say. "You're not going anywhere. You're gonna get drunk, sober up, we'll order a pizza, and then you can go."

"We'll see."

"As a matter of fact, you want to sleep over? I got plenty of room. You can have your own room and your own bathroom. In fact, you can move in. This house is so fucking big I'd probably never see you."

He laughs. "I'll have to go home at some point."

"Yeah. You'll want to see the kids."

"The kids," he says grimly.

I grab the chard by the neck and place it on the coffee table.

Mitch chuckles for some reason and camps on the couch. He leans forward in an improbable position, looking as if he's about to drive. Finally, the wine and the music wash over him and he tips back, landing in the sofa's soft spot.

"Mind if I take off my shoes?"

"Make yourself at home."

He grunts a thanks, pulls off his shoes, places them neatly side by side, and puts his feet up on the coffee table.

"I'm gonna make a fire," I say.

"Great. Listen, do you mind if we jump over to the third song, 'Blue in Green'?"

"You say it, I play it."

I scan over to the third cut. Bill Evans plink-plink-plinks at the piano impossibly slowly, then Miles slides in with his muted horn in a piece that is less a song than a musical interpretation of a wound.

"This song kills me," Mitch says. "Jesus."

I nod weakly. I lift a log from the stack by the side of the fire-place and lay it down on the tiny cabin of kindling I'd con-structed this morning, before the basketball game, anticipating a hot afternoon shower, a glass of wine, a good book in front of a fire, and a nap. Well, got the wine, got the fire. And got Mitch, a man I hardly know, a man trying to make sense of a life that's unraveling, trying to cling to his kids even as his relationship with them is about to become redefined right before his eyes. Mitch's eyelids, heavy with the burden of all this, start to descend like shades. "Blue in Green" ends and Miles's trumpet aches "All Blues" now, and when I finish constructing my fire, I see that Mitch has fallen into a deep, serious sleep, sprinkled with the tiniest rattle of a snore. I want to find a blanket and cover him, but while the thought seems sensible and right, the gesture seems too intimate. He is just a guy I play basketball with, isn't he? A guy who has stayed well past the Sunday game because he has no home to go home to. This is the next best thing. This is a comfort zone, a place to hang a hat, slurp a cup of homemade soup, pour out your problems, curl up on a couch, and fall asleep to jazz.

Yes. There is something about this game.

The next Sunday, Mitch shows up wearing new glasses, black Clark Kents, fastened around his head with a gray athletic strap that looks as if it were ripped from someone's sweatpants.

"You look like a short fat Kurt Rambis," Brick says.

Mitch smirks and brushes past Brick, purposely bumping his shoulder.

"Watch out," Mitch says. "I'm in a *mood.*"

"Whoa," Brick says, laughing. "Not gonna mess with you."

"Don't," Mitch says.

I laugh now; Mitch glares at me, a comic glare, a silly superhero sneer, but I'm not sure he's kidding.

The games begin. Mitch, Brick, and Phil are pitted against Duff, Stewart, and me. Duff, always physical, is on Mitch. Brick tosses the ball to Phil, who scurries right, brushing by a teeth-jarring screen set by Mitch. Without breaking stride, Mitch lowers his shoulder into Duff's throat.

"Sorry," Mitch mumbles. "Take the ball."

I take the ball out, look for Stewart. Stewart grabs my pass, up-fakes left, whirls by Mitch, and drives toward the goal. Mitch barrels toward him and swats futilely at Stewart's uncontested layup. Mitch misses the ball and plows into Stewart. The two men ram into the garage doors.

"I got hit," Stewart says as the ball drops in.

"Count it," says Brick.

"Sorry, Stewart," Mitch says.

"Christ, Mitch," says Duff. "Full contact, huh?"

"Sorry," Mitch says again, delivering his apology into the pavement.

And that's how it goes for the rest of the morning. Guard Mitch and get mugged. I, alone, know the reason Mitch has gone from the quiet, unassuming, bespectacled player with the apologetic air, inaccurate jump shot, and lackadaisical defense to a grunting, growling thug.

"What's with Mitch?" Danny asks me between games.

"What do you mean?"

"Come on. He's a hammer out there. You haven't noticed that?"

I shrug.

"You've noticed it," Danny says. "You guard him. You don't think he's been a little rough?"

"Maybe a little."

"He's probably not getting laid and he's taking it out on us."

"I don't get laid and I don't take it out on you."

"You know more than you're saying," Danny says.

"Why would I know any more than you do?"

"I don't know. People talk to you."

"*Shittt!*" Mitch screams, slams his palm against the metal pole, grabs the basketball, and throws a fastball against the garage.

Danny raises an eyebrow at me.

Done for the day, Mitch rummages through his gym bag, pulls out his wire-rims, and removes his clunky, smudged Clark Kents.

"There. Now I can see. Okay. Well. Next week, huh?"

A smattering of waves and grunts flutter by Mitch as he zips up his bag. He starts to head down the driveway, turns and pauses. His lips move in silent rehearsal, then he says, "Sorry if I played a little rough this week. I'm going through some stuff—"

Satisfied with this, he nods and goes.

"He told me," Phil says when it's clear.

"Me too," says Gabe.

"Yeah," Big Sam says. "Told me too."

"Told you what?" Brick says.

"He and Gracie are splitting up," Stewart says.

"What?" Brick says.

"I think he told every guy he guarded," Jack mutters.

"I didn't guard him so I'm out of the loop?" Brick says.

"That's why he was so rough," Duff says. "He got me a couple of times. Got me but good."

"Tell you this," Danny says, "the guy's hurting."

"He talked to you?" I ask.

"Well, I didn't guard him and you weren't gonna say anything, so I asked him."

"And?"

"He doesn't know what hit him. She came home from work one night and told him she wanted out. Just like that. He tried talking to her but her mind was made up. He offered to go into therapy with her, family counseling, work things out, offered to do *anything.* Nope. She just wants out. Bad, *bad* situation."

"It's the kids," Gabe says. "That's what I worry about."

"Kids are resilient," Duff says.

"Divorce is not good for kids, no matter how resilient they are," Gabe says.

"I only meant that—"

"Look, a lot depends on your relationship with your ex," says Big Sam. "I was lucky. Wife number one and I are still friends. We still have holidays together. I go there for Thanksgiving every year. We made a conscious effort for the kids."

"I don't see that happening here," I say.

"No. Not gonna happen here," agrees Phil.

"I'm not saying the divorce was any picnic," Big Sam says. "Far from it."

"I've told Bobbie a million times that I'll never divorce her," I say. "I'll have her killed."

"I know people," Big Sam says. "Should the time come. Call me."

"I'll keep that in mind. Something quick and painless. Like she'll be out watering the flowers, a guy drives by, *zip*. Instantaneous. Or maybe mix a lethal poison into her glass of wine."

"You seem to have given this some thought," Danny says.

"Haven't you?" I ask.

Duff leans over to Gabe, touches his arm. "What I meant about kids being resilient—"

"We should do something for Mitch," Brick says. "What, I don't know." He reaches into his gym bag. He pulls out a lip balm, pastes on a smile, and spreads the balm across his lips with agonizing slowness and care. I scrunch my forehead and stare at him.

"What are you looking at?" he asks me.

"You're applying *lipstick.*"

"It's not lipstick. It's lip *balm.* My lips get chapped."

"From playing basketball?" Ben asks.

"Mainly from talking to you guys."

"I'm with Brick," Big Sam says. "We have to do something for Mitch. Calm him down. Get him laid."

"Anybody know any women?" I ask.

Silence.

"This is depressing," Ben says finally.

"Gabe knows women," Phil says.

"They're all married and pregnant," Gabe says.

"Probably not into dating," I say.

"Maybe we should take him out to dinner, something like that," Wally says.

"What is something *like* dinner?" Danny asks. "A snack?"

"He definitely needs to lighten up, have a few laughs," Ben says.

"Funny you should mention that," Phil says. "Not funny haha. Funny ironic." He bends over and reaches into his gym bag. He takes out a crumpled newspaper clipping and his reading glasses on a string. He slips on the glasses and holds the newspaper in front of him an arm's length away.

"I have to get to the eye doctor. Anyway . . ." Like a librarian, he peers at us over his glasses. "Jackie Mason. This Tuesday at the Comedy Store. One night only. Anybody here like Jackie Mason?"

"I love him and I'm the token goy," Duff says.

"Ah . . . I'm not Jewish," Jack says.

"I thought you were," Big Sam says.

"No, my wife is."

"Then you're Jewish, too, believe me," Ben says.

"Mazel tov," Phil says.

"Stewart, what about you?" Duff asks.

"I'm agnostic. Haven't we discussed this?"

"To death," says Brick.

"Stewart, you may not believe in organized religion, but you are, in fact, Jewish," I say.

"I suppose so. Culturally."

"Oh, yes. One can tell by your mannerisms, the way you gesture with your hands, the fact that you never put butter on your bagel—"

"What's wrong with butter on a bagel?" asks Duff.

"If you have to ask," Big Sam says.

"Man," Phil says. "Ask a simple question. Jackie Mason. Tuesday night. Cheering up Mitch. Anybody?"

A pause. Then a rush of excuses.

"Tuesday night is tough," says Ben.

"Yeah. It's a school night," says Stewart.

"Dad does dinner," Duff says.

"I can't get away during the week," says Wally.

"I don't get home until eight," Danny says.

"Gabe and I play hockey," says Big Sam.

"I'll do it," I say. "I have no life. Tuesday, Wednesday, they're all the same to me."

"Sounds like you'll be a lot of fun," Brick says. "I wouldn't miss it."

"You'll go?" I say.

"Yeah. Guy needs a pick-me-up. My specialty."

"Oh shit," Phil says. "I can't do it this Tuesday. I forgot. I'm having a colonoscopy Wednesday. Damn."

"Let's bring him to that," I say.

Brick rolls his eyes and springs to his feet. "It'll be easier for us to get him laid."

Every Sunday now, Mitch talks covertly about his crumbling marriage. He speaks in the shadows, in the margins of the morning, between games on the deck, and during games, talking one-on-one with the guy he's guarding. Every other Sunday, Mitch stays behind and hangs out at our house for an hour or more, enjoying Bobbie's soup, listening to jazz, sometimes accompanying me on a couple of Sunday errands. On alternate Sundays, Mitch takes his kids for the afternoon while Gracie stays at home. On those Sundays, Mitch leaves the game early. And on those Sundays, the rest of us talk about him.

"How do you think he's doing?" Danny asks, whirling a basketball around his back.

"Not great," I say. "He's in a lot of pain. It's hard."

"She's not going to move out until the divorce is final," Ben says, rapid-fire. Heads swivel toward him. "That's what he said to me."

"It'll be a lot better once they sell the house and he gets his own place," Big Sam says. "This part now, this is brutal, this is the worst."

"The kids are having a tough time," Gabe says. "That's what he told me. That's what I worry about."

"You're enraged. You hate her. You really hate her," Big Sam says, then stops himself. He removes the baseball cap he's wearing, runs his fingers through his hair like a comb. "I remember I once punched a wall. I was so furious at her, at everything. I punched a fucking wall."

"I thought you and your ex are friends," Jack whispers.

"Not that day we weren't. We are now. But not that day."

"He'll get through it," Stewart says. "He'll be all right. It just takes time."

"That's the thing," Ben says. "Mitch wants this part to be over, wants to move on. You can't make it go any faster."

"I read in a medical journal that it takes five years," Phil says.

"Five *years?*" Duff says.

"Yeah. From the start of a divorce to getting back to normal, emotionally. Five years. That's what I read."

"That seems like an overly long time. Maybe that's at the extreme end," Stewart says.

"No. Five years is about right," Big Sam says. "To go through everything emotionally, physically, financially, to get yourself settled into a new home, get your kids acclimated to a whole new lifestyle, and to get over feeling like a worthless piece of shit so you can function again in society? Start going out, dating? Believe me, it takes five years. A good five years."

No one speaks for a while.

Then Brick stands up, scraping his chair along the deck. "Might take Mitch longer," he says.

We watch Mitch closely, as if he has contracted some terrible disease and we are monitoring him for signs of improvement or decline. We do this because it feels as if one of us, one of our own, has been stricken. We are a strange support group, ragged and clumsy and incapable of talking to Mitch together. We prefer one-on-one face time, man to man. Never men to man. Weekly I see men in games, between plays, talking to Mitch, listening, nodding, and returning to basketball only after placing a caring hand on his shoulder.

As summer approaches, I sense our concern is wearing on him. No longer aggressive, he becomes timid on the court, sometimes downright sheepish. He shoots once a Sunday, plays porous defense, rarely hustles for rebounds. We cut him slack. Brick and Danny, the game's two sergeants at arms, two guys who chew my ass if I make a late cut or slide too far off a pick, are so deferential toward Mitch it's creepy: "That's okay, buddy, nice try!" or "My bad, Mitch. You didn't see it coming."

Hey, I know the guy's going through a divorce and his life is all fucked up, but basketball is basketball.

In October, the week before Halloween, we decide to escape. Our plan is to haul Mitch out of his morass by immersing him in two days of bachelor debauchery in Mexico: basketball, poker, eating until we can't move, and drinking like it's homecoming weekend.

"Road trip," Big Sam says. "That's what he needs. Male bonding South of the Border. He'll come back a new man."

For years now we've been hearing about Big Sam's Mexican hideaway, only four hours away, past the squalor of Tijuana, overlooking the Pacific, just outside of Ensenada, a bustling little seaside city.

"My place is less than a mile from the *universidad,*" Big Sam says. "Plenty of hoops there. I've played ball with a couple of professors and grad students. We get lucky, I might even get us to play *inside.* They just built a brand-new gym."

Inside? On the hardwood? Previously available only in my dreams.

"What would we do down there?" Duff asks. "I mean, besides playing basketball?"

"You want the agenda for the whole weekend? Because I can

do that. I've given this a lot of thought. Believe me, you will not be bored."

"Sure. Break it down," Duff says.

"Okay. I'll get down there Thursday night to set everything up. You guys come down Friday night or Saturday morning, it's up to you. Soon as you get there, you'll crash and fall dead asleep to the sound of waves breaking on the shore, just outside your window. Saturday morning, I'll cook breakfast, Big Sam's famous Mexican hash and your choice of freshly squeezed orange juice or screwdrivers. Sated and possibly hammered, we will then go to the college and play ball. After that, come back, shower, and drive into town for fish tacos on the pier. Then we'll take a walking tour of the city, perhaps explore some of the more notorious saloons. On the way home we will stop at the *farmacia* where you can purchase a supply of prescription drugs over the counter. Valium, Viagra—"

"All the best *v* drugs," I say.

"Right." Big Sam laughs. "Saturday afternoon, we'll come back to the house and imbibe several pitchers of margaritas, mixed by the magical hand of Mr. Mitch himself."

"I feel so wanted," Mitch says.

"You are wanted."

"Don't know if I'm going, though."

"You're going," Phil says.

"Let me finish telling you the schedule, then you decide," Big Sam says. "Okay. After we get plowed on your killer margaritas, we watch the World Series on the dish, catch the incredible sunset—"

"Between innings," I say.

"—between innings. After the game, we will go out for an unbelievable meal at this little place I know, owned by these two gay Spaniards. Incredible food at unbelievably cheap prices. Sunday morning, get up, more ball, shower, lunch, and return to L.A. better and deeper men."

"What about free time?" Brick asks. "I might need to take a shit on Saturday. Did you figure that in?"

"I figured in fifteen minutes of free time a day."

"Good. I was worried there."

"So, Mitch? Mexico?" Stewart asks.

Mitch scowls. His chair creaks as he shifts his weight.

"I don't know, guys. I've got a lot going on. Things are a little bit up in the air—"

"Mexico, Mitch," Phil says. "With us. *Mexico.*"

"Yeah, Mitch, Mexico," Danny says. "Poverty, disease, crime, filth, you can't drink the water, and you'll definitely get diarrhea."

"And you can't get into the bathroom because I'll be in there," Brick says.

"I got more than one bathroom," Big Sam says. "And you can drink the water. It comes from a purified spring. You can drink right out of the tap."

"Who's gonna drink water? You'll be drinking tequila," Phil says.

"I'm having water," I say. "But just enough to swallow the Valiums I'm buying at the Ensenada Sav-On."

"I could actually use some Valium," Mitch says.

"He's going!" Phil says. "You're going, right?"

We begin to chant. Loud and sophomoric, drumming the table with our palms: "*Mitch, Mitch, Mitch, Mitch . . .*"

"Okay, okay, I'll go. I guess," Mitch croaks.

"All rigghtt," Big Sam says, and slaps Mitch five.

"Long as you're going," Danny says, "pick me up a case of Viagra." He whacks Mitch on the back as if he were running for office.

Bobbie wants me to go.

"It'll do you good," she says. "Spend some time with the guys. Change of scenery. You can use the break."

I look at my wife lying next to me, her jade cat's eyes misting. She is so private sometimes, this woman bred from European stock, raised in Connecticut, a mix of Old Country fire and New England reserve. She is at a loss these days. For years, she has endured with grace my incessant complaining and mercurial moods, due to, I explain endlessly, the myriad woes of career, partner, incompetent and cruel coworkers and bosses, and most often, the work itself.

"I'm not doing what I want to do!" has been my continuous, clarion call.

In the end, for the good of her and us, grumbling and miserable, I have always gone back to work, done the best I could, and returned with a fat paycheck. Until now.

I can't do it anymore.

I just don't have it, babe. I lost it at the movies. Or maybe on the set of a sitcom. The problem is, I don't know what I want. Or what to do.

I look for answers late at night. I prowl these rooms like a burglar in my own house. I tiptoe into my children's rooms. I watch them sleep. I approach my son, illuminated by his Teenage Mutant Ninja Turtle night-light. I stroke his hair and kiss his forehead. He dreams blissfully of a world that can be conquered with katana blades. I retreat and walk into my daughter's room, the moonlight a soft white blanket that lies over her. I kiss her, too, and I whisper, "Don't worry, it's going to be all right, Daddy's here."

Crawling back into our bed, I ponder the ceiling, trying to off myself to sleep. When sleep comes, it is fitful and brings with it dreams that exhaust me, dreams of faceless intruders breaking down my door and chasing me into desolate landscapes of smashed metal and frightening, oversize, jagged auto parts looming over me like prehistoric jaws. I escape always, but barely. And when I awake, my body is soaked with the ordeal of the night and I have come no closer to the truth.

So when Bobbie asks, "What's wrong?" and I tell her, "My life," she answers hopelessly in the cavernous silence and sadness of this house, "What are we going to do?"

"I don't know," I say. "Try to think of something before the money runs out."

In the meantime, I'll go to Mexico.

Saturday morning, 6 A.M. Gunning toward the border. Brick, former New York City cabdriver, is at the wheel, pushing ninety. I ride shotgun. Phil and Jack share the backseat. We eat bagels, passing them back and forth through the car. We bitch about the early hour. We second-guess this whole idea. We are married men on the lam.

We are to join four others, the ones who could get away. We will meet at Big Sam's beach house and immediately head over for hoops at the college. Duff, Stewart, and Mitch joined Sam last night, plied by promises of tequila and Cuban cigars.

Outside Tijuana, we weave off the main highway, following a series of signs offering Mexican auto insurance. In Mexico, you can buy insurance by the week.

"Get the insurance," Big Sam insists. "You do not want to get caught with nothing but your American Piece of the Rock collision policy South of the Border. Unless you never want to see your car again and you don't mind spending a week in a Mexican jail."

Near the tip of downtown, we drive into an alley and park next to a portly Mexican in a suit and sombrero and a police officer in a dusty brown uniform. Brick lowers his window. We each pass Brick a couple of twenties, the portly Mexican hands him what looks like a raffle ticket, and we're done, insured. I get the feeling that we could buy insurance by the day if we wanted, or even, for the right price, by the hour.

Back on the road, we follow Big Sam's directions and climb a hill that takes us above the city. The main highway slithers off into one lane, winding and treacherous and packed with a layer of dust as thick as a floor. The poverty here is heartbreaking. Frail men in tattered and stained T-shirts, cigarettes dangling from their lips, congregate in front of their homes, minuscule shacks scarcely bigger than outhouses, thrown together with corrugated aluminum, some topped with rusty TV antennas, many crowned with gleaming new satellite dishes. Stick-figure-thin and filthy children squawk at each other or scuffle in the dirt in front of the shacks. Barefoot teenaged moms stand and sway, hunched over babies fastened to their breasts, their faces stamped with hopelessness.

Solemn, silent, we wind our way back toward the coast. Brick steps on it, trying to put some distance between what we've just seen and the guilt we all feel at being here on holiday. I feel like an intruder. Shaken, I seek comic relief by making fun of Brick's driving, Jack's fear of drinking the water, and Phil's desperate need to pee. In less than an hour we hit Ensenada. Brick slows to a crawl along an unmarked highway as we look for the address of Sam's vacation home.

"This is it," Phil says, navigating, eyes alternating between a cluster of mobile homes on the edge of the sea and the crude map Sam had faxed to him.

"What is?" Brick says.

"*This.* Right here. Turn here."

"This is a trailer park."

"It says here—" Phil removes his glasses and peers at the map, his nose grazing the paper.

"You guys made great time!"

Big Sam in shades, tank top, and a baseball cap jogs toward us. He waves us into a parking space.

"Grab your stuff and I'll show you to your rooms. *Mi casa es su casa.* Well, in your case, my friend's *casa es su casa.*"

"We drove four hours through squalor to spend the night in a trailer park? This is your Mexican dream house?" Brick says.

"Wait until you see the inside, brother. Do not judge a book by its cover. You're talking trailer *deluxe*. All the comforts of home."

"You got a bathroom?" Phil asks.

"Got two. Two where you're staying as well. Come on, I have fresh orange juice, coffee, Mexican pastries."

"We ate," Jack says, patting his stomach nervously.

"What are you gonna do, fast for two days?" I ask him.

"I'm thinking about it."

"Come *on*. The guys are anxious to play some ball," Big Sam says, leading the way.

Inside Big Sam's trailer, Stewart, Duff, and Mitch await us, dressed to play. The trailer is indeed a surprise. A spacious living room overlooks the ocean, one continuous window offering an unobstructed, panoramic view. A giant big-screen TV dominates one wall, a large L-shaped leather couch lined up in front of it. An open kitchen area big enough for an eat-in table pokes in behind the couch, nearly brushing the far arm. Down a hall are two decent-sized bedrooms. Outside, though, is the main feature: a horseshoe-shaped wooden deck connected to the living room, providing an arm's-length view of the Pacific. I gravitate out there and, juice in hand, stare into the sea, swept up by the sound of the waves crashing beneath my feet.

"What do you think, *boychik?*"

Big Sam, hat spun around the other way, joins me on the deck.

"Not bad, Sam."

"Sit."

I do, collapsing into a cloth lounge chair. Big Sam drops into a plastic mesh beach chair next to me and kicks off his shoes.

"I could get used to this," I say.

"Too bad you weren't staying longer. We could go out fishing. Now that is really something. Talk about a relaxing way to spend a day. Guaranteed to catch your dinner, too."

"I'm not that crazy about cleaning fish."

"Don't have to. They got kids on the dock who'll do that for you. Experts. Been doing it since they could walk. They'll clean a whole fish, fillet it, pack it in ice, everything, for fifty cents a fish. Seriously."

The waves roll in below us, a soft, soothing crush. Over and over, again and again. I could actually sleep.

"I come out here at night, have a glass of wine, watch the sunset. Zone out."

"Great place to escape," I hear myself say.

"Yep. And, boy, do I need it. The shit I deal with all week? I need to escape as often as I can. Otherwise I'm either gonna burn out or blow up."

"I hear that," I mutter.

Phil, Brick, and Stewart burst onto the deck. Stewart dribbles a basketball an inch from my head.

"You were right, Sam," Phil says. "Good bathroom. Running water and everything."

"For you, Phil, only the best," Big Sam says.

"Don't spoil him," I say, opening my eyes a slit.

"Well? Shall we?" Big Sam says, heaving himself out of his chair. The plastic seat toots.

The outdoor courts at the university are deserted. A dozen white metal backboards glint in the Mexican sun, causing a head-pounding glare. The rims have no nets and the ground is covered with a layer of smooth, fine dust, almost like silt, the color of coffee ice cream. It is as slick as ice. The seven of us, Big Sam excluded, stand in the center of the courts, hands on hips, trying to hide our disappointment.

"Got our choice," Stewart says brightly. "Wish they had nets, though."

"Little slick here, Sam," Duff says, gingerly sliding his bow-legs through the silt like a child on skates.

"A little *slick?*" Brick says. "You have to be Wayne Fucking Gretzky."

Big Sam grins. "Not to worry, boys." He pops open his trunk, reaches in, and tosses me a brand-new white net still in the package. Then he grunts and drags out a ladder. "There's a broom in there, too. Someone wanna grab it?"

Within minutes, Duff stands on the top rung of the ladder and attaches the net to a hoop. Behind him, I sweep the basketball court futilely. Each flick of my broom causes a tiny ferocious tornado. Phil, darting in and around us, documents all of this with a small gold Olympus camera, his new toy.

"I have the same camera," Mitch says. "Actually, Gracie has it now."

"Someone else want to give this a try?" I say. "I'm just moving the dirt around."

No one moves.

"Anybody?" I say. "It's really a lot of fun."

Stewart sighs, shrugs, grabs the broom.

"So we play in a little dirt," Big Sam says. "We got running water. You'll shower."

"It's not the dirt," Brick says, skating. "I already have one knee brace. Don't need another one."

"Play at half speed," Phil says, snapping a picture.

"How will we know the difference?" I say.

The court can accommodate all eight of us, so we play four-on-four. We're not used to the resulting clutter and confusion. We're also not used to the seemingly endless size of the court.

"Aren't you out of bounds," I huff as Phil curls around me, leaves me in his wake, and catches a perfect pass from Jack.

"He was *out*, wasn't he?" I plead as Phil drops in a layup.

"The out of bounds is over there," Big Sam says, pointing toward a distant horizon.

"Jesus," I say. "Where is that, San Diego?"

Our team of Brick, Mitch, Stewart, and I are overmatched by Jack, Duff, Phil, and Big Sam, partly because Brick and I play tentatively and shoot almost exclusively from the outside, an iffy proposition considering that, if you don't hit the center of the net, the ball recoils off the metal backboard as if shot out of a cannon. After an hour, with the heat beating down and the dust kicking up, we call it quits.

"Getting hungry anyway," Big Sam says, rubbing his hands together like he's about to crack a safe. "Who wants fish tacos?"

"Want a shower first," Brick says.

"What for? You didn't break a sweat."

Our trailer is the same size as Sam's but lacks his view and his taste in furniture and contains only one shower. Phil, Brick, and I allow Mitch to go first mainly because we want to talk about him.

"He seems better," Phil says.

"Definitely," says Brick.

"He doesn't seem so depressed," says Phil.

"Exactly," says Brick.

"He's definitely better than he was," I say.

"Definitely," Phil says.

"What's it been, a couple of months?" I ask.

"Oh, at least," Phil says, then rubs the back of his neck. "Maybe three."

"More like four or five," says Brick.

"That long?" I say.

"Well, let's see, this is October," Brick says. "Figure it out."

"You're right," Phil says. "Might even be closer to six."

"He's definitely less depressed," I say.

Brick scratches his stomach. "We must be doing a good job."

"Ahhhhhh!" Mitch screams from the shower. *"Fuckkkkk!"*

We look at each other for a split second, then dash to the bathroom door. The only sound we hear is the drizzle and slap of the shower running. Phil puts his ear to the door.

"I don't hear him," he says.

"Sheeeyitttt!" Mitch howls from the shower. The shower crashes to a stop and Mitch charges out of the bathroom, a towel wrapped around his middle.

"Good luck, guys," he says. "There's no hot water."

He barrels past us and goes into his room to change.

We begin at a fish taco place located in an alcove tucked off a pier near Ensenada's main wharf. The place consists of two long picnic tables and is run by a mellow Mexican who sees his week made by the eight of us. We order two tacos apiece and two six-packs of Coronas, which Senor Mellow offers to us but doesn't have.

"I will return," he says in Spanish to Big Sam.

He runs down the pier and darts into a liquor store. He emerges with the Coronas and runs back to us, the beers tucked against his side like a portfolio. He lowers the six-packs onto our table and retreats to his skillet. As chunks of Mexican sea bass sizzle behind us, we pass out the brews. We yank off the tops and raise the bottles in a toast.

"Well, you did it," Big Sam says. "I never thought you guys would come down here. I thought you were too tied to your wives' apron strings. You proved me wrong. You're men. All of you. Here's to you."

We clink our bottles and drink.

"I have another toast," Stewart says, pointing his bottle upward toward a dusty and stagnant ceiling fan. "To Sam, our wonderful host."

We cheer, clink, and drink.

"And here's to Alan," Big Sam says. "Without him, we wouldn't be here."

"Here, here," Mitch says.

Clink. Drink.

"And here's to hot water in our shower," Phil says.

Sam laughs. "Not gonna happen this trip, boys."

"Didn't the guy pay his bill?"

"He's been having some trouble."

"Great," says Phil.

"You're welcome to use my shower," Big Sam says.

"We're fine," I say. "You see the four of us here?"

Phil, Brick, Mitch, and I link arms across each other's shoulders.

"We define toughness. We define *manhood.*"

"We define body odor," says Jack.

"Feesh tacos," Senor Mellow sings as he Frisbees our lunch across the table on paper plates.

"Umm," Big Sam says, sniffing his taco before he lowers his jaws into it like a T-rex devouring its prey.

"Excuse me," Mitch says. "Do you have any salsa?"

"Salsa? Sí," Senor Mellow crows, nodding at a small table hugging the wall. A large plastic bowl of soupy red liquid rests on top of the table.

"I'll get it," Mitch says, rising quickly and waving the guy off.

I'm focusing on my fish taco so I miss the first part of the disaster. Out of the corner of my eye, I see Mitch suddenly fly forward as if he's diving into a pool.

"Urnkrfff," he howls, his arms spread-eagled, his feet flailing out from under him. In a desperate, reflexive attempt to keep his balance, he reaches out for the table. Instead, he grabs on to the bowl of salsa and flips it over, spattering salsa everywhere, on to the walls, onto the table, and mostly on Jack.

"Salsa!" Senor Mellow cries.

"Jack," Mitch pleads, crumpling onto the floor, his head lingering a moment above our picnic table, then disappearing from view.

"Wow," Jack says, staring at his formerly white T-shirt, now covered with a bloody red planet.

Mitch emerges from under the table, dazed, salsa pocks covering his face and dotting his hair.

"I tripped," he says.

We lose it. A wave of laughter rumbles through us.

"I just . . . wanted . . . to spice . . . up . . . my . . . taco," Mitch says, gasping between sobs of hysteria.

"Salsa," Senor Mellow moans sadly.

"I really need some," Mitch says.

"Lick the wall," I say.

We clean up the mess, wiping down the walls and floor with paper towels Big Sam finds in the bathroom. When we're done, we pay Senor Mellow for his trouble. The entire meal, including food, beer, tip, and an extra $20 for the salsa, costs the eight of us $40. Five dollars apiece.

"I'm moving here," I announce.

Full, tipsy, and laughing, we walk one short block to the Ensenada Fish Market, a football-field-sized festival of every type of fish imaginable, columns of whole fish with mouths agape, huddles of shellfish with tentacles dangling, all lifelessly packed in ice and laid to rest on tables under faded blue awnings. We stroll through row after row of fish as if we are a high school class perusing exhibits at a museum. As we walk, the relentless fish stench causes my eyes to water. Still, I can't resist purchasing a small slab of smoked albacore, which I munch, while Jack buys a fresh T-shirt from a street vendor. Finally, we emerge out of the odor into the murky sunlight and pile into Big Sam's van.

Next stop, Hussong's, the legendary bar and tourist trap. The place is gorged with Americans, not a native in sight. The eight of us cram into a high wooden booth with Brad and Lila, a couple from Seattle. In record time, Phil and I drain two margaritas apiece that taste like straight Windex. My mouth fills with the flavor of soap. In seconds, the people in the bar are blurry caricatures and the music from the jukebox is a knife into my brain. This is a personal best: hammered at two o'clock in the afternoon. The flash from someone's camera blinds me. I try to smile but the corners of my mouth burn. I haven't been this wasted since Hell Night. We squish together now for a group shot, taken by Brad. We don't find out until we get the film developed a week later that Lila is in the picture, too, behind us. She has pulled her shirt up to her chin, exposing an amply filled-out hot-pink bra.

We stumble out of Hussong's, at least Phil and I do, and collide with a group of tourists streaming out of a bus.

"I'm seriously wasted," Phil tells them, and waves at the air as if he were swatting mosquitoes. He sits down hard on the curb.

An emaciated child, no more than six years old, my son's age, approaches us. The child holds his mother's hand. She is a teenager with chocolate skin.

"Chiclets?" the child says.

With painful deliberation, Phil nods, reaches into his pocket, and hands the child a ten. The boy takes it, gives it to his mother, and offers Phil a small plastic box of gum. Phil shakes his head. The boy then sticks a grubby hand in my face. I hand him a five, all I have in my pocket. I turn down the gum, too. Chattering something in Spanish, could be "Have a good day," could be "Kiss my ass," the mother and child disappear into the flow of people pouring out of the bus and out of Hussong's.

"I'm suddenly sober," Phil says.

I help him to his feet.

We stop at a pharmacy and spend a half hour ransacking the drug bins like looters. We then head back to Big Sam's, where we hibernate for the rest of the afternoon. Big Sam brings out a bowl of chips and homemade guacamole and brews a pot of coffee.

Phil and I silently sip the strong Mexican blend out of oversize latte mugs, the World Series thrumming in the background. The other guys pass in and out of the living room and the deck, stopping to glance at the Series, grab a handful of chips, and return outside to sop up the view.

Some guys stake out a spot. Duff nestles into a recliner and cheers loudly for the Atlanta Braves in between sips of his gin and tonic. Brick, his face obscured by aviator glasses the size of welder's goggles, plants himself in a lounge chair on the deck and vanishes into a novel he's reading by Richard Russo. Stewart, Big Sam, and Jack, drinking rum and Cokes, talk school. I don't want any part of *that*. I turn back to the Series and boo Glavine just to annoy Duff.

We go to dinner at the home-style Spanish restaurant Big Sam has been touting for weeks. We occupy the entire left wall and begin by ordering a couple of bottles of a Chilean red, at $15, the most expensive bottle on the menu. I sit next to Mitch, who is drunk and happy and looser than I have seen him in a year. Suddenly, he stands up and taps his wineglass with his spoon.

"I have an announcement to make," Mitch says, his voice quivering. "Actually two announcements. First of all, though, I just want to thank you guys. You've been terrific, all of you, incredibly supportive. I guess I was kind of surprised at first. Then I was touched, *genuinely* touched—"

"Get to the fucking announcement already," Brick says.

We laugh.

"Okay. All right. The first announcement is, Gracie's getting married."

It's as if he's just scored the winning basket in a play-off game. We shout, cheer, slap him on the back.

"Who's the victim—er, groom?" Big Sam asks.

"Believe it or not, a rabbi," Mitch says.

"A man of the cloth," I say.

"A man familiar with prayer," Mitch says. "A requirement if he is to wed my ex-wife."

"Wish them well," Phil says, a warning.

"Oh, I do, you bet. In fact, to *them*. To Gracie and the rabbi!"

We lift our glasses.

"What's the second announcement?" Stewart asks.

A hush falls over the restaurant. Mitch takes a deep breath. "I met someone."

WOOOOO!

We scream as if Mitch has scored the hoop to win the *championship*. If we were any more drunk, or any less drunk, we might have hoisted him onto our shoulders and carried him out of the restaurant.

"Who is she?"

A nurse, it turns out, related to a close friend of Phil's wife, Madeline.

"Small world," Jack says.

"Amazing," Mitch says.

"Serious?" Stewart asks.

"Nah. She's dating *me*," Mitch says. He roars and we polish off the first bottle of wine.

In Big Sam's van on the way back, Brick says, "So, in other words, Mitch, you're doing fine and we drove all the way down here for nothing?"

"Hey, you're hurting my feelings," Big Sam says.

"I'm really glad we came," Mitch says. "Don't listen to him, Sam."

"I don't."

"I'm glad we came too, Sam," Stewart says. "I think we should come every year."

"Don't get crazy," Mitch says.

• • •

A little after eight in the evening, we settle in for the night in Big Sam's living room. After a minute, Sam offers a victory cigar, and he and Mitch lift themselves to their feet and shuffle outside to light up. Through the living room window, I can make out their profiles. Two sturdy, sizable men standing their ground, sharing a laugh of conspiracy. They bow their heads and tiny bonfires explode six inches from their faces. A cough, a snicker, someone spits. A whiff of sulfur. I close my eyes and hear gulls cawing and the click of a cricket. A warm breeze rustles through the open door and tickles my cheek. The night air smells faintly of cinnamon. On the wall, bathed in blue light, the *SportsCenter* anchor describes the details of a game. He sounds far away, as if he's calling long distance on a crappy cell phone.

I'm aware now of men yawning.

Long soft howls in deep bass notes like foghorns announcing approaching ships.

"I am so tired," says Stewart. "*Exhausted.* I had a very stressful week. You deal with certain parents . . ."

His voice runs away into a cavernous yawn. I yawn in answer, Phil follows, then Jack.

"What time *is* it?" Jack asks.

Aaaooooohhgerrrr blows out of Stewart's throat, another freaky, frightening yawn.

"Eight-fifteen," Duff says, consulting his watch.

"Are you sure?" Stewart asks.

"Eight-fifteen," Duff repeats.

"This is ridiculous," Phil says. "We have to do something. Guys, come on."

"I'm not going anywhere," I mumble.

"I got it," Phil says. "How about a poker game? What do you think?"

"If I don't have to move, I love it."

"Okay, you and me, that's two. Who else wants to play? Duff?"

"I'm not very good. I think I'll pass."

"I hate poker," Brick says.

"Stewart, poker?"

"Sure," Stewart says, and yawns again. "I just don't want to stay up too late."

"It's eight-fifteen," Phil says. "You can't stay up late if you tried. You can play for two hours and it won't be late."

"I won't last two hours."

"Fine. An hour. Jack?"

"I'll play. I'm bad, though."

"Perfect. You're in. Let me see if those guys want to play."

Phil heads outside.

"Well, that does it for me," Brick says. "I'm calling it a night."

"You're *what?*" Duff says.

"You heard me. I'm going to bed."

"You know what time it is, right?"

"Hey, I get up at five o'clock in the morning. Sometimes earlier. I'm in the gym by five-thirty, in the office by seven. By eight o'clock at night, I am dead. Boys, this little jaunt is my vacation. I am going over to Ice Station Zebra, gonna take a crap, and crawl into bed with my book."

"Just don't get those things confused," I say.

"Thanks for the warning," Brick says. "Miss me."

He pulls himself up out of the couch, stretches, yawns, and meets Phil coming in.

"Where you going?"

"Bed."

"*Bed?* Whata you got, a hooker over there?"

Brick winks, yawns again, loud enough for Big Sam and Mitch to turn our way.

"Nighty night," Brick says. He clomps down the wooden stairs that lead away from the trailer and disappears into the dark.

"That is pitiful," Phil says. "Okay. Those guys are in. They're just finishing up a conversation and then we'll play."

"Does Sam have chips?"

"He's got chips, cards, we're all set."

Phil bends down in front of a cabinet next to the TV and pulls out a bottle of liquor. "Grand Marnier. Anybody want a nightcap?"

Stop signs held up all around. Phil shrugs. "A shot before poker? I think that's required. Dude?"

"Hit me."

He finds a couple of shot glasses and pours two fingers for each of us.

"What time is it now?" Jack asks.

"Eight-twenty," Duff says.

"You know what?" Jack says. "I'm gonna turn in, too."

"You're kidding," I say. I lean forward to hear what he has to say.

"Nope. I had a long week. I was in court, dealing with *lawyers*. Besides, I'm reading this fascinating history of the Battle of Gettysburg. The only trouble is, I never get a chance. This is perfect. I'll read for a while then get a good night's sleep."

"No one would believe this," I say.

"So . . . good night, guys," Jack says, and he's out, leaving Duff, Phil, Stewart, and me.

Phil rolls his eyes.

Duff shrugs and sips his drink.

I turn to Stewart. "Stewart, I was wondering about something. Allowing the kids to spell any way they want—"

"*Hugguhhh,*" Stewart says. His nose twitches; he flicks at it with the back of his hand.

Takes me a second before I realize he is fast asleep. I look over at Phil. He shrugs.

"Was there something in the food?" I say.

"I've never seen anything like this," Phil says. "What time is it?"

"Eight twenty-*two,*" Duff says.

"Should we wake him up?" I ask, but before Phil answers, Stewart snaps to attention.

"What time is it?" he asks.

"Jesus, guys, get a watch," Duff says.

"I fell asleep," Stewart says. "I am totally out of it. I don't usually drink this much."

"Nobody does," I say.

"I'll catch you guys in the morning."

Stewart stands up, staggers, and like a bad actor playing drunk, weaves out of the room.

"Last man standing, Duff," I say.

"Don't worry about me. I've got at least ten more minutes in me before I crash."

"What the. . . ?" Phil says. "Those guys just sat down out there. I thought they were coming in—"

He plunks his glass down on the kitchen counter and charges outside. I stare at my glass. At some point it became empty. Don't remember when, exactly. What the hell. I pour another finger.

"Want a nightcap, Duff?"

"I'm good."

I point to Duff's glass. "What are you drinking?"

"Ginger ale. I had a beer with lunch, a gin and tonic this afternoon. I try to go easy."

"I hear you." I belt down the shot. I nearly gag. "That's it. I'm cutting myself off."

"The thing is," Duff says, rolling his glass of ginger ale back and forth between his palms, "my grandmother was an alcoholic."

"Duff, I didn't know—"

"Yeah. She was a pretty bad drunk. I actually have to

watch myself. I don't know if it skips a generation, but I can get, you know, sometimes, uh . . . sometimes I can get carried away."

Duff gets up from his chair and sits down next to me on the couch. With his index finger, he absently taps his glass. "Yep," he says. "I have to watch it."

"What was she like?" I ask.

He lets out a gust of air. "My grandmother, she, well . . . first she would get verbally abusive. Then she would get violent. It was not a lot of fun going over there. After a while, she kinda got sick and she moved in with us. That was not a lot of fun at all."

Duff waits, remembers. He lowers his voice. "It wasn't always bad. She had her moments. We had good times. Holidays, though . . ." His eyes flutter. "Not a lot of fun."

"But you're different. You're not like that."

"No, I'm not. Thank God." He holds his glass up and shakes it gently. He peers into his soda as if he's dropped something of value into its fizz.

"I could be, though," he says. "I could be like that."

"I don't think so, Duff."

"Yeah." He turns and looks at me. His eyes are red and moist. "I could be."

Twenty minutes later, Phil and I sit alone on the deck. Everyone else is in bed. It is Saturday night in Mexico, not yet nine o'clock. To most men, the night is just getting started.

"How do you feel about honeymoon bridge?" I ask.

"Can you believe this?" Phil says. "We couldn't even get a poker game together. Couldn't find five guys to stay up past nine o'clock. I've been to medical supply conventions that were wilder than this."

"When you think about it, though, we are sort of cheating on our wives. We wouldn't dare go to sleep before nine o'clock at home."

"You're right. Why is that?"

"We're men. We have to lock up."

"Plus women cannot comprehend the sheer joy an unscheduled nap brings to a man. They always want you to be doing shit."

"Especially on Sunday," I point out.

"Here's my perfect Sunday," Phil says. "Basketball in the morning, followed by a long hot shower, then up to my roof deck or onto the beach with the Sunday papers, read, and fall asleep. That to me is heaven."

"My perfect Sunday is exactly the same, except for the beach."

"What is it with you and the beach?"

"It's dirty. Tar gets on your feet. Sand gets up your ass. Give me my couch in front of a fire."

"Now, how often do you get to *have* your perfect Sunday?"

"Rarely," I say.

"Almost never," Phil agrees.

"So that's why when we're in Mexico, we eat, drink, and go to sleep at nine o'clock. We're cheating on our wives."

Phil chuckles. "We *bad.*"

I smile. Strange. Despite all I've had to drink, I feel stone-cold sober.

"So, dude, how you doing?" Phil asks after a while.

"Hanging in. Barely."

"Have we decided what you're doing with the rest of your life?"

"Not yet, Philly. I'm working on it."

I hear a plunk in the water, then another. Sounds as if someone is tossing pebbles into the sea.

Phil whistles out a breath. "Are you going to move?"

"It's a possibility. The way I feel, everything's up in the air."

I hold as the thought settles.

"I think about it," I say. "I want to simplify my life. Get rid of the extraneous crap, the mortgage, private school, the *cars* for chrissakes."

Plunk. Splash.

"You know what drives me crazy?" I say. "Choices. We have so many damn choices. Drives me *crazy*. I hate making choices because I usually make the wrong one."

It must be the drink, because I giggle. Phil cocks his head, blows out a laugh of his own.

I say, "I wish I lived in a small town where there was only one school, a bookstore, a movie theater, couple of decent restaurants. I'd walk everywhere or ride a bike. I'd take up cooking."

"Cooking," Phil repeats simply, but in a tone that makes the whole fantasy sound absurd.

"I don't know." I sigh, exhaling a large, desperate gust of air. "I have to figure it out, Phil."

He pauses. "Do me a favor. If you're going to move to a small town or wherever, let me know as soon as you can, okay?"

I nod.

"Because I wouldn't want to get too close to you."

In the morning, we play our second game at the *universidad,* a hazardous slip-and-slide affair featuring several collisions, a few nasty wipeouts, and one or two head bonks. In the interest of safety, we give up after an hour. Back in our trailer, I suck it up and take the icy plunge into our shower, this time not bothering to hold back my scream. Dressed and packed, we scramble down a minor cliff at the foot of Big Sam's trailer and gather by a clump of rocks to pose for a group photo.

"Great weekend," Brick says, always on the run. "Sam, thanks for your hospitality. Maybe next year, huh? Let's go, guys."

"If you want to wait a minute, I'll throw together some lunch."

"No thanks, we'll grab something on the road."

Phil, Jack, and I, riding with Brick, grumble a good-bye to the guys and thank Big Sam.

"Go ahead and hug. I'll pull the car around," Brick says.

"You know him, Sam," I say. "Can't stand still for more than fifteen seconds."

"He's probably right," Big Sam says. "The trip back can take a while, especially on a Sunday afternoon. All depends on how long it takes you at the border."

It takes us two hours at the border. We sit idling in Brick's Taurus, windows down, boxed in by a nation of cars, inching toward an inspection station that looks like a tollbooth manned by the Mexican army. While we wait, mariachi bands serenade us, and roving vendors hawk flowers, fruit, and flimsily stuffed animals. We spend $10 each on rock-hard oranges and half-dead roses, and Phil pays the band $5 to go away. By the time we pass inspection and drive into the States, it's past three o'clock and we are starved and ornery.

We take the first exit off the freeway and end up in a Mexican joint in Olde Towne, a tourist trap outside San Diego. The place is wall-to-wall college-age drunks who have convened here to watch the Chargers play a lackluster game against Kansas City on the big screen. The last thing I want is Mexican food, but every other restaurant has an hour wait. I order squishy cheese enchiladas fresh out of the microwave and a beer, which I vow to the guys is the final alcoholic beverage of my life.

After lunch, we creep back onto I-5 and sit there. By six o'clock we are still an hour away from home and we are hungry again. We pull off the freeway once more and find a place we know in Newport Beach. By the time Brick hangs a right into my driveway, it's eight o'clock. The trip home has taken slightly less than seven hours.

"We must do this again real soon," Brick says. "What did the drive back take, *a month?*"

"Just under. Here."

I hand him two twenties.

"What's this?"

"Gas money."

"Don't insult me." He brushes my hand away as if I were hand-checking him.

"Fine. I'll take you to lunch."

"I'm sure."

I climb out of the car. He barely gives me enough time to grab my stuff before he rockets out of my driveway.

I describe it all to Bobbie: Big Sam's deluxe mobile home, the treacherous basketball games, the ice-cold showers, Mitch knocking over the salsa bowl at the fish taco place, the forty-eight hours of nonstop drinking, the harrowing seven-hour trip back home. I tell her about Gracie's engagement and Mitch's new girlfriend. I even tell her about Duff's grandmother.

"I'm glad things are turning around for Mitch," Bobbie says. "And I'm shocked. You guys *talked.* You're becoming more—"

"Like women?"

"I was going to say open and sensitive and trusting—"

"Okay, okay." I yawn, moosh my face into my pillow. "Man, I am *beat.*"

"Sounds like you had fun."

"Well, fun. I don't know. Yeah, I guess."

"I had fun."

"*You* had fun? What did you do?"

"Went out."

"Where? With who?"

"The ladies. Madeline, Sara, and Faye. We went to a movie, then dinner, then to Shutters for a drink. We sat in the bar and talked for hours. We had a fabulous time. I didn't get to bed until after one. What did you guys do?"

"Saturday night?"

"Yeah. Last night."

"Jesus, it's cold in here. Are you cold? I'm going to put on the heat."

"Quit stalling. What did you do?"

I sit up and look at her. "I'm going to tell you. But you can't say anything to anyone. Especially not to the ladies. And you can't let on to the guys that you know. Promise?"

My wife's green eyes narrow in either concern or fascination, I can't tell which. "Okay. I promise."

"We didn't do anything."

"What do you mean? You didn't go out?"

"We went out to dinner but we were back by eight o'clock."

"And then you did what?"

"We talked for a while. We bonded. Phil and I wanted to play poker, but then everyone else, well, they went to bed. So, we did, too."

Bobbie pauses. Keeps her eyes riveted on my face. "What time was this?"

"It doesn't matter. It was early."

"What time was it? Tell me. I'm curious."

"Ten," I say.

"Ten o'clock? Bachelors alone on a road trip in Mexico packed it in at *ten o'clock?*"

"Everybody was pretty tired," I mutter.

"You were tired. You poor babies. That is pathetic. I can't wait to tell the ladies."

"You promised."

"I promised. I didn't swear."

Like a fish, she flops over to her side and dissolves into an annoying, superior giggle. She comes up for air and flips back to me.

"You're lying. I can feel it. What did you do, go to a strip joint or something?" She looks at me expectantly.

"Okay. This is the truth." I take a beat. "We went to bed at nine-thirty."

Bobbie tilts her head and grins. She arches her torso into a gleeful victorious shriek, which soon explodes into spasmodic, uncontrollable hysterics.

"Unbelievable," she manages between laughs.

"Actually, it was nine," I say under my breath.

But she's laughing too hard to hear.

injured reserve

A caravan of buses and limos surround the caged-in court. A flock of tourists and NBA scouts, noses against the wire, prepare to witness the execution.

I am the Law. I take on all comers, black, white, European, Asian. Their size, speed, or reputation matters not. I will play them all, one-on-one or one-on-three. I break them down with my spin move, cross-over, hops, court savvy, and reindeer games jump shot. I am The Package. I never lose. Hell, nobody scores on me. Unless I'm bored and want to give them false hope, a temporary lead, then I shut them down, run off eight or nine unanswered hoops, crushing their spirit, devouring their will.

One day I am face-to-face with Kobe Bryant.

"Wanna see what you got," Kobe says.

"Just you, alone? Nobody else?"

He grins. We go. He scores first but only because I let him. Winner's outs. He tries a jumper. I swat the rock into the street. The crowd gasps. The NBA scouts scribble on their clipboards and wipe the drool off their chins. Kobe tries a move. Fakes left, fakes right, shake, bake, stutter left. I got him in my sights. I strip him clean, grab the ball, dribble between

my legs, drive, soar, doink *backward over my head. Kobe's jaw drops.*
He puts his hands on his hips. His head slumps down.

"You win," he mumbles. "You're the best ever."

We bump chests.

And then I wake up.

My agent sets up a meeting for me and my partner with a young
African-American woman, call her Janet, who has been hired to
develop movies for a famous rap star. She is a fan of our work,
especially the hit comedy series we wrote in the late seventies,
What's Happening!! Janet is looking for writers to turn the following notion into a full-blown story: a bunch of kids play Little
League sports in different black neighborhoods in Los Angeles.
That's it. And make it funny. She calls a dozen agents, tells them
all that the writer who comes in with the best story will be
awarded a screenplay to write. My partner and I come up with a
plot and tell Janet the story, first over the phone, then in person.
She loves it.

One tiny hurdle.

Before we get the gig, we have to pitch the story to her boss,
Carla, the rap star's wife.

Should be no problem. *It's just a formality.* As I step out of the
shower an hour before the meeting, the phone rings. Squishing
across the bathroom floor, leaking water onto the glimmering
white tiles, I pick up the phone.

"Alan?"

"Janet?"

"Yeah uh." There is trouble caught in her throat. "We have a
problem."

"What is it?"

"Well," Janet says, "the problem is, you're not black."

I hold. "We can be black."

"This is serious."

"You just realized that we weren't black?"

"Of course not. I knew it all along. But Carla, I guess she just . . . oh, this is so embarrassing."

"No. This sucks."

"She likes your story. I've told her the main points. She's just concerned that, well, you know. I don't know what to say."

The weird part is that I agree with her. How can two white middle-aged Jewish men possibly write a meaningful screenplay about eleven-year-old black kids who play Little League sports in neighborhoods that we have never even heard of?

"We can write this screenplay, Janet," I say. "Good writing is good writing. Look, we wrote *What's Happening!!* That was a black show. A black *kids'* show. We're professionals. We can do this. We have a *passion* for this story, Janet. Hell, people are people."

"That's what I told Carla. I think I convinced her to listen to your story with an open mind. But you have to be open-minded, too."

"What do you mean?"

"After you hand in the script, we're going to replace you with a black writer. I want you to know that going in. Is that going to be a problem?"

What a business. What a sick, twisted, compromising, fucked-up business.

"I don't have a problem with that," I say.

We get the job. Carla loves our story. She and Janet laugh at our jokes. I close the deal with a big finish, some bullshit about having different color skin but the same color heart. Moved, Carla smiles and says, "I used to watch *What's Happening!!* with my mom. It was my favorite show in elementary school."

Ouch.

Despite the shadow of the ax held over our heads, my partner and I write the screenplay and turn it in. As promised, we are immediately fired and replaced by a black writer. I find solace by working on my game.

I put myself on a fitness schedule. I increase my running to five miles a day. I purchase dumbbells, two ten-pounders, two fifteens, and two twenties. When I wake up, I hit the carpeting downstairs in the guest room and reel off three sets of push-ups and sit-ups. I limber up, stretch, and do my run. On alternate days, I duck into my garage and work out with the weights twice a day, mornings and afternoons. I do three sets of presses and three sets of curls. Then I shoot a minimum of two hundred jump shots.

After six weeks, I start to see a difference. My flab converts to muscle. I lose ten pounds. My body becomes buff. Well, sort of. Mitch is the first to notice my transformation.

"I can't guard him," he pants one Sunday, hands gripping a fistful of his shorts. "He won't stop running. He's like the goddamn Energizer Bunny. Jesus Christ. You're gonna give me a heart attack."

Next game, Danny puts me on Wally. Wally is bulkier than Mitch. No worries. I body him up all morning.

"Have you been working out?" Wally asks.

"A little."

"I can tell. You're much more physical."

I beam. "Really?"

"Yeah. It's annoying."

Wally rubs a tender pink area above his hip. He winces. I must've whacked him there.

"Next week I'm calling fouls," he says.

This is good but I want more. I want to make an impact. I push myself to six miles a day and cut thirty seconds off my time. I add another set to my presses and curls. I graduate from ten-pound dumbbells to fifteens. Two weeks later I'm routinely hoisting two twenties above my head as if they were stage props. Now I *am* buff. I buy tank tops. I pose in mirrors.

And then one Sunday it happens.

I'm guarding Duff. We are up 2–0, thanks to a tip-in by Danny and a power move by me. I have ripped down two rebounds and on defense I'm on Duff tight as skin.

Our ball. Phil tries a squatter. It shimmies off the rim after a tantalizing dance and drops down into Brick's breadbasket. He whips a pass to Duff, who skips once and shoots. I reach my arm straight up, fingers extended to the sky, going for the block, and . . .

Ping.

Something snaps in the curl of my armpit.

I hear it more than feel it. When I lower my arm and watch Duff's shot bank in untouched, I feel a tug beneath my arm, a soft pull, a minuscule yank, as if someone has attached a tiny weight to my underarm. It doesn't hurt exactly; I'm just aware of it. I picture a tiny door hanging off a microscopic hinge swinging randomly beneath my arm.

I keep playing. No reason to stop. The only thing is—and I'm not sure about this—I don't think I can raise my arm straight up.

So what should I do?

What most men would do: ignore it.

I keep playing the rest of that Sunday, and during the week I run and lift weights as usual. I determine that I've strained a muscle and the weird tugging sensation will disappear after a few days. I'm wrong. The feeling stays. I don't say anything to Bobbie or Phil. I'm convinced that the best thing to do is play through it. The tiny tug persists, set in place in my armpit. On Sunday, between possessions, I rest my left hand on my shoulder and rotate my right arm.

"What are you doing?" Phil asks.

"Nothing. Just trying to stay loose."

"Something wrong with your shoulder?"

"No, I'm fine. This keeps me loose."

"You said that."

"Okay. Whose outs? Come on, I gotta be somewhere *Tuesday.*"

I play in this condition for the next six weeks until I wake up one Sunday morning feeling stiff. I head into the bathroom to brush my teeth, and then, for some reason, I decide to apply deodorant.

I grab my Speed Stick with my left hand and prepare to lift my right arm.

Only . . . I can't.

My right arm remains stapled to my side, limp, dead, without feeling, as if it were asleep. Or worse . . . as if it doesn't belong to me.

I try again.

My arm won't budge.

But this time when I try to force my right arm up, a shooting pain zaps through my biceps like an electric shock. I grit my teeth, don't want to scream, don't want to wake the kids or Bobbie. I take a couple of deep breaths trying to ride it out. But the pain is raging and tears are streaming down my cheeks. I glance in the mirror and see that my right shoulder has risen above my back into an unsightly hump. I look like I am frozen into a permanent shrug.

"What's the matter?"

Bobbie stands in the doorway. One hand is level at her waist, poised and ready to pounce. Her other hand rests on her hip.

"I can't lift my arm." The voice I hear doesn't belong to me. It is small and cracked and defeated.

"You can't lift . . . ?"

Confusion and a hint of terror.

"I can't move it."

"Your shoulder, it's all—"

"I know. I just . . . I don't know what I did. Maybe it's the way I slept—"

I let the lie hang out there. A lie that I know I have twisted into a prayer.

"You shouldn't have played," Bobbie says softly. "I knew there was something. I was so afraid of this. Oh, God."

She reaches out and gently touches my arm. The pain, that electric stab, jolts through my biceps.

"*Shit!*"

I hold on to her hand with my good hand, my left hand, and I watch a tear spatter onto the sleeve of her nightgown. Hers, mine? I can't tell.

"Do you want me to call Phil?"

"No," I say. "He'll be here in two hours."

The guys arrive at ten, staggering in by twos. In street clothes, I greet them on the deck. Phil puts down his gym bag. He nods at my shoulder. "What's this?"

"I can't move my arm."

"Let me see."

He straddles his bag, places one hand gently on my left shoulder, the other on my right wrist. The rest of the guys drift into a semicircle around us like a tribunal. Bobbie squeezes into an opening between Jack and Big Sam.

"Raise your arm as high as you can," Phil says.

I bring my arm up to my waist and stop. My arm is locked. "That's it."

"That's as far as you can go?"

"Yeah."

"Shit," Phil says.

"Don't you take an oath not to use the word *shit* to a patient?"

Random, uncomfortable laughing. Legs shifting nervously.

"Try it one more time."

I do. Same result.

"You might have a tear in your shoulder," Phil says.

"Like I had, Alan," Gabe says. "A torn rotator cuff."

"This is not good, right?"

"No," Phil says. "A torn rotator cuff is not good. Does it sound good?"

"What do I do?"

"If you were a horse, I'd shoot you," Phil says.

"You have to see a surgeon," Gabe says. "But see my guy. Justin Karp. He's great. He won't operate just to operate."

"Do you think he might need surgery?" Bobbie asks.

Eyes now turn to her.

"I don't know," Phil says.

"I wouldn't have surgery," Gabe says.

"You have to see him this week. Like tomorrow," Phil says.

"I'll call him for you," Gabe says.

"Thanks, Gabe. Meanwhile, can I play?"

"*No,*" Phil and Bobbie say together.

"Well, great seeing you, guys," I say to everyone around me. "Thanks for coming. Grab a bagel for the road and I'll see you next week."

Nobody hears me. Or if they do, they don't take me seriously. They're too busy stretching, shooting, and waiting for Stewart to announce the teams for the first game.

Besides, who cares if I play, right?

I just live here.

"You don't have a torn rotator cuff," Justin Karp says.

He studies two X rays, which he has fastened to his wall with magnetic clothespins. Two black-and-white absurdist photographs of the inside of a skeleton. Movie posters for a Corman flick, *Skeleton Killer.* Joke photos you send to an Internet dating service.

The inside of me.

"No torn rotator cuff. So that's good," I say.

Karp turns toward me. He is a surgeon out of the cast of *ER*. Tall, slim, salt-and-pepper beard, kindly smile, a runner's build. Anthony Edwards with hair.

"Actually, it's not so good."

"Really? I mean, well . . . why?"

"If you had a tear, I could operate and repair it. You'd be fine in a couple of weeks probably, three on the outside, four for sure. But what I'm seeing here is a condition called adhesive capsulitis."

He turns back to the far X ray and pokes the picture with his pen. He frowns at my creepy skeletal shoulder.

"Yep. That's what I'd say it is. Ninety percent sure."

"Adhesive . . . ?"

"Capsulitis," Karp says.

I suck in a roomful of air as I attempt to tolerate the pain that's shooting up and down my arm.

Karp opens his hand and cups his fingers. "This is your shoulder socket. Your shoulder bone rests in the center of the socket. For some reason—I'm not sure how, but probably because of an injury you sustained—the blood capsules in your shoulder socket have closed up around your shoulder bone. Locked it up tight. Infused themselves together into a closed, locked *vault*."

To demonstrate, he closes his fingers into a fist.

"What *un*locks it?"

"Time. And a lot of gentle movement. You have to keep the shoulder in motion as much as possible. That's to prevent it from locking permanently. Which can happen if you don't keep the blood flowing to the area. I'll give you a prescription for physical therapy. That'll help. Unfortunately, there is nothing else we can do. We just watch it and wait."

I pause now. Hold my breath. "How long until I, you know, I'm able to . . ."

I can't even say it. I can only manage a tiny croak. Karp asks the question for me.

"Play basketball?"

I nod.

"I'd say we're talking about . . . nine months to a year."

I feel as if I'm swimming underwater and I can't breathe.

"I'm sorry," he says.

"Yeah," my voice replies from somewhere.

"I'd also like you to have an MRI. Small possibility there's a slight tear that the X ray missed. You should have the MRI anyway. To rule out a couple of real long shots."

"Cancer?"

"Well, a tumor, yeah."

"This keeps getting better and better."

"I'd rather be overly cautious."

"Can I run?"

I'm grasping at straws.

"Sure. Run, ride a bike. Let pain be your guide. That reminds me. Let me write a couple of 'scripts for you. One for physical therapy and one for . . ."

He scratches something illegible on a prescription pad. He rips it off and hands it to me.

"This is for Vicodin. An anti-inflammatory and pain reliever. Take it at night." Then Karp adds, sharp as a scalpel, "You're gonna need this shit."

Encased in this narrow torpedo tube, slammed in straight like a refill in a pen, jackhammer-like blasts bludgeoning my eardrums, I decide to review my life.

Let's start here, in the MRI. *Major* fear factor for claustrophobics. We're checking for, at best, a rip in my rotator cuff and, at worst, a tumor. Best-case scenario? A year of physical therapy while I *watch* twelve guys play basketball at my house every Sunday. Sounds fair.

But that's okay because I have so much else going for me right now.

BOMBADA BOMBADA BOMBADA thwacka thwacka thwacka.

"How you doing in there?"

A disconnected voice reverberates through the tube, piercing my skull. I'm lying on a slab in a spaceship, about to be probed by aliens.

"Fine. I'm fine."

"Great. Remember, don't move."

"Got it."

"Gonna boost up the volume a bit."

"No problem."

"Okay. Just relax now."

BOMBADA BOMBADA BOMBADAAAAAAAAAAAAAAAAAA-AAA!

Grit my teeth and hold on. All right. Back to my life. Making a list of what I want.

First item.

I want to stop betraying myself. That's number one. I am living a lie. I have to stop doing that or I'm going to crack up. So put that on top of my list, underline it, set it in bold.

Stop living a lie.

Another way to say it, a more positive way, might be:

Be true to yourself.

Much better. It's a little too Hallmark but fuck it.

Now. Below that write down *Number 2: Make a living* and *Number 3: Avoid a nervous breakdown.*

Right away we have a serious problem, which is:

How does Number 1 get me to Numbers 2 and 3?

All I know is that Number 2 is not happening and Number 3 is nipping at my heels.

Bombada bombada thwacka thwacka.

BOMBADA BOMBADA BOMBADA BOMBADAAAAAAAAAA.

Shit.

• • •

The next day I get the news. I have no tumor and I have no tear. I officially have adhesive capsulitis. My protocol? A year of rest, physical therapy, and absolutely, *positively*, no basketball.

"Are you going to cancel the game?" Bobbie asks me.

"What do you think?"

We are sitting on our deck, overlooking our backyard. A new patriotic net—red, white, and blue, courtesy of Big Sam—dangles from the basketball hoop just off to our right and rustles in a lazy late-afternoon breeze.

"It's up to you," Bobbie says, and means it.

I avoid her eyes. I squint toward the hoop. A small bird settles on the rim, flits, fidgets, then darts off as if she were on a dare.

"Might be nice to have our Sunday mornings back," I say.

"That's true."

I look at her. My right arm throbs. I flinch. "Have to say, though, I do like having the guys here."

She smiles. "I do, too."

Her smile suddenly fades and morphs into a squiggly dark line.

"Promise me you won't play. Until your arm is all healed. *All* healed."

"You think I'm that stupid?"

"Promise me."

"All right, I promise. Jesus."

"Thank you."

Yes. I am that stupid.

On Sundays now, dressed in sweats and sandals, my shoulder frozen into a contorted, immutable hump, I prowl the outskirts of my deck looking for a purpose. It's not that bad, I tell myself. I have several options:

   1. Official greeter and bagel cutter.

I'm pretty good at this. Got the smile down. That's the most important thing. You must be self-effacing yet not too grinny. I don't want to look like I'm in a cult.

"Jack, welcome."

"Oh. Hi."

"How you doing?"

"Not bad. How's the shoulder?"

"Hurts like hell. But no use complaining. Doesn't do any good, right? Ha-*haa*. How was your week?"

"Uneventful. Pretty much the same as last week."

"Great. You're a poppy-seed guy, right?"

"Cinnamon raisin, but I can get it."

"Got it working already. Cream cheese?"

"Okay, sure. Nonfat." Pause. "Are you feeling all right?"

"Yeah. Why?"

"You have this weird smile on your face."

Forget greeter. Let's move on to:

2. Play-by-play announcer.

I lower myself into a beach chair that Stewart sets up for me on the lawn next to the driveway. If I can't play, the next best thing is to announce the games. Keeps me close to the action. I believe I have a talent for this. I've listened to Chick Hearn and Stu Lantz do a million Lakers games. Chick is what, ninety-five? This I can do.

"Here we go. The first game on this beautiful fall Sunday morning. Phil takes the ball out, passes it in to Big Sam. Big Sam fakes, drives, wraparound to Brick . . . *and the mustard's off the hot dog.* Oh *myyyy.* A little too creative for Brick. Ball out to the other team. Stu?"

"Awright," Brick says. "That's enough."

In a deeper, slower voice I say, "Looked to me, Chick, that the ball slipped out of Brick's hand. Guess he wasn't looking. He must have other things on his mind. Maybe he's thinking about his sex life and why he doesn't get as much sugar as he used to.

Has he lost his looks? Is he putting on weight? Is his wife steppin'
out on him? Perhaps he overate last night and his stomach's on
the fritz and he's concerned about passing gas in front of his
teammates . . . *on the World Champion Lakers' Basketball Network.*"

"If you don't shut up, I'm gonna break your neck, too,"
Brick says.

Last option:

3. *Baby-sitter.*

I suck at this. Case in point.

Danny starts showing up with his twin six-year-olds. He
brings a canvas bag filled with toys, games, and books, but they
mainly want to run around and be kids.

"Alan," Danny says, "would you mind playing hide-and-
seek with the twins? It's their favorite game. I'd do it but I'm
playing—"

"You're *it,* Awan," says one of the twins.

"Count to a hundwed," says the other.

"A hundred? That's a lot. Okay. Here goes. One, two, three—"

The twins scream and take off and hide somewhere in the
front yard. And that's the end of the game for me. Like I'm
gonna clop off after them and hunt for them in the bushes with
my one good arm? Fuck that. Hide-and-seek, my way. I count,
you hide, I don't look for you. Deal with it.

All right, the injury has made me surly. Can you blame me?
The guys are playing hoop at *my* house and they barely know
I'm here. I've become furniture. What's even worse is that the
game seems to be thriving without me.

"The games were great today, didn't you think?" Phil says.

"I know. Very competitive, very well played," Stewart says.

"Better than usual," Wally says.

"Why is that?" Big Sam asks.

"I think it's because Alan's not playing," Brick says.

"Shut *up.* Even with one arm, I'll kick your ass."

"Touchy," Brick says.

"Fucking A, I'm touchy." I grimace as the pain blazes out of my shoulder and down my arm. *"Shit."*

Silence as guys rip bagels and dip them into cream cheese.

"That part of the deal?" Big Sam asks, nodding at my arm.

"Sneak attack of knee-buckling pain? Yeah."

"It's a spasm. The shoulder is vibrating out of control," Gabe says.

"Oh, that's great," I say.

"Well, it's in shock. The socket is not used to being locked up like that. I know all about this from my rotator cuff," Gabe says.

"So guys, next week," Danny says, packing up his gear and his kids.

"Next week," I say. "Can't wait. I'm thinking about putting out a buffet. Get some deli, a fine selection of cheeses. Maybe I'll hire an omelette chef, perhaps bring in a caterer. We'll see."

"How long you gonna be out?" Gabe asks.

"Nine months to a year."

"And then there's rehab," Brick says.

Everyone stares at him.

"What? It's true. He's got to get back in shape, get his strength back. Could be a year and a half. Could be two years."

Someone hits him in the face with a dirty sock.

"What?"

"I got a name for you," Big Sam says. "Mike Kim. He's the best chiropractor going. I went to him when I separated my shoulder playing hockey. He's very smart and here's the thing . . . he's not a bone cracker. Some of these chiropractors believe they have to rough you up, crack you like a walnut. Kim isn't like that. He understands sports injuries."

"Thanks, Sam, but I have a prescription for physical therapy. I don't know about a chiropractor—"

"Physical therapists don't know shit. Ever been to one of those places?"

"Not yet."

"They're goddamn factories. They wham you, they slam you, they don't know what they're doing. They do more harm than good. I'm telling you. Mike Kim. He's the guy. And mention my name. I'll call you tonight with the number."

"As long as we're giving referrals, I got a name," Brick says. "Bruce Deukmajian. Faye went to him for her back. This guy is the best. You can ask her. Without him, she'd still be wearing a brace or a corset or whatever the hell that mummy wrap was she wore to bed for what seemed like two years."

"A little too much information," Big Sam says.

"Call him. Bruce Deukmajian. I'll get you the number."

"Is he a chiropractor?"

"Not to disagree with the distinguished attorney from Brentwood, but I would never send you to a chiropractor."

"Why not?"

"They're quacks. Bruce is a physical therapist. But he's different. He's a big guy, about six-three, two-fifty, former hockey player, but he's very gentle. The L.A. Kings, the Dodgers . . . they all go to Bruce."

"What about the pain?" Danny asks.

"I'm popping Vicodins like Tic Tacs."

"Have you considered acupuncture?"

"No way. I can't stand needles."

"These don't hurt at all. They're extremely thin. They look like tiny strands of straw. You barely feel them."

"You've had acupuncture?"

"Off and on for years," Danny says. "I don't know about healing your shoulder, but for the pain, acupuncture is the only way to go."

I consider this. "Bobbie actually goes to a guy sometimes. She has a back thing. She says she gets high during the treatments. She loves it."

"That, my friend, is true. It's better than smoking a joint. Better than 'ludes."

"Huh. I wonder if my insurance covers it."

By the time the guys leave, I have the names of three chiropractors, four physical therapists, two acupuncturists, a rheumatologist, an herbal nutritionist (a Sikh who believes he can cure me by putting me on a diet consisting exclusively of emulsified tree bark), and a psychic healer who determines your treatment by spending two days with an article of your clothing.

The pain in my arm and shoulder is so intense that I call them all.

The next morning, I can't raise my left arm either. I call Karp in a panic. He squeezes me in within the hour.

"This happens sometimes," he says. "The capsulitis travels into the other shoulder. You probably overcompensated by using your left arm and shoulder so much that you developed the condition there, too."

"What do we do?"

"Same deal. Therapy and anti-inflammatories. If you want, I can give you a cortisone shot to relieve the pain. It's short-term. It'll only last two or three days, but you'll get some relief."

"Please," I say.

Karp leaves the room and returns in a few minutes with a needle the length of a ruler. He rubs my shoulder with a wad of cool blue goo and prepares to ram the needle into my shoulder.

"You're gonna feel a bite," he says, doctor language for *You're about to experience the kind of excruciating, hair-curling pain women have in labor.*

"Bring it on," I say.

Plunge.

Compared to the pain I feel in my shoulder, the horse needle is like a soothing shoulder massage.

• • •

Sunday morning, I sit hunched like a comma, watching the guys play basketball in my driveway. Gabe, always the first player to sit out, his choice, pulls his chair next to me.

"Oh, Alan, this must be killing you."

"Yeah, Gabe, it pretty much sucks."

He shakes his head. "Not playing. I can't even imagine how you feel. And now it's in both arms? Did he say how that . . . ?" His voice trails off.

"All he says is that he wishes he could operate."

"He's right. I wish he could."

"What happened to 'Don't go near a cut man'?"

"In your case, you'd be better off."

"I'm trying to shrug, but I can't."

"Can I get you something? Is there anything I can do for you?"

"Would you scratch my ass? I can't reach it."

"Probably a lot of things you can't do."

"Many things. *Many* things."

"A *year?*"

"That's what he says."

Gabe lowers his voice. "What about sex?"

"I can have sex. I just need a spotter."

Gabe throws his head back and roars, a high-pitched, soft, glorious cackle.

"Oh, Alan," he says. "I needed that."

"Me too, Gabe," I say. "Me too."

I begin treatments with Mike Kim the next morning. Kim is short and mysterious, with a permanent five-o'clock shadow and dancing, nervous eyes. The first half of the session he is gentle, almost tentative. He twirls my shoulders in soft, lazy circles.

"Hmm," he says.

I don't like the sound of that. "Are you sure you can help me?"

"Absolutely. Let me try something."

He locks his arms around my shoulder in a half nelson.

"Does this hurt?"

"*Yes.*"

"This tells me you're not ready for even a minor alignment yet. Hmm. This condition is new to me. We're going to have to figure it out by trial and error."

Not exactly what I wanted to hear.

I sort of wanted to work with someone who knew what he was doing.

"How's it going with Kim?" Big Sam asks on Sunday.

"So-so," I say.

"No improvement?"

"Not yet. Maybe it's too soon to tell."

"How many sessions have you had?"

"Three."

"You have to give him time."

"Sam's right. This is going to take a while," Gabe says.

"Waste of time," Brick says. Big Sam dips his substantial head and shakes it once at Brick.

"Hey, you know how I feel about chiropractors," Brick says.

"And how do you feel? Just for the record," Danny says.

"Quack," Brick says. "Quack *quack.*"

"Very fucking mature," Big Sam says.

"They're one step above the WWF," Brick says.

"What about acupuncture?" Stewart asks.

"At this point, I'll try anything."

"Except for the herbal nutritionist who wanted you to drink liquid tree bark," Stewart says.

"Hey, it worked for my ex-wife. Or so she claimed," Mitch says.

"You said she was shitting tree stumps for a month," Jack says.

"Yep," Mitch says, laughing.

"Meanwhile, what are you doing for exercise?" Gabe asks.

I spread cream cheese across my bagel and stuff half of it into my mouth. "You're looking at it."

"You're gonna balloon right up," Phil says.

"I can't run," I say. "I've tried. I'm in too much pain."

"What about a bike?" Phil says. "Can you ride a stationary bike?"

"I guess so. I just hate those leather seats."

"I know. Your balls go numb," Brick says.

We all look at him.

Brick shrugs. "Well, mine do."

"Are you sure it's the bike?" I ask.

He stops his bagel in midair, considers this, and shrugs again.

The next Sunday, as I blast the debris off the court with my electric leaf blower, a bloodred pickup truck backs into my driveway. A screech of brakes and Stewart, at the wheel, and Brick, riding shotgun, climb out. All business, they lower the tailgate and drag an exercise bicycle off the truck. Brick tilts it up and wheels it toward the deck. He stops at the bottom stair, lifts, and heaves the bike onto the redwood.

"Where do you want it?" Brick asks.

I can't speak. I am momentarily struck dumb by their kindness.

"Well? Where do you want it?"

Bobbie, hands on hips, in charge, appears on the deck.

"Put it right there in the corner so he can watch you play. Good. Now angle it a little. No, no, no . . . the other way . . . *facing* the hoop. That's it. Great." She grins at me. "How's that?"

"You knew about this?"

"Sort of."

"It's from all of us," Stewart says.

"I'm . . . I don't know what to say. Thank you . . ."

"Oh. I almost forgot." Brick bounds off the deck and sprints down the driveway. He whips open the front door of the pickup, reaches in, jogs back, and hops onto the deck. "Here."

He hands me a thick, fluffy sheepskin seat cover.

"To protect your balls," Bobbie says with a smile.

Each Sunday, as the guys play, I pedal the exercise bicycle furiously, my ass swaddled and caressed in sheepskin. Eventually little pools of perspiration pop out on my forehead, and a triangle of sweat stains my shirt just beneath my throat. The smell of something sour tickles my nose. I press my eyes closed and drive my legs harder.

And I think about the men in my driveway.

They will not miss this game.

They schedule their *lives* around Sunday morning. If they go on vacation, they leave town Sunday afternoon and return Saturday night so they can be here on time for the game. Gabe, away in Santa Barbara for a weekend alone with Sara, left her in the hotel room, drove two hours to the game (stopping on the way to pick up the bagels), played ball, then drove two hours *back* to Santa Barbara to join her for lunch. Sara, by the way, understood. Big Sam, staying at his place in Mexico, got up at 5 A.M. one Sunday morning and drove five hours to make the 10 A.M. tip-off. Phil, not once but several times, finished his all-night shift at the ER and headed straight to the game, played ball, scarfed bagels, bonded, then went home to collapse. We routinely rearrange travel plans, interrupt corporate retreats, duck out of family functions. We play Christmas Day, Easter Sunday, New Year's Day, the Fourth of July. We play Mother's Day, but in deference to our wives, we end a half hour earlier.

Why? Why do we do this? Why do they come?

It's not for the ball.

The play is fine; it's serious and competitive. We play to win. We break a sweat. I joke that there are moments that actually resemble *basketball*—a snappy give-and-go, an open layup off a back pick or a screen-and-roll, three crisp passes that approximate a set play. We are not high-fliers, and except for Danny, Jack, Big Sam, and Brick, lack creativity and flash, so we exult in these moments of old-time Celtics basketball. Still, these moments remain rare and are what we strive for, not our constant.

So . . . they don't come for the ball.

They don't come for the court.

The driveway is a challenge, lopsided, clipped close on the right by the bed of maple saplings and the gray stucco wall, limited in the front by the garage, which makes full-speed drives to the hoop hazardous, and obscured at the top of the key by the carob tree, making high-arching, long-range jumpers impossible. Every so often someone suggests looking for a gym to rent. This notion is always dismissed, usually by the best players among us:

"I like playing at Alan's house. It's not perfect but it's comfortable. And I like playing outside."

No. They don't come for the court.

I think they come for each other.

Which is odd because we don't know each other all that well.

True, I'll schmooze with Phil and Brick on the phone and occasionally meet one of them for lunch. I've known Wally forever. I really like Jack. Enjoy Danny. Love hanging with Big Sam . . . Hell, I like all these guys.

But except for Phil, Brick, and Gabe, I don't see them outside of the game socially.

Yet why do I feel so close to them?

It could be because of all that has happened—the death of Kyle's wife, Brick's knee injury, surviving the Northridge quake, Mitch's marital troubles, our trip to Mexico. Perhaps sharing these events has cemented us, served as a glue to bring us together. Whatever the reason, I am certain of this one truth: men can achieve closeness without intimacy, while women can achieve intimacy without closeness.

For example, Bobbie knows every intimate detail of her dental hygienist's private life. She doesn't have a close relationship with her, but she knows more about the woman who cleans her teeth twice a year than I do about most of the guys I play basketball with every week. And still I feel a closeness with every one of them. Maybe it's because I don't know too much.

There is one more thing: commitment.

Women know all about that. Women want strength in a man, confidence, sensitivity, wisdom, a sense of humor, and God knows what else. But women *need* commitment.

All these men, all of us, have made a commitment to this game, and for men commitment may in fact equal intimacy.

We play every week. We can all count on that. In life there are few things you can count on. We know we can count on the game.

And so they come to break bread (bagels), to break a sweat, to talk, to swear unchecked, to bitch in peace, to bellow an opinion, to laugh, and most of all, to be. They come because they are committed to the game. And the game is here.

One blinding Sunday morning, Gabe and I walk briskly down my driveway to retrieve his sunglasses, which he's left on the front seat of his car. We match each other stride for stride, as if in a march, caught up in a conversation about his beloved Montreal Expos. We reach his car, a Porsche the color of the sky in *Roger Rabbit*. Gabe snatches the sunglasses off the seat and shuts his car door with a surgeon's flick of the wrist. A BMW convertible stops suddenly in front of us in the street. The driver is an attractive woman, late thirties, short dark hair, a dimple, and a slightly curled lip. She wears a sleeveless top and corduroy jeans with a cuff.

"Gabe!" she calls. "Dr. Gabe."

He looks at her blankly.

"Don't you know me? You're my OB-GYN."

Gabe's eyes move instinctively from her face to her crotch. He stares between her legs for a beat. His face lights up in recognition, as if he has X-ray vision.

"Joanne! Sure . . . *Joanne.* How are you?"

Both Joanne and I break up. Gabe blushes.

"I see so many women," he says, making it worse.

A few minutes later we're back on the deck. I'm pumping the bike and Gabe is sitting out. He scratches the back of his head and slides his chair next to the bike.

"I'm going to sell my house."

I peer at him through sweat-stained eyes.

"Are you serious?"

"Yep. I'm not going to put up a sign or anything. It's going to be quiet. No open house, no ad in the paper, nothing like that. I can't take the idea of all those people tromping through my kitchen, my den, our bedroom. I know I won't be there, but still, the thought of it. Can't *stand* it. Like some kind of cattle call. Nope, not gonna do it that way. Serious buyers only. There's a name for this kind of listing, I forget what it's called."

"A pocket listing."

"That's it." Gabe inches his chair closer so he can whisper. "What I'm paying for that house every month? It's too much, Alan. Do you know what I shell out in landscaping alone? You wouldn't believe it."

"Well, your grounds. Your garden . . . "

"It's another mortgage. That's what it is. A second fucking mortgage."

Gabe sniffs, violently rubs the back of his arm. He speaks deliberately, in a hush, as if what he says is taboo.

"It's not so wonderful being a doctor these days. You know the cliché: marry a doctor. That was before HMOs. It's a lot different now. I need to cut back anyway. I am absolutely exhausted. Between my schedule, deliveries, running the office . . . it's really getting to me. But with that house, those expenses? I have to keep going. I have no choice."

Gabe shakes his head, sniffs.

"I don't want to sell the house. I love it. I love the garden. But it's so expensive to *maintain*."

The game ends and the guys start walking toward us. Without getting up, Gabe hops his chair away from me.

To be continued.

A month later.

I shuffle through my day like a prisoner in an invisible straitjacket. The pain in my shoulders comes and goes in unpredictable ambushes, arriving in undulating waves down and up my arms, often achieving torture status. I visit Mike Kim three times a week but feel no difference. The pain persists and the range of motion in my arms remains at zero. He is stumped; I am frustrated. I am his first failure. I decide to make a change.

"I hate to stop now," Mike says, his voice cascading into a spoiled, irritating whine. "I really think I can heal you. I just need more time."

"Mike, it's been three months. I'm sorry."

"I guess you have to do what you have to do. I am truly sorry." Bobbing his head impotently, he adds, keening like a band saw, "This has never happened to me before."

On my way out, his secretary hands me my bill. For the record, Kim's price per visit is a cool $150. My insurance covers three-quarters of the first twelve appointments, which means I owe $450 for those. The next twenty-four sessions, or $3,600, comes out of my own pocket. Add the $450 I owe, and my balance due to Mike Kim is a whopping $4,050.

For exactly nothing.

Four months into my injury. Gabe and I sit on the deck, watching the first game of the day. He lashes his hands behind his head.

"What's going on with your house?" I ask.

"We've had one insulting lowball offer. That's been it. Nothing else. Not a nibble."

"Why do you think that is?"

"My real estate agent says it's because of the traffic noise from Sunset. Turns people off. I don't hear it. Do you hear it when you're over at my house?"

"I don't hear a thing."

Gabe scratches his neck. "I'm oblivious. She says it's the one consistent complaint. She wants us to build a ten-foot-high concrete wall in front of the house and, get this, put in a *fountain*. Can you believe that? She thinks that will drown out the noise."

"That's crazy."

"I know. This is such a pain in the ass. Maybe I should just pave over the garden."

"If you need a good cement man, I got a name," Brick says, passing through on his way to the bathroom. "Hal McKee, the Cement King. He paved my driveway."

"Is he expensive?"

"He's the Cement *King*. What do you think?"

Brick disappears into my kitchen.

"Gabe, you're not really gonna pave over your garden, are you?" I ask.

Gabe coughs, clears his throat. "I don't know what I want to do." He sniffs. "I'm very off-balance. I need some sort of change, though, I know that. I feel so restless. Feel like I'm on a treadmill." Gabe sniffs again. "I've got to do something. Or I'm telling you"—he puffs out his cheeks and slowly allows the air to escape—"I'm gonna go nuts."

Needles poking out of my arms, shoulders, neck, legs, cheeks—and one sticking out of the center of my forehead, the Unicorn, he calls it. Sitar music gnawing at my eardrums, grating, torturous, because I can't get up to shut it off. Lights on low purple to create a mood. Instead, the effect is sinister and illicit, the kind of lighting you'd find during a drug deal or porno shoot.

"I'll be back in twenty minutes," Robert Nesby, Brooklyn-born, former gang member, now born-again acupuncturist, says in a Barry White love-ballad bass.

That must've been an hour ago. Meantime, my mind races from one potential calamity to the next. What if this is some slow elaborate sadistic torture? What if he forgot me and went home? What if there's an earthquake and, no pun intended, I'm stuck here?

And by the way, when they say you can't feel the needles? They lie. You feel them all right: tiny little pinpricks, teeny pres-surized pinches.

What am I saying? The little fuckers *hurt*.

I want out of this room. I want off this table with the slab of butcher paper sticking to my ass.

Where *is* this guy?

I'm telling you, it's been an hour. Did he go to lunch? Did he go home? I'm serious. He forgot about me. I'm going to be locked in here all night.

I'm just going to pull out these needles myself. How hard can it be? You just give a little *yank* . . .

I can't do that. I'm both squeamish and unmechanical. I'll end up puncturing my spleen.

I can't take this anymore. I'm going to start screaming. I'm just going to holler my guts out. On the count of three.

One . . . two . . .

"Bet you thought I forgot you." Nesby's voice of thunder. He grins in the doorway, arms folded like Buddha.

"Is it twenty minutes already?"

"Actually, a little less. I like to take it slow the first time. How you doing?"

"Great."

"Any discomfort from the needles?"

"Nope. I can hardly feel them."

"Good. Okay, then, let's remove these . . ."

Oh yeah. It also hurts like hell when he pulls them out.

"Any pain as I take them out?"

"Are they out? Didn't feel a thing."

Tough, see? You gotta act tough. I want Nesby to know that I'm as tough as anyone he's ever poked. Plus, the guys at the game are going to ask all about the acupuncture treatment and how the needles felt. I'm going to tell them it was nothing, a walk in the park, a couple dozen flesh ticklers, that's all. I'm not going to tell them I felt like a human shish kebab.

At the reception desk, my head spinning, I write a check for $240: $140 for the treatment and $100 for herbal creams I'm supposed to apply to my shoulders three times a day. At this moment, Nesby could've charged me a thousand bucks and told me to rub my body with camel shit. I wouldn't have blinked an eye. Not only am I relieved to be needle-free, I'm also tripping.

"We are gonna fix this. I have no doubt," Nesby says.

"I have to tell you . . . I feel pretty *good.*"

"Just take it easy. No basketball. I know it's hard not to play. I used to play myself, every Saturday at the Y. Had to stop because of my knees. And old age."

Big booming laugh that rattles the windows.

"I know exactly what you're going through. But we're gonna get you back in the game. Where do you play?"

"At my house."

"At your *house*? We *have* to get you back, don't we?" He speaks now with some awe. "You have room enough for a game?"

"Three-on-three. Come by sometime."

"Like I said, my playing days are over. But you'll be back. What do you do now, just sit and watch?"

"Yeah, it's weird."

"It must be. In the meantime, I'm gonna need to see you three times a week. Next time I'm going to give you some pills that you will take in addition to the creams you're going to apply."

Three times a week? Getting stabbed and jabbed and pricked and poked and skewered and left all alone in dim porno light with that sitar shit grinding my skull to a pulp . . . three times a *week*? No fucking way.

"Sounds good," I say.

"You probably should make your appointments now for the next month or so because I get pretty booked up," Nesby rumbles.

"Good idea," I say.

I make the appointments, leave the office, walk through the parking lot, and cross Wilshire Boulevard. As I walk, sparklers begin dancing in front of my eyes. A wall of them. A TV-screen-ful. Thousands of twinkling, blinking, bouncing stars. My own personal light show. I am dazed. Dizzy. I am *high*. Stoned. Zonked. Zapped. What did Nesby do to me? Those needles . . . were they dipped in hashish? Magical mystery needles. Strawberry needles forever. I am the Walrus Porcupine. I am tripping. And the pain in my shoulders . . . *gone. Gone . . . Gone . . . GONNEERRR . . .*

Uh . . .

Where's my car?

I parked it right here, down this street, across from this park.

Didn't I? I thought I did. Huh. Not there. Wait. Wait. Wait. I'm wrong. I remember now. I parked it one street over. That's right. Absolutely. I cross the street, stutter-stepping, a goofy, stoned-out grin glued on my face. Next street. I see it.

That's not it. That's a truck. Where the hell . . . ?

Oh yeah. Now I remember.

I parked it in Nesby's *lot.*

I wander back across Wilshire, slowly, an inch at a time, loopy I am, my mouth dry, the smell of fresh tar hitting me hard, a distant tinkle from some sprinklers somewhere like an electric-guitar riff exploding in my ear, and there it is, my car, yep, got it, get in, start it up—can I drive?—take a deep breath, clear my head, and . . .

I shiver.

Because the pain is back. Full force. Like a blade thrust into each shoulder. The goddamn . . . *pain.*

Sober as a surgeon I drive home, my shoulders in a demented Ed Sullivan shrug, my mouth flat-lined in a silent holler.

Over the next two months, Nesby sticks me three times a week and I happily purchase $1,000 worth of herbal medications and creams, which I ingest and Bobbie massages into my shoulders with religious fervor. I admit that I probably stick it out with Nesby just because of the five-minute high I experience every time he pulls out the needles. The fact is, nothing has changed. The pain has not gone away, and my range of motion in my shoulders has not improved. I finally make the decision to leave Nesby and try Bruce, Brick's physical therapist. Altogether I have had thirty-six acupuncture treatments at a cost of $140 per, a total of $5,040. Add in the $1,000 for ointments and herbs and we have a grand total of $6,040. I have now spent over $10,000 cash in shoulder treatments.

And I still can't raise my arms.

• • •

Bruce Deukmajian is six-four, wide, muscular, and is partial to pink Izod shirts. He bounces on the balls of his feet when he walks, occasionally breaking into a skip. A field of surfer-blond hair sticks up all over his head in odd angles as if he'd just come out of a wind. I sit at the edge of an examination table in a narrow, dark room as he silently reads my chart. Every so often his lips move as he reads. He stares at the chart for a long time.

"Have you had much experience with adhesive capsulitis?" I ask.

"None. You're my first victim." Bruce's face suddenly lights up. "I see. The symptoms are the same as frozen shoulder. That's basically what you have. I *see.*"

He slaps my chart against his thigh, startling me.

"*Now* I can deal. Here's what we're going to do. First, we get the blood flowing to the area on a consistent basis. Start with very light shoulder movements, very gentle massage. Then I give you exercises to do at home. *Crucial* you do these. Now, let's see where we're at. Huh."

He stares at me, frowns.

"Did you know that your right arm is much more developed than your left?"

"Really?"

"Yeah. You look like a professional bowler. Okay, raise your arms as much as you can."

I do. He tilts his head at a severe angle and stuffs his nose an inch away from my armpit.

"Awright. I'm gonna move your shoulder very lightly."

Deukmajian opens his palms and I see for the first time that his hands are huge. Catcher's mitts. He presses against each side of my right shoulder, enclosing it entirely in his hands. Pain sears through the area.

"Does that hurt?"

"Uh-*huh.*"

"I hardly touched you."

Bruce steps back and tilts his head again, same angle. "We got work to do, brother," he says.

I'm reluctant to give all the credit for my recovery to Bruce Deukmajian—Bobbie's nursing and nurturing and time itself played important roles—but I'm not sure where I would be without Bruce. Three times a week for more than four months (another $10,000, as long as we're keeping score), Bruce coddles, massages, heats up, and rubs down my shoulders and gently, oh so gently, manipulates my arms. There is no cracking, snapping, or stabbing, no herbal potions or mystical creams, no incantations, no abracadabra. It is stripped-down, no-frills physical therapy. A burly, wild-haired, blue-collar worker in a pink Izod shirt focuses all his attention, all his light, and all the magic in his oversize healing hands onto my wounded body and pulls off a miracle. At least it feels like a miracle to me.

I do my part. I throw myself into the homework exercises he assigns. At one point, Bruce presents me with a four-foot-long wooden dowel. He drapes the dowel over my shoulders and runs me through a routine of twists, bends, stretches, shrugs, and twirls. From that moment on, I become fanatical about my dowel. We work out together, my dowel and me, every hour on the hour. My attachment to my dowel eclipses mere devotion; my dowel and I become one.

Gradually I begin to feel and see a difference. The pain abates to a dull ache, then a weak pulsing throb, then a tenuous twitch, then a mere tingle, and finally a sense memory. I am also able to lift my arms subtly, then a little more, then my motion returns to my left arm, and then, after nine months, I am able to raise my right arm.

"I think that's *straight*," I say to Deukmajian, my eyes wide in wonder and hope.

"Pretty close. Try it again."

I lower my hand to my side and lift it, stretching for the ceiling.

"Look at me," I say, giddy.

This is my crowning moment, my graduation.

"You may never have a hundred percent range of motion," Bruce says. "I want you to know that. You may never get it all the way back."

"How much is this?"

"I'd say eighty-five to ninety percent."

"That'll work. I'll take it."

"Good. Keep up the exercises for a while longer, a couple of weeks or so. But you don't have to see me, unless you have a problem."

"What about basketball?"

"I'm clearing you to play, brother."

"Seriously?"

"You're good to go. You might want to play the two guard for a bit, stay off the boards."

"Yes, Doctor." I lower my arm, raise it again. "You have no idea what this feels like. It's like you just released me from prison."

Arm down to my side. Pause. Reach. Stretch. Up, up, up. And hold, hold . . . hold. Waiting for the pain that doesn't come.

"He's *backkk,*" Bruce says, and holds out his hand.

"Thanks. I mean, Bruce . . . *thanks.*"

I hug him.

I spend the next five days preparing for my comeback. I resume running. I jog three miles Tuesday and Wednesday, go to four Thursday and Friday, and do the bike for a half hour on Saturday. I work my shoulders with the dowel faithfully, every hour, and on Wednesday and Friday I do some light weight-lifting. Each day I shoot baskets for an hour in the morning and an hour in the afternoon. I have no pain and no soreness. The one thing that's changed is that I don't have full extension on my jump shot. I feel that I'm heaving the ball up, hurling rocks. Still got my eye, though, and if I have to change my form, I will. I will do anything to play.

Sunday morning I dress slowly. As I lace up my shoes, Bobbie comes into the bedroom. She watches me for a beat. I have been incapacitated for more than nine months. I have been unable to carry the groceries, lift the laundry, or deal with the luggage on our annual trip to the East Coast. Bobbie has done it all, including hauling our suitcases through airports, in and out of rental cars, and up two flights of stairs at our bed-and-breakfast in the Berkshires. Worst of all, for over nine months, I have not been able to pick up my daughter.

"I have to say this," Bobbie says. "But I'll only say it once."

"I know," I say, cutting her off.

She ignores me. "If you hurt yourself again, I will kill you. Please be careful. Please."

I smile. "You know me."

"Yes, I do. Thus the warning."

Gabe is the first to arrive and the first to notice. Clutching his bulging bag of bagels like a baby, he stares at me.

"Alan, you're dressed . . . are you *playing?*"

"I'm back, Gabe."

"This is *great.*" He beams at me, then rubs my back gingerly. "Are you all better? How's it feel?"

"Good enough, Gabe. Good enough."

Phil, Stewart, and Brick emerge from under the carob tree.

"Alan's playing," Gabe says.

"You're cleared?" Phil says.

"I am back, boys."

"What's it been?" Brick says.

"Nine months," I say. "Can you believe it?"

"Wow. Has it been that long?" Stewart says.

"You're *playing?*" Big Sam now, with Duff, Danny, Mitch, Ben, and Jack filling up the driveway. They form a circle around me.

"He's back," Gabe says.

"Bruce came through," Brick says.

"Big time. Came through big-time, Brick."

"So, no pain? Full range of motion?" Phil asks.

"Absolutely no pain. But I don't have full range of motion. I probably never will."

They insist I play the first game. I move tentatively, stay outside mostly, and keep as far away from Duff as I can. With the score tied 1–1, I take my first shot in nine months, a jumper from the left side behind a Brick screen. He anchors himself and, facing me, tucks the ball into my midsection like Warner handing off to Faulk. I set up and measure my shot.

"Don't fuck it up," Brick says.

I launch a moon shot. The ball sails up toward the hoop in slow motion. After what feels like an hour, the ball arcs downward and swishes in. The guys turn to me and applaud.

"Yesss!" Mitch shouts, the victim of Brick's screen.

"Now let's all stop the game and sign the ball," says Brick.

"How'd that *feel?*" Gabe says. "That must've felt great, Alan."

"Actually, it felt weird. Kind of awkward and clumsy and stupid."

"You made the basket. Shut up," Phil says.

"At least you're playing," Gabe says.

"Boychik, that's all that matters," Big Sam says with a clown-sized grin.

"Two–one. Our outs. Let's go," Brick says.

These men, I think.

These men.

How eagerly I wait for the sounds that start each Sunday—
the whap of someone dribbling a basketball, the slap of shoes
on the driveway, and most of all, their voices, their chatter, and
their laughter. Sounds that evoke another time . . .

I am twelve years old.

*Downstairs in my driveway, my best friends, Barry and Eddie, call
to me.*

"Hey, man, let's play some hoop."

"Got homework."

"So?"

Pause. Sigh. "Be right there!"

Hoop was all that mattered then.

It's all that matters now.

7.

the comeback

The summer of '97. Fighting to get back into the rhythm of Sunday, searching for the music of the game.

Playing hoop is jazz, hip-hop, soul, reggae, or the blues. It can be Dylan, the Stones, Springsteen, U2, Ryan Adams, Steve Earle, Moby, Zero 7 . . .

Sitting out is John Tesh.

I'm out of shape. I gasp during games now. The backs of my thighs burn. I need to pick up my running, build up my wind.

My shot's gone, too. I miss short, long, off to the side. I favor my shoulder, fear it will lock. I baby myself, lurching up shots with no extension, all the form of a preschooler. I overcompensate with a loopy rainbow arc. Ball hurtling out of the sky, off course. Not finding the cup. *CLANKKK.* I pile up enough bricks to build a city block.

I'll get it back.

I have to.

A nasty Sunday, I don't know why. The weather's a postcard but the guys are at it today.

Duff, guarding Brick, runs into a pick set by Phil.

"I got a foul," Duff says.

"What?" Phil says.

"You were moving, Phil. That's a moving screen. You can't do that. Our ball."

"I was *set.*"

"No, you weren't. You were like *this.* You can't *do* that. Our ball."

Phil glares at me.

"I didn't see it," I say, and flip the ball to Duff. Duff tosses it to Mitch, who lobs it back to him. Duff backs toward the hoop; Phil's on him, close, standing his ground.

"Foul," Duff says.

"What?" Phil again.

"You're all over me. You're impeding my progress to the hoop."

"Impeding your . . . ? Jesus Christ, Duff, my hands are up here."

"Come on, Phil. You're holding me. That's a foul. Take it out, Mitch."

Phil, hands on hips, shakes his head. Ball in to Duff again. Duff drives, puts up a shot, which is blocked by Phil.

"Foul. You're grabbing my arm."

"This is ridiculous."

"You fouled me, Phil. Come *onnn.*"

"Can we move this along?" Danny says from the deck.

Phil waves his hand at Duff in disgust. "Fine. Just take the ball."

Finally we lose, due mostly to my horrendous outside shooting. We make our way to the deck. Phil is silent, seething.

Duff takes a drag from his water bottle and smiles instantly, warmly. "Guys, I got some news. Guess what Andie brought home yesterday?"

"The clap?"

"No, Alan, a *puppy.*"

"Aww," Mitch says. "What kind?"

"A poodle. Six weeks old. *So* cute."

"Poodles are very smart dogs," says Jack.

"Unbelievable. I had no idea Gracie would be so smart . . ."

"*Gracie?*" Mitch says. "You named your dog after my ex-wife?"

"Shit, Mitch, I didn't realize, the kids named her——"

"Oh, I don't have a problem with it."

"I'm sorry, I didn't mean——"

"It's okay," Mitch says. "Does she bite you and pee on the rug?"

"You're talking about the dog, right?" I ask.

Mitch roars and reaches for another bagel. Phil and I head out for the next game, and Phil mutters, "I'm surprised he didn't name the dog *Foul.*"

A game later, Gabe and I are arranging our chairs to avoid the sun. We're interrupted by a loud crunch.

"Christ, Duff!" Jack screams. "What the *fuck!*"

"Is that Jack?" Gabe asks, stunned. I duck my head and peek through the maze of carob tree limbs. Jack is limping away from the hoop. His face is deep sunburn red.

"I never touched you!" Duff shouts, following him.

"*What?* You threw your leg out. You tripped me!"

"I was getting into position . . ."

"Someday you're going to hurt somebody, you know that? You're dangerous."

"Oh yeah? Fuck you."

"No. Fuck . . . *you.*"

In a blur, Jack whips around and punches Duff, crack, a crisp right to the jaw. Duff stares as if he's been insulted, then lands with a thud onto the concrete. He sits on the driveway, dazed. Shouts. Bodies converge. Duff remains seated in the center of the flurry, dopey, childlike, while Big Sam and Danny lock their arms around Jack and pull him away.

"That's it. I'm through playing here," Duff says, but he stays planted on the ground. After a moment, he gets to his feet and brushes himself off as though he had merely taken an awkward tumble. Chin square, angled up, he strides to the deck. He grabs his bag, doesn't bother to zip it up, and speed-walks down the driveway.

"Go on! And don't come back until you learn how to play!" Jack shouts after him.

Duff whirls and points back at Jack, who's still in the grasp of Big Sam and Danny. "You bet I will!"

I stand at the top of my driveway watching my neighbor tear across the street and disappear from view. Free of Big Sam and Danny, Jack drops his head and sighs. He walks toward me.

"I'm sorry, Alan. There was no excuse for that. Duff just . . . the way he plays . . . he's really gonna hurt somebody. It doesn't matter. I shouldn't have done that. I'm going to go home."

I touch his arm. "Stay."

He looks at me and his eyes fill up.

"It's okay, Jack. He gets out of control."

"He stuck his leg out. He tripped me."

For the first time I notice his leg. A stream of blood from a gash on his knee ripples down to the tip of his sock, soaking it scarlet.

"I lost it," Jack says.

"He's rough," Gabe says quietly. "He almost becomes a different person when he plays."

"I'm surprised this didn't happen sooner," Danny says.

"The thing is," says Phil, "I don't think he knows he's doing it."

"I feel terrible," Jack says. "I never lose it like that. The last time I got into a fight was probably in high school. Not even. Grade school. I don't fight. I'm not a fighter."

"That wasn't a fight. That was a punch," says Big Sam.

"You're proud of Jack, aren't you?" I say.

"I'm beaming," Big Sam says.

"I'm so embarrassed," Jack says. "I really think I should go."

"Forget it. He's a schmuck," Brick says. "Send him flowers,

write him a lovely note. You're not leaving. We need you."

"You could call him," Phil says, heading inside. "Maybe offer to pay to have his jaw rewired."

"Alan, I'm going to leave it up to you. If you want me to go, I'll go. I'll completely understand."

We look at each other for a split second, then Jack turns away and paws absently at his duffel bag.

"Jack, you're not going anywhere. You have to take care of that leg."

"Are you sure?"

"It's okay," I say. "Really."

"I feel terrible," he says.

Phil comes back out on the deck, holding a handful of wadded-up toilet paper. He places the toilet paper compress over the gash in Jack's leg.

"Keep your hand here," Phil says, removing his.

Big Sam grins. "*Helluva* punch."

That afternoon, I go to Duff's house to see how he is.

"Jack called me," he says. "He felt pretty bad. I think he feels worse than I do." Duff forces a laugh.

"Listen, Duff—"

"I'm not coming back. Oh no. Jack was right about one thing. I need to become a better player. My nephew plays in a game on Saturdays. Younger guys, all good players, guys in their twenties and thirties. They play indoors, at a gym. I'm going to play there. I'm going to learn the game and then maybe, *maybe*, I'll come back. When I'm good."

"I'm glad Jack called you—"

"Let's just forget about it."

I nod. Behind us, in a small room crammed with LEGO toys, computer games, and a train set, our two sons play. One of the boys yelps and the other laughs.

"Well, I'd better go. I'm actually gonna try to do some work," I say.

"What are you working on these days?"

"A movie."

"You don't seem too enthusiastic about it."

"Oh, I am," I lie.

"I wish I could write movies or TV. I do a lot of writing but it's technical stuff. Nothing that would make a movie."

I stand up. "Duff, I'm truly sorry about what happened."

"It's fine. I'll live."

I smile weakly and leave.

The next Saturday Duff begins playing in a full-court game at the indoor gym with his nephew. He plays for a few weeks until he crashes into somebody and tears up his knee, requiring surgery. I visit him while he recovers at home. We have a glass of wine and Duff asks about all the guys, including Jack. I invite him to stop over. He shows up one Sunday morning, several months after his surgery. He models his elaborate knee brace, a complex high-tech contraption, jet-black with royal blue highlights. It puts the ones worn by Brick and now Danny to shame. To their credit, they admit it. Duff grins, taking little consolation in winning the battle of best-looking knee brace. We resume play and Duff and Jack sit out together. They shake hands and talk quietly. Duff tells Jack that he has taken up tennis. He plays several times a week and takes lessons from a former UCLA player. He vows to never play basketball again.

"It's *Ruthless People* with a dog."

Eli Decker, king of the one-line movie idea, sits across from my partner and me in Junior's Deli in West Los Angles. Eli has just pitched us a dozen one-liners, things like *"Jaws* with paws," *"The Towering Inferno* in space," and *"Three Men and a Baby Alien."* Our task is to pick out a one-liner we like, develop it into a story, then try to get a deal to write it as a screenplay, with Eli attached as producer. The one-liner that appeals to us most is *"Ruthless People* with a dog."

"There's a kicker," Eli says. He speaks bullet fast as if each sentence were his last. "You know the dog from *The Mask?* The Jack Russell terrier? His name is Max. I think we can get him."

We do. After several laborious weeks of breaking the one-line idea into a full-blown story, Eli, my partner, and I, and Max, begin to make the rounds of the studios.

At one point we pitch the idea to a well-known production company that has its own building on the Universal Studios lot. Eli, my partner, and I are led into a long conference room where we are met by a half dozen eager, young, black-garbed development executives fresh out of the Ivy League, all of whom are introduced to us as vice presidents. We arrange ourselves in squishy leather chairs around a platinum blond conference table polished to a mirror finish. I sneak a look down and see my face. Resting at each of our elbows are a legal pad, a couple of sharpened no. 2 pencils, and a bottle of Evian.

"Is the dog coming?" a vice president asks.

"He should be here," Eli says. "He must've hit traffic."

"Max doesn't actually drive," I say. "He keeps failing the written test."

Polite laughter. The door swings open and Max's trainer, a tall, craggy, bowlegged Marlboro man wearing his good cowboy shirt, the one with the fringe, comes in carrying the dog. He places Max in the leather chair at the head of the table and presses a plastic clicker he has concealed in his hand. Max barks and holds up a paw, which makes him look as if he's waving. The vice presidents all applaud. A door in the corner behind a flowering cactus opens and a photographer crouches into the room. He circles the table like a spy, snapping pictures from every conceivable angle. The trainer places one of Max's paws on a legal pad, the other on an Evian bottle, and puts a pencil in the dog's mouth.

"Aww," says a vice president.

"Let's hear it," another vice president says to me.

"Okay." I clear my throat. "This is a story about two guys—"

"Pet the dog," the photographer says.

I do and he blinds me with his flash.

I tell the story. I don't know what I'm saying. I'm vaguely aware of words spilling out of my mouth in some coherent order, but I can't be sure. My mind has plummeted into a valley of camera clicks, Ivy League giggles, leather-chair squishes, and the crunch and slobber of a canine mauling his rawhide yummy. An eternity, twenty minutes later, I finish the pitch. The trainer presses his clicker several times fast. Max barks again and begins to pant at an alarming speed. It looks like he's grinning.

"He is so cute," a vice president says.

"He was the best thing in *The Mask,*" another vice president says.

"He's a star," a third vice president says.

"I think he has to take a leak," the trainer says.

"In that case, the meeting's over," says a fourth vice president.

"Good story well told," says vice president number five.

"We'll be in touch," says vice president number six.

As I drive off the Universal Studios lot a few minutes later, I start to shiver.

After dinner that night, my head is swimming. I get into bed at eight o'clock, channel surf for a while, settle on a cooking show. I don't know what time Bobbie sneaks under the covers, but the set is off and I'm gazing blankly into space.

"Are you okay?"

"I feel like I'm getting a bug or something."

"You look pale."

"I'm actually sweating."

"Are you sick to your stomach?"

"I'm just out of it. The room is spinning."

She sits up and places her palm on my forehead.

"You're ice-cold. I'm going to call Phil."

"Don't call Phil. It's late. It's just a bug."

I close my eyes. I hear the bedsheets swish as Bobbie changes positions. "So the pitch went all right?"

"Who knows. They loved the dog. I don't think they heard one word of the story I pitched. Course *I* didn't hear one word of the story I pitched. They had a guy taking pictures for the trades."

"No."

"Oh yeah. The trainer kept getting the dog to do cute little tricks. Waving his paw. Covering his ears. It was fucking adorable."

"Do you think they'll buy it?"

"I have no idea. And you know what? I don't want to talk about this anymore."

"Sorry," she says.

I turn over and clutch my pillow. Bobbie sighs, moves off the bed, and pads across the carpet into the bathroom. I flip over on my back and stare up into the wood-beamed ceiling. The wood is honey-colored, hearthlike, calming. Bobbie once said she'd never have to go on vacation because our house, especially our bedroom, was the equal to any five-star country inn. That was years ago. Before the ceiling in our inn started caving in on me.

I close my eyes and will myself to sleep.

I have the attack an hour later.

Bobbie is sleeping next to me, her breath lightly brushing my cheek in tiny cool winds. Suddenly, my eyes pop open, like

headlights coming on, warning lights, alerting me to the overall clamminess covering my body.

And my heart is beating furiously. Slamming in my chest. My
left arm hangs at my side, numb. I clench my fist, unclench,
shake my fingers, try to get the blood flowing, but I can't feel
my left arm, I can't feel it . . .

I start to breathe rapidly, with difficulty, then I'm immediately out of breath. I'm panting. I feel like I'm running and I
can't stop.

"Bobbie."

She sits up. "What's the matter?"

"I can't breathe . . . my heart . . ."

She is out of bed, groping for the phone.

I rest my hand on my chest. The movement of my heart scares
my hand off. I open my mouth to catch my breath. I gasp, suck
in a lungful of air, and I feel now as if I am trapped underwater.

"Phil? Bobbie. I'm so sorry . . . I know how late it is but
Alan . . . he says it's his heart. . . . Yes. . . . Okay . . ."

I don't hear anything else because she walks into the bathroom with the phone and closes the door.

When Bobbie comes out of the bathroom five minutes later, I
am lying in a puddle of sweat. My heart is racing and my eyes
are tearing.

"You're not having a heart attack," she says.

"I'm not?"

"You're having a full-blown anxiety attack."

"It's not a heart attack?"

"You sound disappointed."

"I'm crushed."

"Take slow, deep breaths, and if you're still having symptoms
in the next thirty minutes or so, I'll run over to the pharmacy.
Phil called in a prescription."

I blow out a blast of air.

"*Slow* breaths."

I breathe as deeply as I can and slowly let out the air. My heart is still racing, *thumpa thumpa thumpa,* scary fast.

"It's like I'm running a marathon."

I suck in some air, hold it, let it out. Slowwwly.

"What kind of medication?" I ask weakly.

"He gave me a few choices. I went for Ativan and Valium. He says Ativan will take the edge off."

"And Valium?"

"That's for me."

I smile.

"You feeling any better?"

Another deep breath. My heart slows to a jog.

"A little, now that I know I'm not going to die in my sleep."

She squeezes my hand. "You scared the shit out of me."

"You sound pissed."

She squeezes my hand again and rubs a finger gently across my knuckles.

"I'm not pissed," she says. "I'm worried."

"Whoa," Big Sam says on Sunday, patting his substantial stomach. "A three-bagel morning. You can always tell how much basketball we play by how many bagels we eat."

"Aren't we playing anymore today?" Stewart asks.

No one answers him. Maybe no one has heard him over the din of the bagel bag being crumpled, throats being cleared, and the soothing sound of guys hacking phlegm over the railing.

"Hey, dude, mind if I take a shower?" Phil asks. "I have to go to this family brunch in the Valley—"

"*Brunch.* Now there's a stupid word," says Ben. "*Breakfast* and *lunch,* combined. Whoever came up with that? I say make up your mind."

"It's a woman thing," Danny says.

"Why is it a woman thing?" Wally says.

"Because what man would skip a meal?" explains Danny.

"Ummm," the guys grunt, cavemen chomping.

"Anyway," Phil says, "I have to go to this midday family . . . *meal* . . . and I don't really want to go home, then drive all the way back to the Valley."

"No problem. Shower away," I say.

"Can I shower, too?" Jack asks. "I'm going into the office. If I could shower here, then I can go right downtown instead of going home."

"What am I running, a Marriott?"

Jack's face reddens.

"I'm kidding, Jack. Of course, you can shower here. Anytime."

"Are you sure?"

"I'll be insulted if you don't shower here. I even provide little shampoos and body lotions. You'll be delighted."

"What about a hair dryer?" asks Phil.

"I brought my own," Jack says.

"Use Jack's," I say to Phil.

"It's a nice shower," Phil says. "His brother put in a new space-age showerhead. Excellent spray."

"When was this?" Brick asks. "I took a shower here once and the spray was for shit. It wasn't even a spray. More like a trickle."

"Last time my brother was in town. A few months ago."

"Why didn't you invite me over?"

"For a *shower*?"

"One of the best showers I've ever taken," Phil says. "Very refreshing."

"Your brother's mechanical?" Danny asks.

"Very. Unlike me. He rewired his whole house. He just put in a new bathroom. The fixtures, the tiles, the toilet . . . everything. Did it all in black."

"A black bathroom? Who is he, Batman?" Big Sam asks.

"He's also a gourmet cook."

"What happened to you? Your brother's the catch," Brick says.

"Are we finished playing for the day?" Mitch asks.

"Come on, guys, one more game," Stewart pleads.

"I'm done," Danny says.

"Me too," Brick says.

In unison, like a dance team, they begin unclipping their knee braces.

"They're taking off their legs," I say. "That's a wrap."

"In that case, I have an announcement." Mitch pauses to make sure we're all paying attention. Most of us are. He takes a breath and grins. "I'm getting married."

A spontaneous *"Whoaaaa"* erupts from the group, followed by a jumble of "Great," "Fabulous," and "Holy shit!" tumbling over each other. We mob him, slap him on the back, tousle his hair.

"When?" Gabe asks.

"In about three hours."

We stare at him, stunned.

"We're going to Vegas," Mitch says, then sheepishly adds, "I was wondering if I could take a shower . . ."

We laugh.

"I'm serious," says Mitch, laughing with us.

"What time's your wedding? My brunch is at one," Phil says.

"I can go second. No problem," Mitch says.

"I don't really need to shower," Jack says.

"You're showering. Everybody's showering."

"I don't want to put you out," Jack says.

"If it'll make you feel better, take off your clothes and run through the sprinklers," I say.

"I'd better get in there," Phil says, grabbing his bag. "You might run out of hot water."

"Wait a sec." Mitch reaches into his bag and pulls out a bottle of champagne. "I want to share this with you guys."

"So this is your bachelor party," I say.

"Yeah, I guess it is."

Stewart passes out paper cups and Mitch splashes a finger of champagne into each one. We raise our cups.

"To Mitch," I say.

The guys stand in tableau, cups raised, waiting for more.

"That's all I got," I say.

"To Mitch," Brick says. "Better luck this time."

"I'll drink to that," Mitch says.

"Umm. Champagne and basketball. This is the life, huh?" says Big Sam.

"Helluva bachelor party, Mitch," says Ben.

"Hey, Alan, maybe you can get Bobbie to jump out of a cake," Wally says.

"You ask her. I'll cover you," I say.

"Go ahead, Wally," Phil says. "I think you'd look good wearing a cake."

"Phil, shower. I have to be at a wedding," Mitch says.

"Okay, okay, I'm going," Phil says. "Congratulations, Mitch."

"Thanks, Phil." Mitch and Phil tap paper cups, then Phil heads into the house.

"Hey, Alan," Jack says, "how do you turn on your sprinklers?"

A big laugh, then one by one, each guy shakes Mitch's hand, offers him good luck, and one or two of us hug him.

Think I'll tell them about my panic attack next week.

"Alright, you've sold the movie," Bobbie says.

It's morning. The kids are in school. We walk through a pastiche of pine trees, brisk ocean breezes, and million-dollar homes: our hood.

"Yes. I have sold the dog movie."

"But you're miserable. You're having anxiety attacks. You're not happy with your life. You tough it out because we need the money."

"Yes."

"We can't live on my teaching salary alone."

"No. Unfortunately."

"Can't keep dipping into our savings."

"What's left of it," I say.

"Can't live on love."

"Nope."

"So . . ."

"So I guess I shut up, have my panic attacks, and keep popping those Ativan."

"Until . . . ?"

We walk, saying no more. A car passes, checks us out. A neighbor we don't recognize. Bobbie waves anyway. We crunch through a pile of dead leaves that barricades our path on the sidewalk. We turn a corner and walk up a street completely cloaked by fir trees, a giant arbor. The overpowering smell of evergreen causes me to sniffle.

"You love it here, don't you?" I say.

"I do," Bobbie says. "I really do."

"I know."

"Don't you?"

"Yes. I love it here, too."

I squint at the sun trying to peep through the tangle of pine branches.

Bobbie, looking straight ahead as she walks, says, "It's everything, isn't it? The business. Getting older . . ."

"Yes," I mumble, then blurt out, "Bobbie, I don't know what to do."

"We'll figure it out. I promise," she says, low, almost to herself. "We have to."

"As soon as we figure out exactly what *it* is," I say.

In fact, I do know what *it* is.

I have known all along. It is the emotion that causes my insomnia and my anxiety. It is that which causes me to tread through my days as if I were a visitor in someone else's life.

Its name is Fear.

Fear of hurting my family. Fear of hurting myself. And fear of change.

I fear that most of all.

The following Sunday morning, we sit around the table on my deck, ten of us, the minyan I call us, wolfing bagels, listening to Phil tell us how he bought a used Porsche yesterday over the Internet.

"You never drove the car?" Stewart asks.

"No test drive, nope," Phil says defiantly.

"I could never buy a car without driving it," Wally says.

"I did drive it eventually."

"And you gave all your money to a total stranger?" Ben says.

"Just the down payment. And I talked to him on the phone. He's a very reputable guy. He's done many on-line car sales. I saw pictures of the car, inside and out—"

"Oh, good, you saw *pictures,*" Big Sam says.

"What do you think, he's gonna buy it *blind?*" says Danny.

"What's the risk? If the car's not what he promised, I leave and cancel the check. Meanwhile, I show up with my mechanic and here's this gorgeous '93 Porsche in mint condition, clean as a whistle, with almost no miles on it. My mechanic goes through the car thoroughly. Believe me, he gave the car a rectal exam. It checks out, boom, and I drive it away. I saved thousands of dollars over what I'd pay at a dealership."

"So who's the schmuck, right, Phil?" Gabe asks.

"Would you buy a car on-line?" Stewart asks.

"I don't own a computer," Gabe says with a sniff.

"Alan, would you buy a car on-line?"

"CDs. That's my limit. And porn."

Big Sam roars and holds his hand out for me to slap.

"When do we see this so-called car?" Danny asks.

"Next week," Phil says. "I'm telling you guys, forget car brokers, or schlepping to dealerships in Outer Buttfuck. On-line is the way to go. That's where you get your best deals. It's so easy. And here's the best part. *No used-car salesmen.* That's reason enough for me to buy on-line, right there."

"Ever sell cars, Alan?" Brick asks.

I look at him incredulously. "Ever sell cars? Where do you get that?"

"I don't know. You look like the type."

A little too much chuckling on that one.

"Hey, Gabe," Danny says. "I've been meaning to ask you something. Where do you get these bagels?"

"Manhattan Bagels on Wilshire. Why? You don't like them?"

"I love them. That's why I asked. These are really good bagels."

"Especially the bialys," Phil says. "The best."

"I think they make a damn good garlic bagel," Ben says.

"I like the cinnamon and raisin," Jack says.

"You are such a gentile, "I say.

"I can't help it. I was born that way."

"If you like, I can bring out mayonnaise," I say.

"That's disgusting," says Jack. "But if you have some clam dip . . ."

"Did you always go to Manhattan?" Danny asks.

"We're still talking about this?" Brick says.

"I want to know. Because I think he's only been bringing these maybe the last three years."

"You're right. I used to go to Western Bagel. They were good but it's too far."

"Not as good as Manhattan," Stewart says.

"Western makes a fine cheese-and-onion," I say. "But it's not worth the extra half hour to go there."

"I agree," says Gabe. "Then for a while I went to Noah's."

"Those are not bagels," Stewart says.

"Too doughy," Brick says.

"Rolls with holes," Phil says.

"I kind of like them," Jack says.

"Once I brought some from Von's. The worst. I was running late. I was at the hospital delivering a baby."

"Some excuse," says Danny.

"Oh, I learned. I'll never do that again."

"What, go to Von's or deliver a baby before the game?" Phil asks.

"Both," Gabe says. "Neither."

"While we're on the subject," I say, "should we discuss the cream cheese?"

"I was hoping you'd bring that up," Danny says. He reaches into the bag and pulls out a tub of nonfat cream cheese. "Gabe, with all due respect, this is not cream cheese."

"It tastes like Spackle," I say.

"He's just trying to be sensitive to those of you who are weight conscious," Phil says.

"It's not my weight. It's my cholesterol," Big Sam says.

"How do you know he was talking about you? It's not always about you, Sam," Mitch says, grabbing a handful of flesh from around his middle and jiggling it. Big Sam throws his head back and belts out a laugh.

"The point is," Danny says, spinning the nonfat cream cheese tub on the table like a top, "this stuff is shit."

"It's an insult to the bagels," Wally says.

"It's a sacrilege," says Stewart.

"I kind of like it," says Jack.

"What are we gonna do with you?" Big Sam says.

"I'm with Jack," Mitch says.

"Gentile power," Jack says, and they bump fists.

"I like when Ben comes. He brings me blueberry muffins," Brick says.

"My goal in life is to please you, Brick," Ben says. "It is what I live for."

"I thank you."

"Where do you get these muffins?" Brick asks.

"Starbucks," Ben says.

"Starbucks. Interesting," Gabe says.

"It's the way they dump the whole top into powdered sugar. That's the key," I say.

"I love it so much," says Brick.

"Are we playing any more basketball today?" Stewart begs.

"I'm so stiff. I think I have to stretch again," Big Sam says.

"Yeah, let's play," Danny says.

"I have to go," Ben says.

"Where you going?" Brick asks.

"To get some exercise," I say.

"I got family obligations," Ben says.

"Nikki told him to get home early," I say.

"Also right. Next week, guys."

Ben starts down my driveway and the rest of us chant, "Bennnnnyyyyy," like chefs greeting a customer in a sushi bar.

"I'm gonna miss him," Brick says, ravaging the top of a blueberry muffin.

Later, I sit out with Brick. He picks through the rubble of his muffin and asks, "So, how you feeling?"

"Fine. How you feeling?"

"Phil told me," he says.

"Oh."

"Don't be pissed. He's just concerned."

"I'm not pissed."

"I'm concerned, too."

I look at him. He shrugs.

"You can call me, you know," he says.

"I know. Thanks."

"So how *are* you feeling?"

"Anxious. Out of balance. Wondering what the hell I'm doing with my life."

Brick grumbles, "I hear you. I don't sleep either."

Now I stare at him.

"Yeah, me."

"What's the problem?"

"Money," Brick says. "As in I got more going out than coming in. A fuck of a lot more."

"At least you have a steady income."

"Well, yeah, but the problem is these fucking houses. That's what's killing us. We paid about the same, we have about the same mortgages, wouldn't you say?"

"I'd say so, yeah."

"When did you buy your house?"

" 'Ninety-two."

"At least you didn't buy at the top of the market. That's what I managed to do. I bought mine in '89. Right at the peak. Now we got this downturn. We can't get what we paid."

"No?"

"No way. They say it's coming back, but when? If we sold now, we'd take a huge loss. We'd barely cover our mortgages."

"What do we do?"

"If it were up to me, I'd bite the bullet. I'd sell now. Get out from under. Not gonna happen, though. Faye loves the house. It's beyond that even. The house is part of her identity. That's how she puts it. Frankly, I don't understand it. To me, it's just a house. Four walls and a pain in the ass."

"I could live at the Y," I say. "I think women need to nest."

"Nest this," Brick snorts. "Meanwhile the money's going through me like shit through a goose." He pinches the bridge of his nose. "The other day I had my first migraine."

"And you want me to call *you*?"

We both laugh. We have to.

• • •

Alone on the court, before the last game, I shoot around with
Gabe.

"Phil called me," he says. "You all right?"

"I'm hanging in."

"The movie writing? How's it coming?"

"To be honest, Gabe, it's a struggle."

"Well, I want you to know . . . Sara and I have talked about
this . . . if you need any money, or, really, anything at all . . . we're
here. Anything. You just ask."

"Gabe, I—"

"Don't say anything. I just want you to know the offer is
there, that's all."

He tucks the basketball under his arm and begins to rub my
back gently, in circles, as if he is calming a baby. I nod and swallow.

"Thanks, Gabe," I say.

"Ball game," Stewart says.

A team of Big Sam, Phil, and Gabe faces off against Danny,
Stewart, and me.

"I'll take Alan," Big Sam says.

"Oh no," I say.

Big Sam grins. And why shouldn't he? He's a head taller and
outweighs me by sixty pounds. He is also ambidextrous and slippery quick.

"Hi," Big Sam says to me, still in full-tilt grin.

"I've been running. I thought you should know."

"So have I," Big Sam says.

"*Ball!*" Phil shouts as the basketball trampolines into Klein's
yard.

"I'll get it. I need the exercise," Brick says. Phil tosses him
Klein's key from the redwood table. Brick snags it out of the air and
jogs down my driveway, heading toward Klein's front gate. On the
basketball court, we pair off. I lean against the carob tree, trying to

stretch my thighs. Big Sam, hands on hips, stomach puffed out, saunters over. His grin is gone, replaced by a scowl of concern.

"How you doing?" he asks.

Well, they all know.

"Depends," I say. "I have good days and bad."

"If you want to talk about it, I'm here. I want you to know that."

I actually gulp. I am not prepared for this.

"I also want you to know that if it's about money, I can help you out. I'm offering you a loan, no interest, no questions asked. You just say the word."

I start to say something but I'm not sure what. Big Sam stops me with a hand on my arm.

"Don't think twice about it, I mean it. Just say the word. Or if you're uncomfortable, tell Phil or Gabe or Brick and the money's yours, next day, no questions asked."

I clear my throat.

"Sam—"

"That's what friends are for."

He reaches over and rubs my neck.

The inevitable happens.

My phone rings. "Hello."

"Dude. It's Phil."

"I can barely hear you."

"I'm on the stupid cell phone. Is this better?"

"Kind of. Where are you?"

"Long Beach."

"Long Beach? What are you doing there?"

"Sitting in my car. Waiting for the tow truck."

"Waiting for the . . . oh no."

"Please don't say it. Please. I'm begging you."

"I'm not saying anything. What happened?"

"The goddamn fucking thing *died*. One second the air conditioner's going full blast, beautiful, like a meat locker in here, and all of sudden, *boom*, just like that, the air conditioner shuts off. I can't get it to work. So I drive down to Long Beach where I bought it. No air, it's a sauna in here, sweat's pouring off me, I'm sticking to the leather seats, I'm *dying*. I pull into the guy's place, and, *boom*, just like that, the car dies. So here I am. The Internet guy's mechanic said he'll fix it . . . for twelve hundred bucks."

"*What?* I thought you had a warranty."

"I do. It covers everything but the tires and anything related to the . . . *air conditioning.*"

"Jesus . . . "

"H. Christ," Phil fills in. "Anyway, I called my mechanic in Santa Monica. He'll fix it for five hundred, but I have to get the car towed up there."

"From Long Beach? That's thirty miles."

"Oh, now you're a *Thomas Guide*. I know how far it is. What a fucking pain in the ass. This is not how I wanted to spend my day off."

"It beats pulling cylindrical objects out of strangers' rectums."

"Not by much," Phil says. "Now, I know what you're thinking: 'That's what he gets for buying a used car on-line.' First of all, this could've happened to any car. Second, I could have the car towed and the engine over*hauled* and I'd still be ahead of the game. By a *lot.*"

A garbled voice pierces our connection.

"They're here," Phil says. "The tow truck has arrived. Two guys wearing shower caps."

"Good luck."

"This is such a pain in the ass."

"Just think of all the money you're saving."

Click.

I lose him.

8.

hoop dreams

The beginning of the end—or more accurately, the beginning of the *beginning*—comes in a seven-month burst from January through August 1998. The catalyst, though, the ignition that sets everything in motion, is, of all things, a Little League baseball game in the summer of 1997. The main characters in that game, in the drama that unfolds, are my son, age eight, the starting left fielder, and me, his dad, the umpire.

The first game of the playoffs. My son's Yankees are pitted against their rivals, the dreaded Dodgers. The players are nervous and eager; the parents are tense, tight, frothing. The midafternoon sun is harsh, adding to the tension.

The teams warm up and I watch from my post behind the mound, arms folded, emotions disguised behind clip-on shades. My son is short and mop-haired and scrawny. His glove is ridiculously large, seemingly half the size of his body. He is a smart player, which means he's not the most gifted athlete on the field. Still, he has had a productive season, leading his team in on-base percentage, he tells me. He's run the bases recklessly but effectively. He's had several timely hits, too, including one

Little League home run, a clean single that swerved through all the opposing outfielders' legs as if they were croquet wickets. By the time the other team's center fielder retrieved the ball in a clump of weeds and tossed it vaguely in the direction of the infield, my son had slid into home well ahead of the tag (my son loves to slide, whether he needs to or not). In the field, he's been an effective stopgap, preventing several home runs, once by throwing his glove at the ball. Admittedly, he's made his share of errors due to a combination of bad luck, bad hops, poor depth perception, and sheer boredom.

The game begins and I know that today I'm going to be tested. For openers, there are two bang-bang plays at the plate. *Two.* I haven't had a play at the plate all season. Today, when it matters, I have two. One involving my son, who follows a ground ball over third into his glove and, in one fluid motion, slings the ball into the cutoff man, who turns and guns out the runner at home. Incredibly, an inning later, the same play happens *against* the Yankees, in which I call our best player out at the plate.

My son, meanwhile, is playing the game of his life. He singles, steals second, steals third, then races home on an infield single for the first run of the game. The Dodgers pull ahead 2–1, and in the last inning, with two runners on, one out, they bring in a freckle-faced Opie look-alike, a flame-haired, flame-throwing right-hander with a windmill motion and pinpoint control. He blows away the first Yankee he faces for the second out. Up to the plate, the game on the line, two outs, his bat on his shoulder, walks my son.

What happens next invokes literature from *Oedipus* to "Casey at the Bat." Standing behind this eight-year-old Mariano Rivera, I watch helplessly as the Dodgers' reliever gets my son to flail limply at two rockets on the outside corner, then freezes him with a laser right down the middle.

"Strike three," I whisper.

The parents from both teams gasp. Amid a gloom and

silence that rips at me somewhere near the pit of my stomach, my eyes focus on a throng of mini-Dodgers mobbing each other while my son and his Yankee teammates walk hangdog back to their bench. Parents I know rush me, shake my hand, and one dad, a movie producer, a man unfamiliar with integrity, says, "I could never have done that. Strike out my own son? *Never.*"

I'm sandwiched then by the parents of our star player. Their faces are dripping with compassion and promise.

"Wow," the mom says. "What a story. You know you have to write that."

I'm too stunned to speak. I'm stunned by what's just happened, what I've just done, and by the truth in what she has said.

"She's right," the dad says. "It's a helluva story. You *must* write it, man."

I don't remember how or if I responded. I vaguely remember leaving the field. I do know that this story is the start. The start of the new.

In the car on the way home, I look at my son, who, as always, is reading a book.

"I had to call you out," I say. "I had no choice. It was a strike, right down the middle."

He never takes his eyes off his page.

"I thought it was high."

On New Year's Day, 1998, Bobbie and I walk along the bluff at sunset, overlooking the Pacific Ocean, the sky the color of a fresh sunflower. Our kids are with Phil and Madeline. We have stolen this hour to be alone and to invite each other into our dreams.

"I always wanted to get a Ph.D. and teach college," Bobbie says, eyes shaded toward Hawaii.

"Was that your fantasy?"

"I don't know. I just always knew I would do it."

"My fantasy?" I say, lost momentarily in the shadow of a palm tree. "I've wanted to be a writer since the sixth grade. I wrote a novel when I was eleven."

She smiles. "What was it about?"

"It was a science-fiction comedy detective thing. *The Hardy Boys Go to Mars,* something like that."

She laughs, a booming, glorious cackle as if she were being viciously tickled. There is never a mystery about what my wife is feeling. She is incapable of hiding even the most minuscule emotion.

"I have always dreamed of being a writer, of writing on my own. Living the writer's life. Like David."

Here it comes. The refrain that's drumming in my head.

"I got sidetracked. Got caught up in having to make money. In *wanting* to make money. Wanting the big house, the lifestyle. I guess. I don't know. I don't know what I want anymore."

I slow my pace. My feet kick up dust on the dirt path. I watch them shuffle through the cloud of brown, watch my own feet with exaggerated fascination.

"I think maybe I'm losing my mind."

"What about writing movies? Isn't that what you want to do?"

"I love movies. Always have. But writing them with my partner? I mean our day . . . we spend our day planning lunch, having lunch, and doing errands. Shit. I feel like I'm in fucking quicksand."

I let go of Bobbie's hand and kick a pebble soccer-style. I top it and the pebble barely moves. Screw it. I stuff my fists into my pocket. I tremble but it's not that cold.

In a soft, casual child's voice Bobbie asks, "Would you be willing to end your partnership and go off on your own?"

"The thought of that scares me to death."

We ease down onto a concrete bench overlooking the Pacific. From this angle, the light pulses in mesmerizing orange, engulfing the sky and stinging my eyes.

Bobbie slides close to me and drops her head onto my shoulder. "Want to know something? One of the first things that attracted me to you was your writing."

I scrunch my head toward her and get a whiff of her hair. The ends tease my throat.

"I never knew that."

"It's true."

"Well," I say. "I bet you're not attracted to my writing now. These movies, the TV shows . . ."

She says nothing.

"You can't be," I say.

"Those . . . are not you."

"No," I say. "They're not."

I pause and sop up the smells around us. Eucalyptus maybe, gasoline from the street, a faint tinge of urine from the night before.

"You didn't do a bad thing," Bobbie says. "You made money for your family. You made a living."

Not a *life*, I say to myself. "I thought that's what you were supposed to do," I say aloud. "Suck it up, do your job, be a man. That was how I was brought up. I didn't know any better."

"Neither did I. Hey," she says, a finger tapping my cheek, "I'm in this, too. We chose this lifestyle together. We bought that house together."

"Regrets? I have a few," I say.

"The house."

"The house. Paying for it, keeping it up, repairs . . ."

"So much money . . ."

"So much pressure," I say.

A woman jogs by pushing twins in a baby stroller. She's wired into a headset attached to music or a cell phone. Another jogger passes her, running backward with his eyes closed. A guy all in yellow breezes by on a racing bike. Curled up over the handlebars, he looks like a banana. I feel as if I've been plunked down in the middle of a circus. I shake my head. Bobbie presses my arm.

"So," I say into the air, "what do we do?"

"Well." I can feel Bobbie's face crinkle into a frown. "I think we're talking about starting over. Isn't that what this is all about?"

I squint into the dying sun.

Starting over.

Try that on for size. I'm looking around the corner at turning fifty. Got two little kids. No guarantees of work. Hell, no *prospects.* How would I even do it? Boot up and jump in? Put my twenty-five-year partnership to bed and begin again, alone?

Can I start over now? As in a children's game, can I ask for a do-over?

I think of Kyle and the time I saw him years ago in David's gym, his newly shaved head a symbol of both solidarity with his wife and a shiny new beginning. Kyle had to start clean; he had no choice. The old was filled with pain and grief.

"It's an opportunity," Bobbie says. "We have to look at it that way."

"That's one way to look at it. It's also a bloody *crisis.*"

She grins. "I just had a student tell me that, in Chinese, crisis and opportunity are the same word."

I have to smile at that. "I like that."

After a beat, Bobbie says, "We should probably get back to the kids."

"Yeah. It's time."

"We'll keep talking," she promises. "This is just the beginning."

I nod. And neither of us moves.

"I don't think we're moving to New England," Bobbie says after a moment.

"Nope. We're going to need our friends."

"It's about simplifying life, isn't it?" she says. "Finding out what's really important. The things that matter. Our friends . . ."

"Family," I say.

"That's first."

"And work. I want work to matter." I look at her. The night has begun to sneak in and I'm cold. "You know what I've lost?"

Bobbie starts to speak but I hiss the words: "My voice."

She nods, knowing. "You have to get that back."

I swallow now, choking on the cold.

We sit in silence on the concrete bench, watching the vanishing light, holding on to each other. Then, without saying a word, two people in sync, in perfect step, we stand and walk, hand in hand, back to our car.

"I know this sounds weird," I say, "but except when I'm with you and the kids, the only place I hear my voice is at the game. I am so comfortable with those guys—"

Bobbie smiles. "That's why I come out every Sunday for a few minutes. It's not just to say hello. It's to see you with the guys."

"The game has been my salvation," I say.

We arrive at our car. I start to pull my hand away but Bobbie won't let me.

"I'm here, you know," she says.

"I know."

And then she says, "Try not to be afraid."

I cough and I feel my nose begin to run. I sniff. "This conversation," I say, "this changes everything."

"I know," she says.

And right then, on the first day of the New Year, I make a decision, a decision made possible by my wife's giving me permission to break away from the vise of tradition, to not be The Man of American myth and American culture and the man of my dreams, but to be the man that I am.

I decide then to do it.

I decide to live my life on spec.

• • •

Crisis and opportunity. To begin with, the movie career just *ends.*

I mark its death with the demise of the dog movie. As we struggle to complete it, a battalion of executives and producers lie in wait, leg-pumping, Armani-clad assassins with good hair, populating studio bungalows and trendy restaurants, their cell phones and laptops lethal weapons, preparing to ambush us with their litany of better ideas, notes we *must* incorporate into the script if we have any intention of (a) getting this movie made or (b) writing another screenplay in this town.

The story as we conceive it is simple:

Two idiots kidnap a famous movie-star dog only to discover that the dog is much smarter than they are. Complications ensue.

A *few* of their actual notes, as we fall into the Hollywood abyss known as Development Hell:

"Do they have to be *idiots?* They should be *smart.* Or, okay, what if one's an idiot and the other one's smart?"

"Make one a woman. Love interest. Sexual tension. That always works."

"Why *two* idiots? What are we doing here, *Dumb and Dumber with a Dog?* Make it one guy and don't make him an idiot. Think Adam Sandler."

"Maybe it should be a woman and a dog. You know, a romantic comedy without the sex."

"Does the dog talk? I hate talking-dog movies. I don't want to see the dog talk. Instead I want cartoon bubbles. Yes. Cartoon bubbles above the dog's head. I want to know what the dog's thinking. What is on the dog's mind? I've always wondered what dogs were thinking. I think everyone does. But do not make the dog talk."

"Don't make the movie too broad. I hate broad comedies. This should be a sophisticated comedy, like *Caddyshack* or *Stripes.*"

"Give the dog a girlfriend. Steal the scene from *Lady and the Tramp*. You know, the spaghetti scene. Rip that off. No one will know."

"Does it have to be a movie-star dog? Nobody likes Hollywood movies. Maybe it should be a police dog, or a bomb-sniffing dog. Those movies always work."

"Does it have to be a *dog*? Maybe it should be a cat. Or a dog and a cat. How about a monkey? Two idiots and a monkey. That's not bad."

"Good news. We're thinking of turning this into a musical . . ."

Mercifully, at last, we put the dog to sleep.

Holed up in my office one night, my movie career at sea, my life on hold, a bottle of good red wine halfway killed, I decide to take a crack at the story of umpiring the Little League baseball game in which I called my son out on strikes. I click on my computer, close my eyes, and begin to type. The words gush unchecked, unguarded, tumbling and tripping over each other as they rush to their places on the page. I don't write; I *spew*. I finish the piece that night in one joyful sprint. I spend the next five days staring at the ten pages I have written, poring over each word with a lump in my throat. I don't know if it's any good. I just know that it's *me*.

I decide to see if I can get the story published. On a whim, I call Alice Short, the editor of the *Los Angeles Times Magazine*. She answers her own phone on the first ring. After a brief conversation, she asks me to fax her the article. I do. Alice calls me fifteen minutes later and in five words changes my life:

"I'm going to publish this."

The call comes on a Thursday morning in mid-March. I am in my office compiling notes for a new article I'm about to begin.

Bobbie suddenly appears on the stairs, the phone cupped against her thigh.

"Dave is on the phone," she says. "He wants to talk to both of us."

Dave is our accountant. He rarely calls and he never wants to talk to us together. I take the phone, knowing what he is about to say.

"You both on?" he asks.

"We're both here," says Bobbie.

"Look, guys—" Dave says.

"No hello?" I say.

"Hello." He clears his throat. "Okay. I've been going over your finances, which is what I do."

He tries a laugh, gives up, and speaks in a gravelly trill. "The fact is, you've run up a lot of debt, and, Alan, let's face it, since you've been writing movies, the cash flow is down."

"Way down," I say trying to make this easier.

"Well, yeah. So we need to right the ship, so to speak. What I'm trying to say is, um . . ."

"We have to sell the house," I say.

He whistles out a sigh. "That's what I would recommend, yes. I think you should strongly consider it. I really don't know where else. I mean, your income . . . I think it's the only way *out* . . . unless you want to go back to TV . . ."

"I'm not going back to TV," I say. "I won't do that."

I look at Bobbie. She sits on the floor of the office cross-legged, her back slumped against one wall of the handmade pine bookcase we had built six years ago by the temperamental Italian carpenter-artist. Despite being on the phone, she holds a hand over her mouth.

"We should've called you, Dave," Bobbie says. Her voice is muffled. "We want to make some changes . . . big changes . . . life changes . . ."

"Okay . . . we're talking about. . . ?"

I say, "I want to write on my own. Articles, books . . ."

Dave laughs gently, nervously. "So you're talking about even *less* cash flow?"

"It's what Alan's always wanted to do," Bobbie says.

"We talked about this once, remember?" I say. "A long time ago."

"It's vaguely familiar. I didn't take you seriously at the time," Dave says.

"Well, it's serious. I'm going for it. Following my dream. Pick any cliché you want."

He sighs. "Guys climb mountains, fly around the world in a hot-air balloon, move in with the Dalai Lama. People do a lot of crazy things."

"Yeah," I say.

"Career change at our age." I can hear Dave scratching his head through the phone. "I'll say this. You got guts."

"It's kind of now or never," I say.

"It does make things a little clearer. In order to finance this new career, you really are going to have to sell the house. I don't see any other choice."

"We know," Bobbie says. "I wish we'd called you sooner."

I look over at her. Her eyes are jammed shut.

"Now's actually an opportune time," Dave says. "You can get good value. Especially in Santa Monica, which has appreciated significantly this year. We work with a wonderful real estate agent. If you want, I'll call her for you."

Bobbie shifts on the floor. A rustle escapes from her throat.

"Let us talk about it first, Dave," I say, a glance at my wife. "This is a big step."

"Sure, of course. I know this is a huge decision. Make sure it's what you want to do. And if you want to talk, I'm here. Call me anytime."

"Thanks, Dave."

"I'm not sure what to say," Dave says. "Hang in there, I guess."

"That'll do," I say.

"Call me," he says.

I hang up. Bobbie's head sags forward. It looks almost as if she's been shot. After a full minute of silence, she raises her head and blinks at me through eyes that are filled with tears.

"I know this is what we're going to do. What we *want* to do. I know that. It's just . . . I didn't expect to feel this way."

She lets out a sob. I can't speak. I swallow and join my wife on the floor.

"I'll be all right," she says. "I will. We have to sell the house. But when you hear it from someone else—"

She chokes back another sob. A train of tears streaks down each cheek.

"This is *hard,*" she says.

She lowers her chin and her long brown hair flops down, the ends nearly sweeping the floor. I can no longer see her face. When she speaks, her voice comes from a distance, reprising a plea she uttered six years ago in an escrow office, her tear-soaked words now diving into the whitewashed wood.

"We never should've bought it," she says.

A month later we prep the house for sale. Our real estate agent, Nicole, an oddity in her business because she seems to have a heart, oversees several simultaneous beautification projects: the painting of the exterior trim, the touch-up of a couple of rooms inside, the addition of four blooming potted trees to the line of French doors in the front, a row of tropical plants to augment the maple saplings along the stucco wall that borders Klein's house.

Inside, we work on dispensing with clutter. Over the years, our living room has become a repository for the overflow, a foster home for unwanted and ignored *stuff.* After six years, we haven't found the time to deal with it all. It appears now that we never will. Our task at hand is to let go.

Each night, in our new ritual, Bobbie and I rummage through the room, plucking an occasional gem from a pile, tossing it aside, rescued.

"I called Madeline, Faye, and Sara," Bobbie says, lifting an armful of books from the floor to a more secure position on the couch. "They were wonderful. We're very lucky. We have great friends. Faye and Brick invited us for dinner the night we move."

I nod, scan the stuff in the room. Bobbie wants a garage sale. If it were up to me, I'd have a bonfire.

"When are you going to tell the other guys?"

"I thought I'd wait for the moving van to show up, let them figure it out," I say.

Bobbie *hmms,* meaning she's not in the mood for me right now.

"You have to do it Sunday," she says.

I decide to tell them after the first game, during a bagel break. I'm not sure exactly what I'll say. I know I'm not going to make a big deal about it. This is a time to revert to the way most guys announce sensitive and personal news: report it, explain it as concisely and inarticulately as possible, and move on. No point in getting bogged down in a lot of unnecessary details.

Game one completed, we gather around the redwood table. Words float in the air. Something about an overpriced meal and rude service at the so-called restaurant of the moment. Some talk about someone getting burned with a stock tip from his brother-in-law. Someone else says, "These two old ladies are sitting on a park bench . . ."

I can't focus on any of this. Instead, I tune in to the uniqueness of their laughs: Jack's begins as a giggle, then cascades into a rumble; Brick's is a long pant, dissolving into a series of breathless gasps; Gabe's is a screech, muffled and tentative, as though he doesn't want to bother you with the noise.

The laughs roll away. I drift over toward the hoop to practice my shot and regroup. Stewart joins me, bouncing across the driveway on the balls of his feet. My shot rams off the rim and the basketball rolls against one of Nicole's new tropical plants that hug the stucco wall. Stewart jogs over to retrieve it.

"Wow, I never noticed these before. Alan, these plants are beautiful. Really adds some nice color over here. Did you get a new gardener?"

"Actually, Stewart, no, I'm selling the house."

I squeak the words out, my voice cracking slightly.

"You're . . . ?" Stewart's jaw has dropped. He's not sure he's heard correctly.

"Yeah. I'm selling. Uh."

The talking on the deck stops.

"I had a feeling," Big Sam says. He dips his head toward Phil, Gabe, and Brick. "They were acting funny."

"Huh," Stewart says. "When?"

"It's probably going on the market in a couple of weeks."

"You're *selling?*" Danny says.

"The house is just too big. I have rooms I've never been in. Seriously. I never go into my living room, ever."

There is a silence that seems to last an hour.

"I know exactly what you mean," Ben says finally, his motor idling, slow. "We never go into our living room, either. Never."

"And we have six bathrooms," I say. "Six bathrooms? Why do I need six bathrooms?"

"Huh," Stewart says again. "I didn't realize you had so many bathrooms. Six, huh?"

"Yeah. Way too many."

"Six is a lot," Mitch says.

"Boy, are you doing the right thing," Brick says. "I should do it, too. Unload that white elephant, grab the cash. Smart move."

"Where are you going to go?" Danny asks.

"I don't know. We're open. We want to scale down."

"Now's the time. Definitely," Gabe says.

"Absolutely. You never know when the market's gonna turn around again," says Phil.

"The only thing is . . . the game," Wally says with a strained laugh. "Alan, you're taking away our game. Where we going to play?"

"Any chance you'll buy a house with a driveway big enough for a hoop?" Stewart asks.

"If I move to Ohio, maybe. Or back to New England."

"He's not moving back East," Phil clarifies.

"So that's the story," I say.

"You're selling the house," Big Sam says, and clears his throat.

"Yeah."

"Well," says Phil, clapping his hands, giving us all a start. "The house is not even on the market yet. Who's got next?"

"Yeah," Danny mutters, "let's play while we can."

They call that night, one after another. They want to know if I'm all right. When I tell them I am, that I'm fine, they want to know what they can do. They want to help. Phil, Gabe, and Big Sam once again offer money.

"You can pay me back when you sell the house," Phil says. "I'm in no rush."

"I am," I say. "But thanks."

Brick offers to help me move; Jack, Ben, and Wally offer to take me to lunch and remind me that they are always there to talk to. Stewart offers regret and sympathy. Mitch offers anything, anything at all.

Danny calls because he is confused. "I don't understand. Why are you selling your house?"

"It's the right time," I say. "The market's good now. I can sock away some serious cash."

"But you live in the best neighborhood in the city. Everybody wants to live here. If you wait a couple, three years, your house will be worth twice what it is now."

"Maybe so but I want to take advantage now—"

"I don't get it. Don't you like your house?"

"It doesn't really work for us. It's too big, too many bathrooms—"

"You were serious about that shit?"

"Oh yeah."

"I don't believe this," Danny says in a tiny, wounded voice. "You're going to lose the game. What about that? I thought you loved having the game at your house."

"I do."

"Is everything all right with you and Bobbie?"

"Yes. Look . . ."

He waits.

I ram my eyes shut. "I wrote TV for something like twenty years. Made some good money. Bought this big house. This is a television writer's house." I swallow. "That's not who I am anymore. I'm making a career change. Changing how I spend my days. I feel like I've been wasting a lot of *time.*"

Now I swallow hard.

"So, I'm starting over. I'm gonna do what I always wanted to do. Write my own stuff. Try that out. See if I can make that work. I'm gonna take a shot." And then, too loudly, too urgently, I say, "I can't do that unless I sell the house."

"Oh," he murmurs. He sounds stunned and defeated, like someone who has been informed of an unexpected, untimely death. "I'm . . . I'm going to miss coming on Sundays."

"Danny, you can play anywhere. Any playground, schoolyard, Y . . . you'd rule anywhere."

"I don't want to play at the Y," he says heavily.

There it is. Finally. I have found Danny's dark side: the goddamn guy is *sensitive.*

I drop my chin to my throat and wait. Fumbling with the language, wanting to put reality behind us in a hurry, he says, "Big changes in your life."

"Yeah," I say.

"Huge," he adds quietly.

"So," I say.

I pause, mark time to Danny's short, rapid breaths humming through the phone.

He says, "Have you looked in Cheviot Hills?"

"No."

"We used to live there. Some beautiful houses. You can probably find one at a good price because it's not as desirable as Santa Monica or Brentwood . . ."

"Cheviot Hills, huh?"

"Great neighborhood."

"I'm going to look into it."

"You should. Definitely."

"We're gonna keep playing for a while," I say. "The house isn't even on the market yet."

"Oh yeah, I know that."

"So," I say again, riding through another pause.

"Well," Danny says, his voice ringed with sadness. "Good luck, Alan."

A week later, Nicole plants a For Sale sign in front of our house. Within hours, I am visited by neighbors I have seen only in passing. One neighbor, a woman I recognize but whose name I don't know, tells me she is shocked that we're moving, that we have been wonderful neighbors and that she will miss us.

Among the other neighbors who visit is Duff. I return the tepee to him, admit that my son didn't get as much use out of it as we had hoped, and express regret that we will be moving, especially on behalf of our sons, who have become good friends.

"What's going to happen to the game?" Duff asks.

"We haven't talked about it. Someone's supposed to look into renting a gym."

"Not that easy to do."

"We have to figure something out," I say.

"Shame to give up your game."

The words sting.

Nicole holds an open house on a warm Sunday afternoon in late June. The house sells three days later. The buyers want us to move as soon as possible so they can rip out the kitchen and my office and begin remodeling. They insist on a sixty-day escrow. I do the math. We will have to move just before Labor Day. The last game at my house will be Sunday, August 30, 1998.

I spend most of the summer frantically searching for a place to live. Nicole, Bobbie, and I trek through a hundred houses but find nothing that we'd sink our money into. Finally, we decide to rent a futuristic apartment in a concrete-and-steel lump overlooking an inlet in Marina Del Rey.

"Something new just came on the market," Nicole tells us as we leave the apartment with our kids. Her hand cups the mouth of her cell phone. "It sounds cute. It's small."

We drive into the Pacific Palisades section of the city and pull up to a 1940s bungalow on a narrow street. An arbor of flowers bursting with color envelops a minuscule front yard, partially obscuring a dramatic sandstone walkway leading to the front door. Ravenous Realtors, snoopy neighbors, and a few slobbering prospective buyers swarm in and out of the house.

"This is it," Bobbie says as soon as she walks inside. "I have to have this house."

Despite the size, I love it, too. I love the warm colors the owners have painted the walls, the restaurant-quality appliances in the kitchen, and the flow from the dining area to the living room to the bedrooms. I can see my family here, the four of us cozying up by the fireplace, happily living with half the number of bathrooms, half the square footage, and half the mortgage. I'm knocked out by the location, a few blocks from the Palisades village, a three-street grid of coffeehouses, restaurants, boutiques, a Blockbuster, a bookstore, a library, and a recreation center. Of course, the driveway is slim, the width of a car, impossible to accommodate a basketball hoop, much less six middle-aged men. We put in an offer—we're one of four—and Bobbie writes the sellers an impassioned letter imploring them to choose us.

They do. The countdown begins. Only eight more Sundays left.

Bobbie throws herself into packing, organizing the move, coordinating and supervising the minor repairs we've agreed to make, and discarding a chunk of our possessions. We donate to charity racks of clothes and boxes of toys the kids have outgrown or lost interest in. We have not one but two garage sales. We donate furniture to friends with unfurnished apartments and growing families, and people who need couches, a dining room table, a dollhouse, a crib, a changing table. I give away the leather chair in my office, the one my partner inhabited for six years. Bobbie is a tornado of motion and drive, her emotions held in check, no time to take a breath, second-guess, or grieve over the loss of her New England farmhouse. In shadows, though, late at night, when I feel sleep descend over me like a cool sheet, I hear her distress, her pain, her fear. I hear her get out of bed, go into the bathroom, and cry.

Sundays, it's hoops as usual. I notice no change in any of the guys or in the dynamic among us. Danny still dominates the games, Phil squats, Jack bombs from outside, Mitch and Gabe continue to bang me under the boards, Wally arrives an hour late. Between games and at the end of the morning, we talk and gobble up our bagels, same as always, no hint that a major change is looming.

A few days before the last game, I sit on the floor above the garage and pack the last few remnants of my office into a box. Empty, the office seems surprisingly small. I flash back to designing the floor-to-ceiling bookcases, now naked and forlorn without books, and laying out the way I wanted the built-in work area to curve around and enclose me like an embrace. I stare into space for a long time, no thought crossing my mind really, just memories, and for the first time, I have regrets. I regret that I wasn't more frugal with money. I regret that I relied so much on a business that I never believed in. I regret that I wasn't truer to myself sooner.

Other than the white box at my feet, the only object that remains in the office now is a copy of the *Los Angeles Times Magazine* that contains the story I wrote about my son. I flip to the article and begin reading my words.

"Great office."

I look up and see a man standing in the doorway. I blink. It is Doc Rivers, former New York Knick. I remember Nicole asking me if she could send someone over to see the house even though it had sold.

"Wish I'd seen this house before," Doc Rivers says. "I would've bought it for this office."

I smile. "I bought it because there was room for a hoop. It was my dream to have my own basketball game."

"And did you?"

"Every Sunday for five years."

"Why did you sell?"

"Things change."

Doc nods. "It was my dream to play in the NBA," he says.

"You had a better dream," I say.

He laughs, then rubs his palm along the smooth surface of the barren built-in pine cabinets.

"I really missed one here," Doc says.

"There's always another one," I say.

"Yep. Always. Take care," Doc Rivers says, and I shake hands with the future NBA Coach of the Year.

He climbs down the stairs of the office. Through the window, I watch him walk down the driveway. He stops for a moment and squints up at my basketball hoop.

I close the *Los Angeles Times Magazine* with my article in it. Instead of packing it away in the box, I fold it up and carry it with me inside.

They come up the driveway Sunday morning at ten: Phil, Gabe, Brick, Jack, Big Sam, Danny, Ben, Mitch, Stewart, and Wally.

They come up the driveway as they have every Sunday for the past five years, laughing, groaning, gossiping, swinging a bag of bagels, and dribbling a couple of basketballs.

But this Sunday, the last Sunday, Danny is lugging a tripod and has a video camera hidden in his gym bag, and as I come out of my house and onto my deck, there is a hush, followed by strained and mumbled hellos. We slip on wristbands, stretch, grab a bagel in silence. Nobody knows what to say. Danny attaches the camera to the tripod.

"Well, come on, let's play," I say. "I have to be somewhere Tuesday."

"Stewart, make teams," Brick says.

"Okay, let's see . . . Danny . . ."

"I'm filming. I got next."

"If we look grainy or fuzzy, it's because we *are* grainy and fuzzy," I say.

"I don't like this shot." Danny picks up the tripod and jockeys for position between Gabe and Sam.

"Excuse me," he says, setting up between them. "Making memories."

"Fucking Fellini," says Big Sam.

"I can't work like this," Danny says, winking into his camera.

We play. I swish in a couple of jumpers, grab two boards, intercept a pass, rifle a no-look bounce pass into Brick for a layup. We win 7–3. We break for bagels, but this week, Big Sam and Gabe don't hang around on the deck. They're up, shooting, getting ready to play the next game.

"Boys," a voice shouts from the bottom of the driveway. I bob my head below the carob tree and identify Buddy, the stand-up comic, and Duff, who waves shyly, striding toward us. Cameo appearances.

"Last game," Buddy says. "Had to make a guest shot."

"Me, too," Duff says.

"Duff," Jack says.

"Hey, Jack. Don't worry, I'm not playing."

"Good," Brick says. Jack and Duff laugh and shake hands.

"All we need now is for Kyle and Ivan to show up."

Stewart cackles too loudly.

"I loved his beer," Phil says.

"Don't forget Monk," Ben says. "I liked Monk."

"And Ivan and Barry. Remember Barry?" I say.

"Barry," Phil says. "Sure. The filmmaker."

"He never played but he loved to climb over the wall," Ben says. "Him I remember fondly."

"Where are the muffins?" Brick says, scrounging through the bags on the deck.

"I didn't stop. I didn't want to be late. Next week," Ben says.

"Next week?" Brick says, stunned. "Where's your *head?*"

"Oh yeah. Sorry," Ben says.

"I was really looking forward to my muffins," Brick says. "I'm crestfallen."

"You better turn the sound off," Mitch says to Danny behind his camera. "This is too incriminating."

"Hey, Fellini, you playing?" I say.

"You think I can leave the camera running?"

"Sure. Cinema *verité,*" Big Sam says.

"Guys, I'm tightening up," Phil says.

"I guess I'll have a bagel," Brick says.

"Do you want me to go get you muffins?" Ben says.

"Would you?" says Brick.

"I feel like I'm visiting my parents," Buddy says to Duff.

"Brick, you playing?" Stewart asks.

"Yeah, yeah, I'm playing," Brick says, jogging onto the court, an onion bagel jammed into his mouth.

I drill in three long-range rainbows in game two, but Danny shakes, bakes, and overcomes Jack and Brick's double team, and Danny's team wins, 7–5. I sit out the third game, mugging for the camera and bullshitting with Buddy and Phil. At one point, I retreat into the kitchen, a warehouse now of boxes packed with plates, silverware, and small appliances. Bobbie folds newspaper around coffee cups, lies them neatly into a brown moving box.

"Anybody talking out there?"

I search her face for clues.

"You know, about the move, the new house? The end of the game? Memories? Feelings? That sort of thing?"

"Feelings," I say, and shake my head.

"Hey, you guys talked about your feelings. In Mexico. And here. You guys talked about your feelings a lot."

"Yeah," I say. "Before."

I head back outside.

The morning gets hot and we talk less. Buddy leaves. We shake hands, promise to stay in touch.

Ben picks up his black Casio runner's watch from the table and checks the time. He clicks his tongue. "Gotta go, man. Sorry about the muffins, Brick."

"I'll live," Brick says. "Not as happily, but I'll live."

"Hey, Alan," Ben says.

"Take it easy, Ben."

"We're talking about playing at Cloverfield Park next week, over by M-G-M," Stewart says. "You available?"

"Next week?" Ben scratches his head. "I think I'm on call."

"Well, if you're available," Stewart says.

"I'm pretty sure I'm on call," Ben says. "But, well, hey, see you guys."

"*Bennnyyyy,*" we howl as he gallops down the driveway.

"One more," Phil says, a statement, not a question.

"I'm done," Danny says, unhinging his knee brace, then packing away the camera and tripod.

We choose sides for the final game. I'm not sure whether it's a setup or whether I'm on fire, but I score six straight baskets and my team wins, 7–0. I'm going out on top. I swagger back toward the deck. And then I'm pelted by backslaps and handshakes, and one by one, each guy hugs me.

"Dude," Phil says, "we'll talk."

"Bye, Alan," says Gabe.

"Okay," Brick says.

"Take it easy, boychik," says Big Sam.

A cascade of muffled "See you's" and "Thanks" swirling around me, I watch the basketball players walk down my driveway for the last time. The air vibrates with a few last rants about mortgage rates and the ineptitude of the Dodgers, but soon their footsteps fade and their voices trail off. Car doors open, swing shut. Engines turn on, rev up, hum, and the cars roll out. The sounds echo and linger. Then, an eerie silence.

I stand riveted to my spot at the top of the driveway, and an imaginary photograph album opens up in my mind's eye. Moments that have mattered in this driveway come rushing forward: a five-year-old boy's birthday party, children squealing at lizards and reptiles crawling up their arms; my son and daughter playing backyard soccer and baseball and performing plays on the deck; my friend Joey, the professional magician, doing his act in my garage; my daughter, now an all-league player in middle school, picking up a stray basketball and making her first basket ever, at age six; washing the car with my family, sloshing each other with soapsuds and jousting with hoses; shooting baskets with my wife, watching her hit ten in a row, giddy as a little girl; rebounding my eighty-year-old father's two-handed set shots, while my mother watches from the deck, remembering when she saw him play in high school. The album closes. I hold it in my head, the end of an era.

I move off my spot and walk up to the deck. I begin cleaning up the dozens of crushed paper cups and cream cheese stains on the redwood table. I brush off the remains of the last game and I suddenly feel nothing but loss. A tear mixes with the sweat on my cheek. I choke back a sob.

I stand over the table and wipe it in circles, over and over, long after it's clean.

9.

next

The Sunday after the last game at my house, the guys play at a small public park next to M-G-M Studios in Santa Monica. This new game is marred by a blinding, relentless midmorning sun, a slippery surface that retains water from aggressive sprinklers that leap over an adjacent patch of grass and douse the court, and an influx of players, most of them young, some of them *teenagers,* who congregate impatiently along the sidelines waiting for next. This game is all-business, all-ball. Nobody cares what you have to say. No one listens to your jokes. Nobody wants to bond. Nobody knows your name.

I play off and on for a few months, but I can't get used to the lack of interaction. Some of the guys try to connect in the same ways we did at my house. Phil still recounts his weekly gruesome and funny ER story, Danny tells a joke, Stewart shouts encouragement when any of us makes a halfway decent play, Big Sam attempts to arrange another trip to Mexico. Occasionally a couple of the players I don't know stare curiously at us, a hint in their eyes that they wouldn't mind an invitation to join us. Most of the players look at us as if we're a weird support group, recovering somebodies, playing basketball at the park instead of attending a meeting.

Attempting to keep tradition intact, Gabe brings bagels to the first game at the park. It's awkward. There is no place to sit, no deck, no redwood table, and the bagels remain in the bag, ignored, shunned, a symbol of a different kind of game, perhaps even of different men. Gabe never brings bagels again.

Mitch and Ben stop coming, citing conflicts in their schedules. After a couple of months of playing irregularly at the park, I, too, decide to take a hiatus, maybe a couple of weeks, a month. I want to experience what it's like to have my Sunday mornings back. I'm looking forward to hanging out with the kids, taking walks with Bobbie, reading the Sunday papers, and just vegging out. Before I know it, a year passes, then another. I write a book, then another.

Bobbie and I remain close with Phil, Gabe, Brick, and their wives, seeing them often, with families, and without, couples dating, going out to dinner, a movie, the theater. We mark birthdays, anniversaries, and holidays together. Phil and Gabe keep playing in the game in the park, but Brick stops one Sunday when his good knee buckles. At least that's the first report. Phil tells me that Brick stormed off the court after nearly getting into a fight with a jack-off half his age who wouldn't stop trash-talking and hanging on to his shirt.

"Pummel him," Big Sam reportedly said. "I'll back you up. I might have to take out his two friends first."

"Fuck it," Brick said, and walked away.

On the phone the next night, when I asked him about the fight, or near-fight, Brick shrugged it off.

"I left before there were any punches thrown. The game's gotten rough, but that's not why I left. I left because you have to wait a half hour between games. You sit around doing nothing. It's so boring. There's no one to talk to."

One night, a few months later, out to dinner with Phil, Gabe, and their wives, Phil says, "Hey, dude, guess what? We're not playing at the park anymore. Starting tomorrow, we're playing *inside,* at that new high school gym."

I lift an eyebrow. "Inside?"

"It's gonna be great," Gabe says. "We only invited a few people from the park."

"They're mostly nice guys. We couldn't avoid asking a couple of jackasses," Phil clarifies.

"That's true," Gabe says. "I guess every game has a couple of assholes."

I say, "What's the old saying? There's always one asshole in the room. If you can't pick him out, it's you."

Phil and Gabe laugh, then Phil says, "You should come. For research."

"The guys would love to see you, Alan," Gabe says.

"I'll think about it," I say.

I do think about it, every Sunday morning for the next six months. For some reason, I just can't get it together to play in the new game. I do miss the guys and I miss playing. I have also learned to love leisurely Sunday mornings. There is something to be said for idleness.

Then, one Sunday morning, I wake up itching to play. I roll out of bed and search for my basketball shoes. I find them buried at the bottom of a wicker basket stuffed with other retired footwear: hiking boots caked with dried mud, and sandals with the soles detached and flapping like dog tongues. The tread on the sneakers is gone and the rest of the shoes are covered with a misty white dew I identify as a form of killer mold. I toss them into the trash, run out to my local shoe store, and buy a brand-new pair of New Balance.

I arrive at the gym at ten-thirty, a Wally-like hour late. I approach the gym door and hesitate, fighting both a catch in my throat and the urge to turn back. I had not expected this sudden bout of nerves. Not even sure what it's from. And then I realize that in the two-plus years since I've played with these guys, I've changed. My relationship to them has changed. Everything's changed.

But I started this game, I tell myself. *Get in there.*

I blow out a gust of jittery air and stride inside on a wave of manufactured confidence as if I own the place. The gym floor is a warm honey color, and the squeak of sneakers and the bounce of the ball immediately soothe me. At the far end of the court, eight guys play four-on-four. One player drives to the hoop, stops, squats, and shoots. Phil. Unmistakable. The ball squirrels around the rim and rolls off. A large guy with a military haircut yanks down the rebound and rifles a pass to Danny, who dribbles between his legs to avoid another guy I don't know. The looks on these eight faces are all the same and far removed from any I ever saw at my house. These guys are *focused.* I try a small wave to Phil and Danny. They don't seem to recognize me. I pick out Jack and Wally on opposite teams. They don't notice me either. I withdraw my hand, scratch my cheek as if that's what I intended to do all along. I walk along the bleachers feeling as if I'm breaking in.

"Damn it!" Danny shouts as his shot bops off the rim. He slaps his hands in disgust, then slides over to guard his man, his body coiled in a crouch, his fingers flicking at his opponent's dribble. No one looks anywhere but at his man or the ball. This is beyond playground competitiveness; this is playoff intensity.

I approach the far end of the court, see five guys sitting in the two bottom rows of the bleachers waiting to play, only three of whom I know.

"I got next," I say.

"I don't believe it," Big Sam says, looking up. "It must be a ghost."

"Hey!" Stewart says, standing up, pumping my hand. "Great to see you."

"Alan, I didn't think you'd ever come back," Gabe says, rubbing my shoulder.

I nod at the others, the strangers. They nod back.

"Nice guys," Gabe assures me in a whisper.

That's it. Nothing else is said. I sit down and watch the game. A couple of shots, an argument over a charging call, a snazzy Danny no-look pass off a drive to the hoop resulting in the game-winning layup.

"Let's go," Stewart says, and he, Gabe, and Big Sam charge onto the court. I follow, trailing like someone's little brother.

Then the others see me.

"Dude!" Phil shouts.

"Heyyy!" Danny says. "When did you get here?"

"Just now," Gabe says. "You're playing, right?"

"Gonna try," I say. "It's been a while."

"Like two years, right?" Jack says.

"Something like that," I say.

"How you doing?" Jack says, banging me on the back.

"I'm good. You look great, Jack."

"Hey, Alan," Wally says, bulldozing his way in. "You look like you've put on some weight."

"Let's go," Stewart says, clapping his hands, and adds, tossing this over his shoulder, "We only have the court until noon."

"Come on, play!" someone shouts from the bleachers, annoyed.

"Hurry *up!*" someone else shouts, even more annoyed.

We start. I'm on Phil, who I happen to know has been running more and working out with a personal trainer. He's quicker and stronger than he's ever been and has added a nifty ball fake and power drive to his signature squat shot. I lay off him, don't want to fall prey to the drive, preferring instead to give him the outside jumper. He quickly hits two bombs.

"You hef to get up on heem!" a guy on our team with a thick accent hollers. "Guard heem close!"

This guy seems disgusted. Then, pissed at seeing me getting torched twice by Phil, he switches with me and takes Phil himself. Phil fakes, blows right by him, and finger-rolls in the winning basket.

"*Sheet*," the guy snarls.

"And that's why you don't guard him close," I say.

He ignores me. We sit. We're losers.

"How do you feel?" Big Sam asks, sitting next to me.

"Crappy. I'm out of shape. But you look great."

"Well, I've been exercising, watching what I eat." Big Sam takes a belt from his water bottle. He nods at the gym floor. "What do you think?"

"Really nice."

"It's a different game," Big Sam says.

"I can see that."

"Lot more intense. The conversation is kept to a minimum. Not that we talked much after you stopped coming."

"After I stopped coming?"

"Oh yeah. People liked to talk to you, *boychik*."

"*Boychik,*" I say, "I'm probably older than you are."

"I wish," Big Sam roars. "Plus, this is a gym, you know? It's not your house. That makes a big difference. Yep. A lot of changes."

He looks straight ahead, trains his eyes on the players in front of us. Big Sam clears his throat. His Adam's apple bobs in his throat like a buoy.

"I'm thinking of making some big changes myself."

I try to catch his eye but he's staring off.

"What kind of changes?" I ask into the air.

"Career changes. Life changes. I'm seriously thinking about quitting the public defender's office in two years, when my youngest goes off to college."

He peeks around, then lowers his voice. "I actually had this conversation with Carol last night. I told her what I wanted to do. She's totally into it. Much to my shock. This is the plan. I'm going to move to Italy and get a Ph.D. in Roman history. It's my dream. I want to teach and write about that period of history and the origin of our laws."

"That's quite a change," I say.

"I know. It's nuts. Starting over in my late fifties. But why not? The kids will be out of the house. The timing's perfect. What do you think?"

"I think I'd love to come visit you in Italy," I say.

He smiles, bends his head down, sighs, and takes another hit from the water bottle. In front of us, someone howls, someone else swears, and someone hisses, "Fine, take it *out.*"

"What do these guys think?" I ask him.

Big Sam's mouth snakes into an embarrassed smile. "I haven't told them yet."

The smile fades and Big Sam fights off a sigh.

"It's a much different game," he says.

A few minutes later I'm back on the court, playing in my second basketball game in two and a half years. I check the three other guys on my team, scan the four guys we're playing. Every man on the court, all eight, including the ones who played in my backyard, sport exact looks of determination and focus. Long and lean faces with eyes narrowed in competition. Grim, humorless warriors in battle.

My team takes the ball out. Jack gathers in the pass, fakes, and drives toward the rack. I duck behind a screen set by a load of a guy named Charlie and sneak into the corner. My defender, concerned with Jack, steps toward him, leaving me alone.

Jack flips me the ball.

I catch and shoot.

BANG.

On the bleachers, Phil and Gabe stand and applaud.

Like Kobe, I blow on my fingers as if they are on fire.

"Guard heem!" the thick accent screams from somewhere.

• • •

After the last game of the morning, Phil, Gabe, and I collapse onto a bench on the sidewalk outside the gym.

"I am so sore," Phil says.

"You know what I love to do after basketball?" Gabe murmurs. "I love to go home, get into a nice hot bath, soak for at least an hour, and read a good mystery. I look forward to it all week. First basketball, then a bath and a book. I love that."

Big Sam and Stewart come out of the gym, see us, and stop.

"Look at this," Big Sam says.

"You guys waiting for a bus?" Stewart says.

"You look like poster boys for a funeral home," Big Sam says.

"I wish I had my camera," Jack says, arriving now on the scene.

"I'm glad you don't," Phil moans.

"Well, I have to pick up my daughter. Good seeing you, *boychik*. Come back," Big Sam says, thumping off, his wrestler's chest thrust toward the sun.

"Are you a regular now?" Stewart asks.

"It's possible," I say, though I know immediately that I probably won't be. "We'll see."

"Okay, well, hope to see you soon."

"See you, Stewart," I say.

He flashes a smile behind his bushy mustache and walks briskly into the parking lot, his hands shoved into his shorts' pockets.

"Well, guys," says Gabe, "I am about to stand up and attempt to walk to my car. Wish me luck."

"Good luck," Phil and I say in unison.

Gabe whistles a breath, then lifts himself to his feet. "Man, I'm stiff as a board. I am really gonna soak today. We have theater tickets next week, don't we?"

Phil nods. "Saturday night."

"Good. I look forward to the nap."

Heads veered toward Gabe, Phil and I watch him snail toward the parking lot. We turn back and sit silently, our sweat-soaked shorts clinging to the bench like plastic wrap. Neither of us moves. I suddenly regret playing today. I feel like an outsider, as if I've forced my way into a private club, long after my membership has expired.

And then Phil says heavily, "You know what I miss? The bagels. That was the best part. Sitting around. A bunch of guys bullshitting, making each other laugh, once in a while getting serious . . ."

He looks off, his head turned in such a way that he is sure to avoid my eyes. My eyes search the sky, and I second-guess myself. Should I have held on? Should I have not sold the house?

No.

Regrets? This time I have none.

"I like playing here, sure," Phil says. "The games are good. You get a great workout. The gym is terrific. The guys are nice, mostly . . ." His voice putters out. His eyes are stationed on a Dumpster across the street. "It's not the same, though. It's good . . . it's different, that's all."

And then I say, just because I need to hear it, "Let's suppose . . . I bought another house with a hoop."

"That's not happening."

"Humor me. Let's *suppose.*"

"Fine. You got a new house. You got a big driveway. No stucco wall, no carob tree. And you got a hoop. Make it fiberglass this time."

"Would the guys come back?"

"Oh."

Phil pauses. For the first time, he turns and looks at me. He locks his eyes into mine.

"In a heartbeat," he says. "In a heartbeat."